Black Briar Advisors

The Leadership Edition
Titans of Industry
Visionaries Who Shaped Modern Business

Stephen L. Nalley DBA., CHA
American Business Magnate, Entrepreneur, Veteran and Author

Black Briar Advisors

Copyright © 2024
All Rights Reserved
ISBN: 9798332677861

Acknowledgment

I would like to acknowledge everyone who has ever wronged me, betrayed me, doubted me, gave up on me and/or ever tried to cheat me. You are my compelling "WHY" that has driven me to such heights. Your hate, negativity and disrespect has always motivated me to barrel through any setback and every adversity I have ever faced in my life.

I would never have set the bar so high and gone so far if it were not for you and your actions. You know who you are, and I would like to thank you all for providing me with the inspiration that I needed to drive my passion and achieve my own definition of success in my life.

About the Author

Stephen Nalley is an American Business Magnate, Entrepreneur, Investor, Veteran and Author. He is best known as the principal founder of Inner Circle Capital, Breanna Bailey Investments and Black Briar Advisors.

Over the course of Nalley's 30-year professional career, he has started and/or participated in hundreds of corporate ventures and managed over $2 Billion in Real Estate Assets.

Prior to his professional pursuits, Nalley served his country honorably in the United States Army as a Non-Commission Officer and Commando with the Army's Elite 10th Mountain Division.

After serving his Country, Nalley went on to obtain academic degrees from several prestigious colleges. Nalley earned a Bachelor of Science Degree in Healthcare Administration from the University of North Florida, Master's Degree in Business Administration and Doctorate Degree in Business Administration from the University of Atlanta and a Law Degree from the Washington University School of Law.

Stephen is a Certified Hotel Administrator through the American Hotel & Lodging Association and is a Member of the Forbes Business Council, as well as, a Writer for the Entrepreneur Leadership Network

Preface

In the annals of history, certain individuals stand out not merely for their success, but for their transformative impact on industries and societies. This book delves into the lives and legacies of such figures—visionaries who redefined the parameters of their fields, reshaped markets, and left indelible marks on the fabric of modern business and technology.

Our journey begins with Henry Ford, whose innovations in mass production revolutionized the automobile industry and manufacturing at large. Ford's introduction of the assembly line not only made cars affordable to the average American but also set new standards for production efficiency. His pioneering labor practices, including the unprecedented five-dollar workday, sparked both admiration and controversy, setting the stage for modern labor relations.

Next, we explore the life of John D. Rockefeller, the mastermind behind Standard Oil and one of the most influential figures in the petroleum industry. Rockefeller's methods of horizontal and vertical integration, coupled with his strategic business practices, allowed him to dominate the oil market. Yet, his story is also one of philanthropy and public scrutiny, providing a complex portrait of ambition and altruism.

The narrative continues with Andrew Carnegie, whose ascent from humble beginnings to steel magnate showcases the quintessential rags-to-riches story. Carnegie's innovations in steel production and his business strategies played a pivotal role in the industrialization of America. His later life as a philanthropist, advocating the "Gospel of Wealth," left a legacy that extends beyond industry into education and public welfare.

We then turn to Thomas Edison, an icon of American ingenuity and entrepreneurship. Edison's prolific career, marked by inventions such as the phonograph, the incandescent light bulb, and advancements in motion pictures, underscores his relentless pursuit of innovation. His establishment of General Electric and his approach to intellectual property set benchmarks for future generations of inventors and entrepreneurs.

Sam Walton's story is one of retail revolution. By founding Walmart, Walton transformed the retail landscape with his focus on discount pricing and supply chain efficiency. His innovative approach to employee management and customer service helped build one of the largest and most influential companies in the world.

The narrative shifts to Walt Disney, whose creative vision and entrepreneurial spirit built a media empire. Disney's innovations in animation, the creation of iconic characters, and the expansion into theme parks and television redefined family entertainment. His legacy continues to influence the entertainment industry and corporate culture.

We also examine the transformative impact of Steve Jobs, the co-founder of Apple Inc. Jobs' vision for personal computing, combined with his design-centric approach, led to groundbreaking products like the Macintosh, iPod, iPhone, and iPad. His story is one of overcoming setbacks and driving market disruption, leaving a lasting impact on consumer electronics and technology.

Mary Barra's ascent to the helm of General Motors marks a significant chapter in the automotive industry. Her leadership and strategic initiatives in electric and autonomous vehicles are steering GM towards a sustainable future. Barra's efforts to build a strong corporate culture and her approach to diversity and inclusion offer valuable lessons for modern business leaders.

The tale of Robert Noyce, the co-founder of Fairchild Semiconductor and Intel, highlights the birth of the semiconductor industry. Noyce's innovations in integrated circuits and microprocessor technology paved the way for the digital age. His leadership style and collaborative culture at Intel have had a profound influence on modern technology companies.

Finally, we explore the story of Fred Smith, the founder of FedEx, whose vision for overnight delivery revolutionized logistics and global commerce. Smith's development of the hub-and-spoke distribution model and his focus on customer service set new standards in the industry. His strategies for rapid growth and innovation continue to influence logistics and supply chain management.

Each chapter of this book provides a detailed exploration of these extraordinary individuals—

examining their early lives, career milestones, innovative contributions, and enduring legacies. Their stories offer valuable insights into the principles of leadership, innovation, and strategic thinking that remain relevant in today's rapidly changing business landscape.

Through these narratives, we aim to inspire and inform, shedding light on the minds and strategies that have shaped the modern world. Whether you are a business professional, a student, or simply someone fascinated by the stories of great innovators, this book offers a comprehensive look at the titans who have driven progress and transformation across industries.

Welcome to an exploration of vision, ambition, and impact. Welcome to the lives of the leaders who revolutionized the world.

With Resilience and Hope,

Stephen Nalley

Contents

Acknowledgment: ii
About the Author: iii
Preface: iv

Chapter 1: Henry Ford - Innovating Mass Production

Chapter 2: John D. Rockefeller - Building a Petroleum Empire

Chapter 3: Andrew Carnegie - Steel Magnate and Philanthropist

Chapter 4: Thomas Edison - Innovator and Entrepreneur

Chapter 5: Sam Walton - Revolutionizing Retail

Chapter 6: Walt Disney - Creating a Media Empire

Chapter 7: Steve Jobs - Transforming Technology

Chapter 8: Mary Barra - Leading General Motors

Chapter 9: Robert Noyce - The Integrated Circuit Pioneer

Chapter 10: Fred Smith - Revolutionizing Logistics

Page Left Blank Intentionally

Chapter 1

Henry Ford Innovating Mass Production

Henry Ford was born on July 30, 1863, in Greenfield Township, Michigan, on a farm owned by his family. His father, William Ford, was an Irish immigrant, and his mother, Mary Litogot Ford, was of Belgian descent. Henry was the oldest of six children. His early life was shaped by a strong work ethic instilled by his parents and a deep fascination with machinery.

From a young age, Ford exhibited an intense curiosity about mechanical devices. At the age of 12, he received a pocket watch from his father, which he promptly dismantled and reassembled. This early tinkering earned him a reputation as a watch repairman among his neighbors. Ford's mechanical aptitude was evident, and he spent his free time working on machinery and exploring how things worked.

In 1879, at the age of 16, Ford left home to work as an apprentice machinist in Detroit. He gained experience at James F. Flower & Bros. and later at the Detroit Dry Dock Company. These formative years provided

Ford with hands-on experience and a deeper understanding of the mechanics of machinery, laying the groundwork for his future innovations in the automotive industry.

Entry into the Automotive Industry

Ford's entry into the automotive industry began with his fascination with internal combustion engines. In 1891, he became an engineer with the Edison Illuminating Company in Detroit. By 1893, he had been promoted to Chief Engineer, which provided him with the time and resources to experiment with gasoline engines.

In 1896, Ford completed his first self-propelled vehicle, the Quadricycle. This vehicle had four bicycle wheels and was powered by a two-cylinder, four-horsepower engine. The Quadricycle was a significant milestone for Ford, as it demonstrated the feasibility of his ideas and solidified his resolve to pursue automobile manufacturing.

Ford continued to refine his designs and, in 1899, left Edison to join the Detroit Automobile Company. However, the company faced financial difficulties and was dissolved in 1901. Undeterred, Ford designed a 26-horsepower automobile and raced it, winning a competition and gaining investor interest. This success led to the establishment of the Henry Ford Company in 1901, which he eventually left d
ue to differences with his financial backers.

Founding the Ford Motor Company

In 1903, Henry Ford founded the Ford Motor Company with 11 investors and $28,000 in capital. The company's first car, the Model A, was assembled at a rented factory on Mack Avenue in Detroit. Ford's vision for the automobile industry was centered on producing affordable, reliable cars for the average American.

The Ford Motor Company's early years were marked by several key innovations and business strategies. Ford focused on improving the efficiency of production processes, which was crucial for reducing costs and making automobiles more accessible to the public. One of his early successes was the Model N, which sold for $600 and became popular due to its affordability and reliability.

Ford's vision was not just about creating affordable cars but also about transforming transportation and society. He believed that the automobile could democratize mobility, allowing people to travel greater distances and connect with others more easily. This vision guided his relentless pursuit of innovation and efficiency in manufacturing.

Vision for the Automobile Industry

Henry Ford's vision for the automobile industry extended beyond mere production. He imagined a world where automobiles were not just luxury items for the wealthy but essential tools for everyday life, accessible to the average person. This vision was revolutionary in an era when cars were largely considered luxury items.

Ford's commitment to affordability and quality led to the development of the Model T, introduced in 1908. The Model T was designed to be simple, durable, and easy to operate. It featured a rugged design that could handle the rough roads of the time and was priced at $850, significantly lower than many of its competitors.

To achieve his vision of mass affordability, Ford realized that he needed to revolutionize the manufacturing process. This realization led to the development of the moving assembly line, which dramatically increased production efficiency and lowered costs. The assembly line allowed Ford to produce cars at an unprecedented scale, making the Model T affordable for a broader audience.

Ford's vision also included better working conditions and wages for his employees. In 1914, he introduced the $5 workday, doubling the average wage of autoworkers at the time. This move was not only a response to high turnover rates but also a strategic decision to ensure a stable, motivated workforce that could produce high-quality automobiles efficiently.

Initial Challenges and Setbacks

Despite his eventual success, Henry Ford faced numerous challenges and setbacks in his early career. His first ventures in automobile manufacturing, including the Detroit Automobile Company and the Henry Ford Company, were fraught with financial difficulties and disagreements with investors.

One of the major challenges Ford faced was skepticism from investors and the public. Many people doubted the viability of affordable automobiles and were reluctant to invest in his vision. Additionally, Ford's early prototypes had technical issues that needed to be resolved, requiring significant time and resources.

Ford also encountered resistance to his innovative production methods. The introduction of the assembly line faced pushback from workers who were unaccustomed to the monotonous, repetitive nature of the work. Managing labor relations and maintaining morale became critical issues as the company scaled up production.

Another significant challenge was competition from established automobile manufacturers. Companies like General Motors and Chrysler had more resources and market presence, making it difficult for Ford to gain a foothold in the industry. However, Ford's relentless focus on innovation, efficiency, and affordability eventually allowed him to overcome these obstacles.

Henry Ford's early life and career were marked by a series of influential experiences and pivotal moments that shaped his approach to the automotive industry. His early fascination with mechanics, hands-on experience as a machinist, and relentless pursuit of innovation laid the foundation for his success. Despite numerous challenges and setbacks, Ford's vision for affordable, reliable automobiles and his revolutionary production methods transformed the industry and left an enduring legacy.

The Assembly Line Revolution

The introduction of the assembly line by Henry Ford marked a revolutionary transformation in manufacturing, fundamentally altering the way products were made and setting the stage for modern mass production. This section delves into the key aspects of this transformation, exploring the concept and implementation of the assembly line, its impact on production efficiency, cost reduction, the challenges and resistance faced, and its long-term implications for manufacturing.

Concept and Implementation of the Assembly Line

The concept of the assembly line is rooted in the idea of dividing labor into simple, repetitive tasks to increase efficiency and productivity. Henry Ford did not invent the assembly line, but he perfected its application in the automotive industry. The inspiration for the assembly line came from various sources, including the continuous-flow production methods used in flour mills, breweries, and the disassembly lines in meatpacking plants. However, Ford's most significant innovation was applying these principles to the complex process of automobile manufacturing.

Ford's vision for the assembly line was to create a system where the car would move from one workstation to the next, with each worker performing a specific task. This method differed from the traditional craft production, where individual workers built entire vehicles or large parts of them. By breaking down the manufacturing process into smaller tasks, Ford aimed to reduce the time and effort required to produce each car.

The first moving assembly line was introduced at Ford's Highland Park plant in Michigan in 1913. The initial implementation was for the production of magneto coils, but the success of this experiment quickly led to the application of the assembly line to the entire manufacturing process of the Model T. The assembly line consisted of a conveyor belt that moved parts along a predetermined path, with workers stationed at various points along the line to perform specific tasks. This innovation drastically reduced the time required to assemble a car from more than 12 hours to just about 90 minutes.

Impact on Production Efficiency

The implementation of the assembly line had a profound impact on production efficiency. By standardizing and simplifying tasks, the assembly line allowed Ford to produce cars at an unprecedented rate. The efficiency gains were evident in several areas:

- Increased Speed of Production: The assembly line significantly reduced the time needed to assemble a car. With each worker performing a specific, repetitive task, the production process became much faster. This increase in speed enabled Ford to produce more cars in a shorter amount of time.

- Consistency and Quality: The standardization of tasks ensured that each car was assembled in the same way, reducing variability and improving the overall quality of the final product. Consistency in the manufacturing process also meant that defects were easier to identify and rectify.

- Labor Efficiency: The division of labor into simple tasks allowed Ford to employ workers with less specialized skills, reducing the dependency on highly skilled craftsmen. This approach not only lowered labor costs but also made it easier to train new workers.

- Inventory Management: The continuous flow of parts along the assembly line reduced the need for large inventories of finished components. This just-in-time approach to manufacturing minimized waste and optimized the use of materials.

- Innovation in Tooling and Equipment: To support the assembly line, Ford invested in specialized tools and equipment that further enhanced productivity. Innovations such as automatic screw machines and conveyor belts were critical in maintaining the efficiency of the assembly line.

Reducing Costs and Making Cars Affordable

One of the most significant outcomes of the assembly line was the dramatic reduction in production costs.

The efficiency gains achieved through the assembly line allowed Ford to lower the price of the Model T, making it affordable for a broader segment of the population. This democratization of the automobile had far-reaching social and economic impacts.

- Economies of Scale: The ability to produce cars in large quantities reduced the per-unit cost of production. These economies of scale allowed Ford to pass on the savings to consumers in the form of lower prices.

- Reduced Labor Costs: By simplifying tasks and employing less skilled labor, Ford was able to reduce labor costs. The introduction of the $5 workday, while initially increasing labor costs, ultimately led to higher productivity and lower turnover rates, further reducing overall labor expenses.

- Lower Material Costs: The efficient use of materials and the reduction of waste through the just-in-time production model lowered material costs. Ford's vertical integration strategy, which included owning raw material sources and transportation networks, also contributed to cost reductions.

- Increased Market Demand: The affordability of the Model T made it accessible to the average American, leading to a surge in demand. The increased sales volume further reinforced economies of scale and drove down costs.

- Consumer Financing: Ford's innovative

approach to consumer financing, including installment payment plans, made it easier for consumers to purchase cars, thereby expanding the market and increasing sales.

Challenges and Resistance Faced

Despite its success, the implementation of the assembly line faced significant challenges and resistance. These obstacles came from various quarters, including workers, competitors, and even within the Ford Motor Company.

- Worker Resistance: The monotonous and repetitive nature of assembly line work led to high turnover rates and dissatisfaction among workers. Many workers found the work dehumanizing and physically demanding, leading to resistance and strikes.

- Management Challenges: Implementing and maintaining an efficient assembly line required rigorous management and oversight. Coordinating the flow of parts and ensuring that each station operated smoothly was a complex task that demanded constant attention.

- Technical Issues: The introduction of new machinery and equipment often led to technical problems that needed to be resolved. Ensuring that all components fit together seamlessly required precision engineering and frequent adjustments.

- Competitor Reactions: Competitors quickly recognized the advantages of the assembly line and sought to implement similar systems. This increased competition put pressure on Ford to continually innovate and improve its processes.

- Quality Control: Maintaining consistent quality across a rapidly moving assembly line was a significant challenge. Ensuring that each car met Ford's high standards required stringent quality control measures and constant monitoring.

- Economic Fluctuations: The cyclical nature of the economy posed challenges for maintaining steady production levels. Economic downturns led to reduced demand for automobiles, necessitating adjustments in production schedules and workforce levels.

Long-term Implications for Manufacturing

The introduction of the assembly line by Henry Ford had long-term implications that extended far beyond the automotive industry. The principles of mass production and efficiency that Ford pioneered became the foundation of modern manufacturing.

- Standardization and Efficiency: The assembly line set a new standard for production efficiency and standardization. The principles of dividing labor into specialized tasks and using assembly lines were adopted by various industries, from electronics to consumer goods.

- Industrial Growth: The efficiency gains achieved through mass production contributed to the rapid growth of industries and economies. The ability to produce goods quickly and at lower costs fueled industrial expansion and economic development.

- Labor Practices: The assembly line revolutionized labor practices, leading to the development of new labor management techniques and employee welfare programs. The $5 workday introduced by Ford became a benchmark for fair wages and employee benefits.

- Technological Innovation: The need to maintain and improve assembly lines drove technological innovation in machinery, tools, and production techniques. Advances in automation, robotics, and information technology can trace their roots back to the innovations sparked by the assembly line.

- Global Impact: The principles of mass production and assembly line techniques spread globally, influencing manufacturing practices worldwide. Countries around the world adopted these methods to boost their industrial capabilities and compete in the global market.

- Consumer Culture: The mass production of affordable goods, starting with the Model T, helped create a consumer culture centered around accessible, standardized products. This shift transformed how products were marketed, sold, and consumed.

The assembly line revolution spearheaded by Henry Ford transformed the manufacturing landscape, setting the stage for modern mass production. The concept and implementation of the assembly line drastically improved production efficiency, reduced costs, and made automobiles affordable to the masses. Despite facing significant challenges and resistance, the long-term implications of the assembly line extended far beyond the automotive industry, influencing labor practices, technological innovation, and global manufacturing standards. Ford's pioneering work laid the foundation for the industrial growth and consumer culture that characterize the modern world.

Labor Relations and the Five-Dollar Day

The introduction of the $5 workday by Henry Ford in 1914 was a groundbreaking moment in labor management and industrial history. This section explores the rationale behind this decision, its impact on employee welfare and productivity, the controversies and criticisms it sparked, Ford's relations with labor unions, and the enduring legacy of this revolutionary approach to labor management. Introduction of the $5 Workday

On January 5, 1914, Henry Ford announced that he would more than double the daily wage of his workers from $2.34 to $5. This move was not just an increase in wages; it also included a reduction in the workday from nine hours to eight. The announcement sent shockwaves through the business community and made headlines worldwide.

- Rationale Behind the Decision: Ford's decision was driven by multiple factors, including the high turnover rates and absenteeism that plagued his factories. By offering higher wages and shorter hours, Ford aimed to attract and retain a stable, loyal, and efficient workforce.

- Economic Incentive: Ford believed that by paying his workers better, they would, in turn, be able to afford the products they made, thus driving demand for the Model T. This concept was a practical application of the principle of "Fordism," where higher wages for workers lead to increased consumption and economic growth.

- Public Relations Strategy: The announcement also served as a brilliant public relations move. It portrayed Ford as a progressive employer who cared about the welfare of his workers, enhancing the company's public image and helping to distinguish it from competitors.

- Production Efficiency: By increasing wages and reducing working hours, Ford anticipated an increase in productivity. A well-paid and well-rested worker was expected to work more efficiently, with higher motivation and better focus.

- Social Experimentation: The $5 workday was also part of Ford's broader social experimentation, where he sought to engineer a more orderly, disciplined, and productive workforce through better pay and strict behavioral guidelines.

Impact on Employee Welfare and Productivity

The introduction of the $5 workday had profound and immediate impacts on employee welfare and productivity at Ford's factories.

- Reduction in Turnover and Absenteeism: One of the most significant effects was a dramatic reduction in employee turnover and absenteeism. Prior to the increase, the turnover rate at Ford was extremely high, with many workers leaving due to the grueling conditions and low pay. The $5 workday created a stable workforce, with workers more inclined to stay due to the attractive wages.

- Increased Productivity: The increase in wages and the reduction in working hours led to a significant boost in productivity. Workers were more motivated and could maintain a higher level of focus and efficiency throughout the workday. The promise of higher pay also incentivized employees to perform better.

- Improved Living Standards: For many workers, the $5 wage meant a substantial improvement in their living standards. They could afford better housing, education, and overall quality of life. This uplift in living standards had a positive ripple effect on the communities where

Ford's workers lived.

- Enhanced Loyalty and Morale: The wage increase fostered a sense of loyalty and morale among the workforce. Workers felt valued and appreciated, which translated into a stronger commitment to the company and its goals.

- Economic Stimulus: The additional income earned by workers also acted as an economic stimulus. As Ford's employees spent their higher wages, demand for goods and services in the local economy increased, contributing to broader economic growth.

Controversies and Criticisms

Despite its benefits, the $5 workday was not without its controversies and criticisms.

- Business Community Backlash: Many business leaders criticized Ford's decision, fearing that it would lead to wage inflation across the industry. They were concerned that other companies would be forced to raise wages to compete, which could increase costs and reduce profits.

- Worker Scrutiny: The wage increase came with conditions. Ford introduced a Sociological Department that monitored workers' lifestyles to ensure they adhered to certain standards of behavior, including sobriety and cleanliness. This intrusion into workers' private lives was seen by many as paternalistic and invasive.

- Labor Union Skepticism: While the wage increase was beneficial for workers, it was also viewed with skepticism by labor unions. They feared that Ford's actions were an attempt to undermine union influence by directly addressing worker grievances and needs.

- Public Perception: Some critics argued that the wage increase was more about public relations than genuine concern for workers. They saw it as a strategy to attract media attention and create a positive public image for Ford.

- Economic Concerns: Economists debated the sustainability of such high wages. They questioned whether the productivity gains and increased sales would be sufficient to offset the higher labor costs in the long term.

Relations with Labor Unions

Henry Ford's relationship with labor unions was complex and often contentious. Despite the seemingly worker-friendly $5 workday, Ford was staunchly anti-union.

- Anti-Union Stance: Ford was a firm believer in direct negotiation between employer and employee, without the intervention of unions. He felt that unions were unnecessary and counterproductive to the efficient operation of his factories.

- Union Avoidance Strategies: To keep unions at

bay, Ford employed various strategies, including providing high wages and good working conditions to keep workers satisfied. He also used surveillance and hired spies to identify and weed out union organizers.

- Labor Disputes: Despite his efforts, labor disputes were inevitable. The most notable was the Battle of the Overpass in 1937, where Ford's security forces violently clashed with union organizers. This incident drew national attention and highlighted the growing tension between Ford and labor unions.

- Unionization of Ford Plants: It wasn't until 1941, under pressure from the UAW (United Auto Workers) and amidst broader labor movements, that Ford Motor Company officially recognized the union. The recognition of the UAW marked a significant shift in labor relations at Ford.

- Legacy in Labor Management: Ford's complex relationship with unions left a lasting legacy in labor management. While his high-wage policies were progressive, his anti-union stance created a contentious atmosphere that persisted for years. The eventual unionization of Ford plants underscored the importance of collective bargaining in labor relations.

Legacy in Labor Management

The introduction of the $5 workday had a profound and lasting impact on labor management practices, not just at Ford but across industries.

- Setting Wage Standards: Ford's decision to raise wages set a new standard for industrial labor. Other companies, in an effort to attract and retain workers, were compelled to raise wages and improve working conditions.

- Human Resources Development: The focus on employee welfare and productivity at Ford laid the groundwork for the development of human resources as a distinct management function. Companies began to see the value in investing in their workforce through better wages, benefits, and working conditions.

- Corporate Responsibility: Ford's approach to labor management emphasized the role of corporations in ensuring the welfare of their employees. This principle became a cornerstone of corporate social responsibility, influencing how companies interacted with their workforce and communities.

- Labor Relations Framework: The challenges and successes of Ford's labor management strategies contributed to the development of a more structured labor relations framework. The recognition of unions and the establishment of collective bargaining practices became integral to labor management in the industrial sector.

- Influence on Modern Practices: The principles underlying the $5 workday continue to influence modern labor management practices. The emphasis on fair wages, good working conditions, and employee welfare remains central to contemporary human resources strategies. Companies today recognize that a well-compensated and motivated workforce is crucial for long-term success.

The introduction of the $5 workday by Henry Ford was a landmark moment in labor management, with far-reaching impacts on employee welfare, productivity, labor relations, and corporate responsibility. While it faced its share of controversies and criticisms, the innovative approach to wage management set new standards and left an enduring legacy in the world of business. Ford's strategy not only transformed his company but also influenced labor practices across industries, shaping the modern landscape of labor management.

Market Strategy and Competition

Henry Ford's innovative market strategies and response to competition were pivotal in establishing Ford Motor Company as a dominant force in the automotive industry. This section explores Ford's market positioning strategies, his response to competitors like General Motors, innovations in marketing and sales, building the Ford brand, and lessons for modern competitive strategy.

Ford's Market Positioning Strategies

Henry Ford's market positioning strategies were groundbreaking and transformed the automobile industry. He focused on making cars affordable and accessible to the average American, a vision that guided his market strategies and differentiated Ford from competitors.

- Affordability and Accessibility: Ford's primary market positioning strategy was to make cars affordable for the average American. By introducing the assembly line, he significantly reduced production costs, allowing him to lower the price of the Model T. This strategy made car ownership possible for the masses, not just the wealthy.

- Standardization and Simplification: Ford believed in standardizing production to achieve economies of scale. By producing a single model (the Model T) with limited variations, he simplified the manufacturing process and reduced costs. This standardization was a key component of his market positioning, as it allowed for consistent quality and reliability at a lower price.

- Focus on Reliability and Durability: Ford positioned the Model T as a reliable and durable vehicle that could withstand rough roads and long distances. This focus on reliability resonated with consumers who needed a dependable means of transportation. The slogan "Built Ford Tough" encapsulated this positioning and became synonymous with the brand.

- Innovative Financing Options: To make cars

even more accessible, Ford introduced innovative financing options, including installment plans. This allowed more people to afford cars by spreading the cost over time. These financing options expanded the market and increased sales.

- Geographic Expansion: Ford's market positioning also included a focus on geographic expansion. He built assembly plants in different regions, including international locations, to reduce shipping costs and adapt to local markets. This expansion helped Ford reach a global audience and establish a strong international presence.

Response to Competitors Like General Motors

Ford's success attracted competition, most notably from General Motors (GM). GM, under the leadership of Alfred P. Sloan, implemented strategies that challenged Ford's dominance. Ford's response to this competition was crucial in maintaining its market position.

- Product Diversification: Unlike Ford's one-model strategy, GM introduced a multi-brand strategy, offering a range of vehicles to cater to different market segments. Ford eventually responded by diversifying its product line, introducing new models to compete with GM's offerings.

- Adoption of Annual Model Changes: GM's strategy of annual model changes appealed to consumers' desire for new and updated features. Ford, initially resistant to this approach, eventually adopted annual model changes to keep up with consumer expectations and remain competitive.

- **Improving Customer Service:** GM focused on improving customer service and building a strong dealer network. Ford responded by enhancing its dealer relationships and investing in customer service initiatives to improve the overall buying experience and customer satisfaction.

- **Technological Innovations:** GM's investment in technological innovations, such as automatic transmissions and advanced safety features, pressured Ford to accelerate its own technological advancements. Ford increased its R&D efforts to introduce new technologies and stay competitive.

- **Marketing and Branding Strategies:** GM's aggressive marketing and branding strategies highlighted the lifestyle aspects of car ownership. Ford responded by refining its marketing strategies, emphasizing the practical benefits of its vehicles while also incorporating elements of lifestyle branding.

Innovations in Marketing and Sales

Henry Ford's innovations in marketing and sales played a significant role in establishing Ford as a household name and driving the company's success.

- Mass Marketing Campaigns: Ford was one of the first companies to use mass marketing campaigns to reach a wide audience. His use of newspapers, magazines, and later, radio advertisements helped build widespread awareness of the Ford brand and its products.

- Branding and Corporate Identity: Ford understood the importance of branding and created a strong corporate identity. The blue oval logo and the consistent use of the Ford name in marketing materials helped create a recognizable and trusted brand.

- Public Relations and Media Engagement: Ford actively engaged with the media to generate positive publicity. His public appearances, factory tours for journalists, and strategic press releases helped shape public perception and build a favorable image of the company.

- Innovative Sales Techniques: Ford introduced several innovative sales techniques, including the "Ford Times" magazine, which featured stories about Ford vehicles and their owners. This publication helped build a community around the Ford brand and fostered customer loyalty.

- Dealer Network Expansion: Ford's strategy of building a strong dealer network was crucial for its sales success. By establishing dealerships in various locations, Ford ensured that customers had easy access to its vehicles and services. The company also provided support and training to dealers to maintain high standards of customer service.

Building the Ford Brand

Building a strong brand was central to Henry Ford's strategy for long-term success. The Ford brand became synonymous with innovation, reliability, and affordability, values that were meticulously cultivated through various initiatives.

- Consistency in Quality and Messaging: Ford emphasized consistency in the quality of its vehicles and in its marketing messages. This consistency helped build trust with consumers and established Ford as a reliable and dependable brand.

- Community Engagement and Social Responsibility: Ford's efforts to engage with communities and demonstrate social responsibility further strengthened the brand. Initiatives such as the $5 workday and contributions to public projects positioned Ford as a company that cared about its employees and society.

- Innovation and Technological Leadership: The Ford brand was closely associated with innovation and technological leadership. The introduction of the assembly line and continuous improvements in manufacturing processes reinforced the image of Ford as a pioneer in the automotive industry.

- Customer-Centric Approach: Ford's focus on understanding and meeting customer needs was a key aspect of its branding strategy. By offering affordable and reliable vehicles, Ford positioned itself as a customer-centric company that prioritized consumer satisfaction.

- Leveraging Media and Publicity: Ford skillfully leveraged media and publicity to build and maintain its brand image. Positive media coverage of Ford's innovations, business practices, and philanthropic efforts helped create a favorable public perception of the brand.

Lessons for Modern Competitive Strategy

Henry Ford's strategies and responses to competition offer valuable lessons for modern businesses. His innovative approaches to market positioning, competition, marketing, branding, and labor relations provide timeless insights for today's competitive landscape.

- Embrace Innovation and Efficiency: Ford's success was built on continuous innovation and efficiency improvements. Modern businesses should prioritize innovation in products, processes, and business models to stay ahead of the competition.

- Focus on Customer Needs: Understanding and addressing customer needs was central to

Ford's strategy. Businesses today should adopt a customer-centric approach, using data and feedback to tailor products and services to meet evolving consumer demands.

- Build a Strong Brand Identity: Ford's emphasis on branding and corporate identity helped create a lasting legacy. Companies should invest in building strong brand identities that reflect their values, mission, and unique selling propositions.

- Adapt to Market Changes: Ford's ability to adapt to competitive pressures and market changes was crucial for its success. Modern businesses should remain flexible and responsive to market dynamics, continuously assessing and adjusting their strategies.

- Invest in Employee Welfare and Corporate Responsibility: Ford's introduction of the $5 workday and focus on employee welfare demonstrated the importance of valuing and investing in the workforce. Companies today should prioritize employee well-being and corporate social responsibility to build a motivated and loyal workforce.

Henry Ford's market strategies and competitive responses were instrumental in shaping the automotive industry and establishing Ford as a dominant player. His innovative approaches to affordability, efficiency, branding, and labor relations offer enduring lessons for modern businesses navigating today's competitive landscape. By embracing these principles, companies can achieve long-term success and build lasting legacies in their respective industries.

Case Study: The Model T

Development and Design of the Model T

The Ford Model T, introduced in 1908 by Henry Ford and his team, marked a pivotal moment in automotive history. Designed to be affordable, reliable, and easy to maintain, the Model T represented a departure from the luxury status of early automobiles. Henry Ford envisioned a car that could be mass-produced using assembly line techniques, making it accessible to the average American family.

The development process was a culmination of Ford's innovative spirit and his commitment to engineering simplicity. With its sturdy chassis, high ground clearance, and robust tires, the Model T was tailored for the rough roads of the time. Its four-cylinder engine provided sufficient power while maintaining efficiency, setting a new standard for automotive design.

Production and Sales Success

Ford's implementation of the moving assembly line in 1913 revolutionized manufacturing, significantly reducing production time and costs. This breakthrough allowed Ford to scale up production of the Model T dramatically. By 1927, when production ceased, over 15 million Model Ts had been manufactured, making it one of the most widely produced cars of its era.

The affordability of the Model T—initially priced at around $850—further bolstered its popularity. As production efficiencies drove costs down, Ford passed on savings to consumers, eventually reducing the price to just $260 by 1925. This price reduction made car ownership feasible for a broader segment of the population, transforming the Model T from a novelty into an essential commodity.

Influence on American Society

The Model T's impact on American society was profound and multifaceted. It democratized mobility, enabling individuals and families to travel greater distances with ease. This newfound mobility spurred the growth of suburbs and facilitated urbanization, as commuting became more practical. The automobile also catalyzed economic opportunities, fostering industries such as tourism, roadside accommodations, and the petroleum sector.

Socially, the Model T catalyzed a cultural shift, symbolizing freedom and independence. It became a status symbol, signifying upward mobility and modernity. Its ubiquity in everyday life reshaped American norms, influencing leisure activities, dating customs, and even family dynamics.

Evolution of the Automobile Market

The success of the Model T catalyzed rapid evolution within the automobile industry. Competitors sought to emulate Ford's mass-production techniques and affordability. Innovations in design and engineering proliferated, leading to improvements in safety, comfort, and performance. The Model T's dominance spurred the development of a diverse range of vehicles catering to different consumer preferences, from luxury sedans to rugged trucks.

Moreover, the Model T's success encouraged automakers to innovate in marketing and distribution. Advertising campaigns promoted cars as symbols of modernity and adventure, appealing to a broader audience beyond traditional elites.

Enduring Legacy of the Model T

Despite ceasing production in 1927, the Model T's legacy endures as a testament to automotive innovation and industrial prowess. Its assembly line production techniques became a benchmark for efficiency in manufacturing across industries. The Model T's affordability and mass-market appeal laid the foundation for Ford's continued success and established the United States as a global leader in automotive manufacturing.

Culturally, the Model T remains a nostalgic icon, celebrated in museums, vintage car shows, and popular media. Its legacy as the car that "put America on wheels" resonates with historians and enthusiasts alike, reminding us of its pivotal role in shaping the modern world.

Chapter 2:

John D. Rockefeller - Building a Petroleum Empire

John Davison Rockefeller was born on July 8, 1839, in Richford, New York. His father, William Avery Rockefeller, was a traveling salesman and a somewhat dubious figure who often dabbled in various schemes. Known for his charm and persuasive abilities, William Avery often sold goods, including elixirs and remedies, to earn a living. In stark contrast, Rockefeller's mother, Eliza Davison Rockefeller, was a devout Baptist who instilled in her children values of thrift, hard work, and morality.

Growing up in a household with six siblings, John experienced a life of modest means. Despite the financial instability caused by his father's unpredictable ventures, Eliza ensured that the household ran smoothly. She taught John the importance of saving and prudent financial management, lessons that he would carry throughout his life. John's upbringing was a blend of his father's entrepreneurial spirit and his mother's ethical grounding, setting the stage for his future success in the business world.

Entry into the Oil Industry

Rockefeller's entry into the oil industry began after a series of ventures in various businesses. At 16, he started working as a bookkeeper for a small produce commission firm, Hewitt & Tuttle, in Cleveland, Ohio. This experience honed his skills in finance and taught him the intricacies of business operations. By 1859, he had saved enough to venture into a business partnership with Maurice B. Clark, forming Clark & Rockefeller, a commission merchant business dealing in hay, grain, meats, and other goods.

The same year marked the discovery of oil in Titusville, Pennsylvania, which sparked the Pennsylvania oil rush. Recognizing the burgeoning opportunity, Rockefeller and his partner invested in a refinery in 1863. They established the Andrews, Clark & Co. refinery with Samuel Andrews, a chemist with refining expertise. This move marked Rockefeller's official entry into the oil industry.

Founding of Standard Oil

In 1870, Rockefeller took a significant step by founding the Standard Oil Company with his brother William Rockefeller, Henry Flagler, Samuel Andrews, Stephen V. Harkness, and O.B. Jennings. The company was established in Ohio, with Rockefeller as its driving force. The aim was to consolidate the fragmented oil industry and bring order and efficiency to its operations.

From its inception, Standard Oil focused on refining oil rather than drilling, as Rockefeller believed

refining offered more stable and lucrative opportunities. The company quickly expanded its refining capacity by acquiring competitors and investing in technological advancements. Standard Oil's systematic approach to refining, distribution, and sales soon set it apart from its competitors.
Vision for the Petroleum Industry

Rockefeller's vision for the petroleum industry was comprehensive and ambitious. He aimed to create a vertically integrated company that controlled every aspect of the oil business, from production to distribution. His belief in efficiency and economies of scale drove this vision. By owning and controlling the entire supply chain, Rockefeller sought to minimize costs, improve product quality, and ensure stable market conditions.

He envisioned a standardized and reliable supply of petroleum products that could meet the growing demands of industrialization and urbanization. Rockefeller's strategic foresight included the development of infrastructure, such as pipelines, tank cars, and storage facilities, which would facilitate the smooth transportation and distribution of oil products. He also recognized the importance of byproducts, investing in research to develop new products from refining residues, further maximizing profitability.

Early Business Strategies

Rockefeller employed several innovative and aggressive business strategies to achieve his vision:

- Horizontal Integration: Rockefeller's early strategy involved horizontal integration, which entailed buying out competing refineries. By consolidating multiple refineries under Standard Oil's control, he could achieve economies of scale, reduce competition, and increase market share. This approach allowed Standard Oil to dominate the refining sector and set industry standards.

- Vertical Integration: Rockefeller also pursued vertical integration by acquiring businesses involved in every stage of the oil production process. This included purchasing oil fields, pipelines, tankers, and retail outlets. By controlling the entire supply chain, Standard Oil could better manage costs, ensure product quality, and stabilize prices.

- Cost Efficiency: Rockefeller was a master of cost management. He introduced rigorous cost-cutting measures, negotiated favorable deals with suppliers and railroads, and invested in technology to improve refining efficiency. His focus on reducing production costs allowed Standard Oil to offer lower prices than competitors, driving many out of business.

- Rebates and Transportation Deals: One of Rockefeller's most controversial strategies was negotiating secret rebates with railroads. These rebates reduced Standard Oil's transportation costs and gave it a significant advantage over competitors. Additionally, Rockefeller secured preferential rates and drawbacks (refunds on standard rates paid by competitors), further consolidating Standard Oil's market dominance.

- Predatory Pricing: Rockefeller didn't hesitate to engage in predatory pricing. Standard Oil would temporarily lower prices in specific markets to drive competitors out of business. Once they had monopolized the market, they would raise prices to recoup losses. This strategy was effective in eliminating competition and expanding Standard Oil's influence.

- Innovation and Research: Recognizing the value of innovation, Rockefeller invested in research and development. Standard Oil's laboratories worked on improving refining processes and developing new products. Innovations like the Frasch process for sulfur removal and the development of kerosene for lighting revolutionized the industry and opened new markets.

- Legal and Corporate Strategies: To manage its vast operations and mitigate legal challenges, Standard Oil adopted a trust structure in 1882. This structure centralized control under a board of trustees, enabling Rockefeller to manage the company more efficiently and circumvent state-level regulations. The trust structure set a precedent for future corporate governance.

John D. Rockefeller's rise from humble beginnings to the founder of Standard Oil epitomizes the transformative power of vision, strategic thinking, and relentless pursuit of efficiency. By employing innovative business strategies and leveraging his keen understanding of the industry, Rockefeller built a petroleum empire that revolutionized the oil business and set new standards for industrial operations.

His legacy is multifaceted, reflecting both the remarkable achievements and the ethical controversies that accompanied his methods. While Rockefeller's monopolistic practices drew criticism and led to significant legal challenges, his contributions to industrial efficiency, innovation, and philanthropy remain influential.

The Standard Oil Company not only shaped the petroleum industry but also left an indelible mark on American business practices, corporate structures, and economic policies. Rockefeller's life and career offer valuable lessons in leadership, strategic planning, and the complexities of balancing business success with ethical considerations.

Monopolization and Expansion

Techniques for Gaining Control of the Oil Market

John D. Rockefeller's strategy for gaining control of the oil market was multifaceted, combining innovative business tactics, strategic acquisitions, and a relentless pursuit of efficiency. Rockefeller and his associates at Standard Oil employed several key techniques to dominate the oil industry:

- Strategic Acquisitions: Rockefeller strategically acquired competing refineries and oil companies across the United States. This aggressive expansion was aimed at consolidating the market and eliminating competition. By purchasing rivals, Standard Oil could control a larger share of the market and achieve economies of scale, which allowed for more efficient operations and lower costs.

- Predatory Pricing: Standard Oil often engaged in predatory pricing to drive competitors out of business. By temporarily lowering prices to unprofitable levels, Standard Oil could undercut competitors who lacked the financial resources to sustain losses. Once the competition was eliminated, Standard Oil would raise prices to recoup its losses and establish a monopoly in that market.

- Exclusive Transportation Deals: Rockefeller secured preferential rates and rebates from railroads for transporting Standard Oil's products. These secret deals gave Standard Oil a significant cost advantage over competitors, who had to pay higher transportation fees. By controlling the transportation network, Standard Oil could further consolidate its hold on the market.

- Pipeline Networks: Standard Oil invested heavily in building its own pipeline network to transport crude oil from production sites to refineries. By owning and controlling the pipelines, Standard Oil could bypass the railroads and ensure a steady supply of oil to its refineries at a lower cost. This vertical integration further strengthened its market position.

- Innovative Refining Techniques: Standard Oil continuously invested in research and development to improve refining processes. Innovations such as the Frasch process for sulfur removal and advancements in cracking technology allowed Standard Oil to produce higher quality products more efficiently, giving it a competitive edge in the market.

Horizontal and Vertical Integration

Rockefeller's strategy of horizontal and vertical integration was instrumental in Standard Oil's monopolistic growth:

- Horizontal Integration: Horizontal integration involved the acquisition of competing refineries and oil companies to consolidate the market. By bringing multiple refineries under the umbrella of Standard Oil, Rockefeller could streamline operations, reduce redundant costs, and achieve greater control over pricing and production. This approach allowed Standard Oil to dominate the refining sector and create a near-monopoly in the industry.

- Vertical Integration: Vertical integration extended Standard Oil's control across the entire supply chain, from oil extraction to distribution. This strategy involved acquiring or developing businesses at every stage of the oil production process, including drilling, refining, transportation, and retail distribution. By owning the entire supply chain, Standard Oil could ensure a consistent supply of raw materials, control production costs, and maximize profits.

Expansion into Refining and Distribution

Standard Oil's expansion into refining and distribution was a key aspect of its growth strategy:

- Refining Expansion: Standard Oil systematically expanded its refining capacity by acquiring existing refineries and building new ones. This expansion allowed Standard Oil to process a larger volume of crude oil and produce a greater variety of refined products, such as kerosene, gasoline, and lubricants. By controlling the majority of refining capacity in the United States, Standard Oil could influence market prices and supply.

- Distribution Network: Standard Oil developed an extensive distribution network to ensure its products reached consumers efficiently. This network included storage facilities, tank cars, pipelines, and retail outlets. By controlling distribution, Standard Oil could reduce costs, maintain product quality, and ensure a reliable supply to meet market demand.

Anti-Competitive Practices

While effective, many of Standard Oil's business practices were deemed anti-competitive and drew significant criticism and legal scrutiny:

- Price Fixing: Standard Oil engaged in price fixing to eliminate competition and maintain its monopoly. By artificially manipulating prices, Standard Oil could force competitors out of the market and discourage new entrants. This practice undermined free market competition and led to public outcry.

- Market Division: Standard Oil often made agreements with railroads and other oil companies to divide markets and territories. These agreements allowed Standard Oil to operate without competition in specific regions, further consolidating its control over the industry.

- Political Influence: Standard Oil used its financial resources to influence politicians and regulators, lobbying for favorable legislation and regulatory practices. This political influence helped Standard Oil maintain its monopoly and stifle attempts at regulation or competition.

- Rebates and Drawbacks: Standard Oil negotiated secret rebates and drawbacks with railroads, giving it preferential treatment and lower transportation costs. These agreements were often not extended to competitors, giving

Standard Oil an unfair advantage in the market.

Impact on the Oil Industry

The impact of Rockefeller's strategies on the oil industry was profound and far-reaching:

- Industrial Standardization: Standard Oil's emphasis on efficiency and innovation set new benchmarks for the industry. Its investments in refining technology and distribution infrastructure improved the overall quality and reliability of oil products, benefiting consumers and other industries reliant on petroleum.

- Economic Influence: The success of Standard Oil made Rockefeller one of the wealthiest individuals in history, and the company became a cornerstone of the American economy. Standard Oil's dominance in the market influenced economic policies, business practices, and the development of corporate structures.

- Regulatory Responses: Standard Oil's monopolistic practices eventually led to significant legal and regulatory responses. The Sherman Antitrust Act of 1890 was enacted to combat monopolies and restore competition in the market. In 1911, the U.S. Supreme Court ruled that Standard Oil violated antitrust laws and ordered its dissolution into 34 smaller companies. This landmark case set a precedent for antitrust enforcement and corporate regulation.

- Legacy: Despite its dissolution, Standard Oil's legacy endures through its successor companies, such as ExxonMobil, Chevron, and BP, which continue to dominate the global oil industry. The strategies and innovations pioneered by Standard Oil have shaped modern business practices and industrial operations.

John D. Rockefeller's monopolization and expansion of the oil industry through Standard Oil exemplify the transformative power of strategic business practices and industrial innovation. By employing techniques such as horizontal and vertical integration, strategic acquisitions, and innovative refining processes, Rockefeller built a petroleum empire that revolutionized the industry.

However, the aggressive and often anti-competitive nature of Standard Oil's practices also highlights the complexities and ethical challenges of achieving market dominance. The legal and regulatory responses to Standard Oil's monopoly underscore the importance of maintaining competitive markets and safeguarding against monopolistic behavior.

Rockefeller's legacy is a testament to the impact of visionary leadership, strategic planning, and relentless pursuit of efficiency. His contributions to the oil industry and American business practices continue to influence modern corporate governance, economic policies, and industrial operations.

Philanthropy and Public Perception

Rockefeller's Philanthropic Efforts

John D. Rockefeller, one of the wealthiest individuals in history, dedicated a significant portion of his fortune to philanthropy. Motivated by his Baptist faith and the belief that his wealth was entrusted to him for the good of humanity, Rockefeller embarked on a journey to use his resources to address social issues and advance scientific knowledge. His philanthropic efforts were extensive and diverse, spanning education, medical research, public health, and social welfare.

Rockefeller's approach to philanthropy was systematic and strategic. He believed in addressing the root causes of social problems rather than merely alleviating symptoms. This philosophy led him to support initiatives that aimed to create long-term, sustainable improvements in society. His philanthropic endeavors were guided by the principle of "scientific philanthropy," which emphasized data-driven decision-making and the application of scientific methods to charitable work.

Establishment of Charitable Organizations

To institutionalize his philanthropic efforts, Rockefeller established several major charitable organizations that continue to have a profound impact on the world:

- The Rockefeller Foundation: Established in 1913 with an initial endowment of $100 million, the Rockefeller Foundation aimed to "promote the well-being of humanity throughout the world." The foundation's initiatives focused on public health, medical research, education, agriculture, and the arts. It played a pivotal role in eradicating diseases, advancing scientific research, and promoting international development.

- The General Education Board (GEB): Founded in 1902, the GEB was dedicated to improving education in the United States, particularly in the rural South. It funded the construction of schools, supported teacher training programs, and advocated for educational reforms. The GEB's work helped modernize and standardize the American education system.

- The Rockefeller Institute for Medical Research (now Rockefeller University): Established in 1901, this institute was one of the first research centers in the United States dedicated to biomedical research. It made significant contributions to the understanding and treatment of infectious diseases, including the discovery of the yellow fever virus and advances in immunology.

- The University of Chicago: Founded in 1890 with substantial funding from Rockefeller, the University of Chicago quickly became one of the leading research universities in the world. It emphasized rigorous academic standards and was a pioneer in various fields, including sociology, economics, and law.

Influence on Education and Medical Research

Rockefeller's philanthropic investments had a transformative impact on education and medical research:

- Education: Rockefeller's support for education extended beyond the GEB. He funded the establishment and expansion of numerous institutions, including Spelman College, a historically black women's college, and several other universities and schools. His contributions helped shape modern educational practices and increased access to education for marginalized communities.

- Medical Research: The Rockefeller Institute for Medical Research was at the forefront of scientific discovery. Its researchers made groundbreaking contributions to understanding diseases, developing vaccines, and advancing medical knowledge. The institute's work laid the foundation for modern biomedical research and influenced the creation of similar research institutions worldwide.

- Public Health: Rockefeller's interest in public health led to significant investments in efforts to combat diseases such as hookworm, malaria, and yellow fever. The Rockefeller Foundation's International Health Division conducted extensive public health campaigns, improving health outcomes in many countries and advancing the field of epidemiology.

Controversies and Criticisms

Despite his philanthropic achievements, Rockefeller's legacy is not without controversy and criticism:

- Monopolistic Practices: Critics argue that Rockefeller's wealth was amassed through monopolistic practices that exploited workers, stifled competition, and manipulated markets. Standard Oil's aggressive tactics led to public outcry and legal challenges, culminating in the company's breakup in 1911.

- Tainted Money: Some viewed Rockefeller's philanthropy as an attempt to sanitize his image and distract from the unethical business practices that built his fortune. The term "tainted money" was used to describe his donations, with detractors arguing that the ends did not justify the means.

- Social Engineering: Rockefeller's philanthropic efforts sometimes faced criticism for promoting social engineering and paternalism. His focus on systemic change and scientific philanthropy was seen by some as an attempt to impose his values and vision on society, raising concerns about democratic accountability and local autonomy.

Balancing Public Perception and Business Interests

Rockefeller's philanthropic activities were, in part, a response to the negative public perception of his business practices. Balancing his reputation and business interests required careful navigation:

- Public Relations Strategies: Rockefeller employed public relations strategies to improve his image. He engaged in high-profile philanthropic activities, such as funding educational institutions and medical research, to highlight the positive impact of his wealth. These efforts were designed to counteract the negative publicity surrounding Standard Oil's monopolistic practices.

- Transparency and Accountability: To build public trust, Rockefeller emphasized transparency and accountability in his philanthropic work. He established independent boards to oversee his foundations and ensure that funds were used effectively. This approach helped legitimize his charitable efforts and mitigate criticism.

- Legacy and Impact: Despite the controversies, Rockefeller's philanthropy left a lasting legacy. His charitable organizations have continued to advance education, medical research, and public health long after his death. The positive impact of his philanthropy on society has, to some extent, overshadowed the criticisms of his business practices.

John D. Rockefeller's philanthropy represents a significant chapter in the history of American philanthropy. His strategic and systematic approach to charitable giving set new standards for philanthropy, emphasizing the importance of addressing root causes and creating sustainable change.

While his business practices and the source of his wealth remain subjects of controversy, Rockefeller's contributions to education, medical research, and public health have had a profound and lasting impact on society. His philanthropic legacy continues to influence modern philanthropy, demonstrating the potential for wealth to be used for the greater good.

Rockefeller's life and work illustrate the complex interplay between business success and social responsibility. His story is a reminder that philanthropy can be both a tool for positive change and a means of navigating public perception and legacy. Through his charitable endeavors, Rockefeller left an indelible mark on the world, reflecting both the possibilities and the challenges of using wealth to shape society.

Legal Challenges and the Breakup of Standard Oil

Legal Battles and Antitrust Cases

John D. Rockefeller's Standard Oil Company dominated the oil industry in the late 19th and early 20th centuries through aggressive business tactics, strategic acquisitions, and innovative practices. However, its monopolistic approach and control over the market attracted significant legal scrutiny and public outcry.

The legal battles against Standard Oil were driven by increasing concerns over the company's anticompetitive practices and its dominance in the industry. Critics argued that Standard Oil's strategies—such as predatory pricing, securing exclusive deals with railroads, and using rebates to undermine competitors—violated the principles of free competition and harmed consumers.

One of the earliest significant legal challenges came in 1890, when the Ohio Supreme Court ordered Standard Oil of Ohio to dissolve due to its violation of state antitrust laws. In response, Rockefeller and his associates reorganized the company under the Standard Oil Trust, which centralized control over numerous subsidiaries. This move allowed Standard Oil to continue operating as a monopoly, despite state-level legal challenges.

The Sherman Antitrust Act

The federal government's response to monopolistic practices like those of Standard Oil was the Sherman Antitrust Act of 1890. Named after Senator John Sherman, this landmark legislation aimed to promote fair competition and prevent monopolies and trusts from restraining trade.

The Sherman Antitrust Act had two main provisions:

- Section 1: Prohibited contracts, combinations, and conspiracies in restraint of trade.

- Section 2: Made it illegal to monopolize, or

attempt to monopolize, any part of trade or commerce.

Despite its passage, enforcement of the Sherman Antitrust Act was initially weak. The federal government lacked the resources and political will to pursue major corporations aggressively. However, public pressure and political changes in the early 20th century led to more vigorous enforcement.

The Breakup of Standard Oil

The turning point in the legal battle against Standard Oil came with the administration of President Theodore Roosevelt, known for his "trust-busting" efforts. Roosevelt's administration took a more proactive stance in enforcing antitrust laws, targeting major monopolies, including Standard Oil.

In 1906, the federal government filed a lawsuit against Standard Oil under the Sherman Antitrust Act, accusing the company of maintaining a monopoly through unfair business practices and restraining trade. The case, officially titled Standard Oil Co. of New Jersey v. United States, culminated in a landmark Supreme Court decision in 1911.

The Supreme Court ruled that Standard Oil was indeed guilty of monopolistic practices and ordered its dissolution. The Court mandated that Standard Oil be broken up into 34 independent companies, effectively dismantling the monopoly. Some of the companies that emerged from the breakup included Exxon (originally Standard Oil of New Jersey), Mobil (originally Standard Oil of New York), Chevron

(originally Standard Oil of California), and others.
Long-term Impact on Business Practices

The breakup of Standard Oil had profound and far-reaching implications for business practices in the United States and beyond:

- Regulatory Framework: The case set a precedent for the enforcement of antitrust laws and shaped the regulatory framework governing corporate practices. It demonstrated the federal government's commitment to curbing monopolies and promoting fair competition.

- Corporate Behavior: The breakup sent a strong message to other large corporations about the consequences of monopolistic behavior. Businesses became more cautious in their strategies, avoiding practices that could be seen as anti-competitive to prevent legal repercussions.

- Market Competition: The dissolution of Standard Oil fostered greater competition in the oil industry. The newly independent companies competed against each other, leading to innovations, improved efficiency, and better services for consumers.

- Economic Policy: The case influenced economic policy, emphasizing the importance of maintaining competitive markets. It reinforced the role of government regulation in preventing monopolies and protecting consumer interests.

Lessons in Regulatory Compliance

The legal challenges and breakup of Standard Oil offer several valuable lessons in regulatory compliance for modern businesses:

- Adherence to Antitrust Laws: Companies must understand and comply with antitrust laws to avoid legal pitfalls. Engaging in practices that restrain trade, create monopolies, or undermine competition can lead to significant legal consequences and reputational damage.

- Transparency and Accountability: Maintaining transparency in business operations and being accountable for corporate actions are crucial. Companies should establish robust compliance programs, conduct regular audits, and ensure that their practices align with legal and ethical standards.

- Corporate Governance: Effective corporate governance structures can help prevent anti-competitive behavior. Independent oversight, clear policies, and ethical leadership play a vital role in guiding corporate conduct and mitigating risks.

- Stakeholder Engagement: Engaging with stakeholders, including regulators, consumers, and the public, can build trust and demonstrate a commitment to fair practices. Open communication and collaboration with regulators can also help address concerns and ensure compliance.

- Proactive Legal Strategy: Businesses should adopt a proactive legal strategy, seeking legal counsel to navigate complex regulatory environments. Staying informed about changes in laws and regulations and anticipating potential challenges can help companies mitigate risks.

The legal challenges and breakup of Standard Oil represent a pivotal moment in the history of American business and antitrust law. John D. Rockefeller's empire, built through innovative yet often controversial practices, ultimately faced the full force of federal antitrust enforcement. The Supreme Court's decision to dismantle Standard Oil reshaped the oil industry, promoting competition and setting a precedent for future regulatory actions.

The case underscores the importance of regulatory compliance, ethical business practices, and the role of government in maintaining fair markets. The lessons learned from Standard Oil's rise and fall continue to resonate, guiding modern businesses in navigating the complex landscape of antitrust laws and corporate governance.

Rockefeller's legacy, while marked by both immense achievement and significant controversy, provides a nuanced perspective on the balance between business ambition and regulatory oversight. The story of Standard Oil serves as a reminder of the enduring principles of fair competition and the critical role of regulation in safeguarding the interests of consumers and the broader economy.

Case Study: Standard Oil

Rise and Dominance of Standard Oil

Standard Oil, founded by John D. Rockefeller in 1870, rapidly ascended to become one of the most powerful and influential companies in the history of the United States. Rockefeller, alongside partners like Henry Flagler and Samuel Andrews, established the company with the vision of bringing order and efficiency to the chaotic and fragmented oil industry. From its inception, Standard Oil focused on refining oil rather than drilling it, which allowed the company to control a critical stage of the oil supply chain.

By the late 1870s, Standard Oil had achieved a dominant position in the oil refining industry, primarily through a strategy of aggressive acquisition. The company systematically purchased competitors, consolidating refining capacity under its control. This approach was coupled with innovative business practices that enhanced operational efficiency and reduced costs, further solidifying its market dominance. By the early 1880s, Standard Oil controlled approximately 90% of the refining capacity in the United States.

Business Strategies and Practices

Standard Oil's dominance was built on a foundation of several key business strategies and practices:

- Horizontal Integration: One of the primary strategies employed by Rockefeller was horizontal integration. This involved acquiring competing refineries to consolidate market share and eliminate competition. By absorbing smaller refineries, Standard Oil could achieve economies of scale, reduce redundant costs, and exert greater control over pricing and production.

- Vertical Integration: Rockefeller also pursued vertical integration to control every aspect of the oil production process, from extraction to distribution. Standard Oil acquired pipelines, railcars, and storage facilities to ensure a steady supply of crude oil to its refineries. This strategy minimized dependency on external suppliers and allowed for greater control over the entire supply chain.

- Innovation and Efficiency: Standard Oil invested heavily in research and development to improve refining processes. Innovations such as the Frasch process for sulfur removal and advancements in cracking technology enabled the company to produce higher-quality products more efficiently. These technological improvements gave Standard Oil a competitive edge in the market.

- Negotiating Rebates and Transportation Deals: Rockefeller negotiated favorable deals with railroads to secure rebates and preferential rates for transporting Standard Oil's products. These secret deals gave Standard Oil a significant cost advantage over competitors, who had to pay higher transportation fees. The company also built its own pipeline network, further reducing transportation costs and enhancing logistical efficiency.

- Predatory Pricing: Standard Oil employed predatory pricing strategies to drive competitors out of business. By temporarily lowering prices to unsustainable levels, the company could force smaller competitors to sell out or go bankrupt. Once competition was eliminated, Standard Oil would raise prices to recoup losses and maximize profits.

- Corporate Structure: To manage its vast operations and mitigate legal challenges, Standard Oil adopted a trust structure in 1882. This structure centralized control under a board of trustees, enabling more efficient management and coordination across the numerous subsidiaries. The trust model set a precedent for future corporate governance practices.

Legal Challenges and the Breakup

Despite its success, Standard Oil's aggressive business practices drew significant legal scrutiny and public outcry. Critics argued that the company's monopolistic tactics stifled competition, exploited workers, and manipulated markets to the detriment of consumers and the broader economy.

The Sherman Antitrust Act of 1890 was a federal

response to the growing concern over monopolies and trusts. Named after Senator John Sherman, the act aimed to promote fair competition by prohibiting contracts, combinations, and conspiracies in restraint of trade, as well as monopolization of any part of trade or commerce.

The federal government, under President Theodore Roosevelt's administration, took a more proactive stance in enforcing antitrust laws. In 1906, the U.S. government filed a lawsuit against Standard Oil under the Sherman Antitrust Act, accusing the company of maintaining a monopoly through unfair business practices.

The case, Standard Oil Co. of New Jersey v. United States, culminated in a landmark Supreme Court decision in 1911. The Court ruled that Standard Oil had indeed engaged in monopolistic practices and ordered its dissolution. The company was broken up into 34 independent entities, which included major companies such as Exxon, Mobil, and Chevron. This breakup aimed to restore competition in the oil industry and curb the monopolistic power of Standard Oil.

Impact on the Modern Energy Industry

The breakup of Standard Oil had a profound and lasting impact on the modern energy industry:

- Increased Competition: The dissolution of Standard Oil fostered greater competition in the oil industry. The newly independent companies competed against each other, leading to innovations, improved efficiency, and better services for consumers. This increased competition helped drive advancements in technology and exploration, contributing to the growth of the global energy sector.

- Regulatory Framework: The case set a precedent for the enforcement of antitrust laws and shaped the regulatory framework governing corporate practices. It underscored the importance of government intervention in preventing monopolies and protecting consumer interests. The legacy of the Sherman Antitrust Act and the breakup of Standard Oil continues to influence antitrust enforcement and corporate regulation today.

- Corporate Strategies: The breakup of Standard Oil influenced corporate strategies and behaviors. Companies became more cautious in their business practices to avoid antitrust violations. The case highlighted the need for transparency, accountability, and ethical conduct in corporate operations.

- Global Influence: The successor companies of Standard Oil, such as ExxonMobil and Chevron, grew to become major players in the global energy industry. These companies expanded their operations worldwide, contributing to the development of the international oil market and shaping the global energy landscape.

Rockefeller's Enduring Influence

John D. Rockefeller's influence extends far beyond the rise and fall of Standard Oil. His legacy is multifaceted, reflecting both his immense contributions to the business world and the ethical controversies surrounding his methods:

- Business Innovation: Rockefeller's innovative business strategies, including horizontal and vertical integration, set new standards for industrial operations. His emphasis on efficiency, cost control, and technological innovation continues to inspire modern business practices.

- Philanthropy: Rockefeller's philanthropic efforts had a transformative impact on education, medical research, and public health. He established several major charitable organizations, including the Rockefeller Foundation, the General Education Board, and the Rockefeller Institute for Medical Research (now Rockefeller University). These institutions have made significant contributions to scientific discovery and social progress.

- Corporate Governance: The trust structure implemented by Rockefeller at Standard Oil influenced the development of modern corporate governance practices. His approach to centralized management and strategic oversight remains relevant in today's complex corporate environment.

- Antitrust Legacy: The breakup of Standard Oil and the legal battles surrounding its practices have had a lasting impact on antitrust law and enforcement. The case highlighted the importance of maintaining competitive markets and the role of government regulation in preventing monopolistic behavior.

- Public Perception: Rockefeller's legacy is also marked by the complex interplay between his business success and public perception. While he is celebrated for his contributions to industry and philanthropy, he is also criticized for the ruthless tactics used to build his empire. This duality underscores the ethical challenges faced by powerful business leaders and the importance of balancing ambition with social responsibility.

The rise and dominance of Standard Oil, driven by John D. Rockefeller's visionary leadership and innovative business strategies, represent a pivotal chapter in the history of American industry. The company's aggressive pursuit of market control and efficiency revolutionized the oil industry but also led to significant legal challenges and its eventual breakup.

The dissolution of Standard Oil had far-reaching implications, fostering greater competition, shaping regulatory frameworks, and influencing corporate behaviors. Rockefeller's enduring influence is evident in the continued impact of his business innovations, philanthropic contributions, and the lessons learned from the antitrust battles that reshaped the landscape of American industry.

Rockefeller's story is a testament to the transformative power of strategic vision and the complex ethical considerations that accompany immense economic power. The legacy of Standard Oil and its founder continues to resonate, offering valuable insights into the dynamics of business, regulation, and social responsibility in the modern era.

Chapter 3:

Andrew Carnegie Steel Magnate and Philanthropist

Andrew Carnegie was born on November 25, 1835, in Dunfermline, Scotland, to William Carnegie, a handloom weaver, and Margaret Morrison Carnegie. His family lived in modest circumstances, and the advent of the industrial revolution significantly affected their livelihood. The introduction of mechanized looms displaced many weavers, including Andrew's father, leading the family into financial hardship.

Seeking better opportunities, the Carnegies decided to immigrate to the United States in 1848. They settled in Allegheny, Pennsylvania, a suburb of Pittsburgh. This move marked a turning point in young Andrew's life. At just 13 years old, he began his journey in America, a country that offered the promise of opportunity and success.

Early Jobs and Entry into the Steel Industry

Andrew Carnegie's early years in America were marked by hard work and a determination to support his family. His first job was as a bobbin boy in a cotton factory, where he earned $1.20 per week. Despite the long hours and difficult working conditions, Carnegie's work ethic and ambition were evident. He took every opportunity to learn and improve his situation.

Carnegie's big break came when he secured a position as a telegraph messenger boy with the Ohio Telegraph Company. His keen interest in learning and exceptional memory allowed him to quickly master the telegraph system. By 1851, he had become a telegraph operator, which opened the door to more significant opportunities.

In 1853, Thomas A. Scott of the Pennsylvania Railroad hired Carnegie as his personal telegraph operator and assistant. This position was pivotal for Carnegie, as it provided him with invaluable exposure to the business world and a network of influential contacts. Scott became a mentor to Carnegie, teaching him the intricacies of business management and investment.

Carnegie's entry into the steel industry began with his investments in the iron industry during the 1860s. He recognized the potential of steel, a stronger and more versatile material than iron, especially for the expanding railroad industry. By the early 1870s, Carnegie had focused his efforts on steel production, laying the foundation for his future empire.

Founding of Carnegie Steel Company

The official founding of Carnegie Steel Company in 1892 was a culmination of years of strategic planning and investment in the steel industry. Carnegie had already established the Edgar Thomson Steel Works in Braddock, Pennsylvania, in 1875, named after the president of the Pennsylvania Railroad. This mill was among the first in the United States to use the Bessemer process, which revolutionized steel production by significantly lowering costs and increasing output.

Carnegie's approach to the steel industry was marked by innovation and efficiency. He believed in controlling every aspect of the production process, from raw materials to the finished product. This strategy, known as vertical integration, ensured that Carnegie Steel could minimize costs, maximize profits, and maintain a competitive edge.

Under Carnegie's leadership, the company rapidly expanded. He reinvested profits back into the business, continually upgrading technology and increasing production capacity. By the end of the 19th century, Carnegie Steel had become the largest and most profitable steel company in the world.

Vision for the Steel Industry

Andrew Carnegie's vision for the steel industry was revolutionary. He foresaw the critical role that steel would play in the industrialization of the United States. His vision encompassed several key principles:

- Efficiency and Cost Reduction: Carnegie was relentless in his pursuit of efficiency. He implemented the latest technologies and production methods to reduce costs and improve output. The Bessemer process, for instance, allowed for the mass production of steel at a fraction of the previous cost, making steel an affordable and essential material for construction and manufacturing.

- Vertical Integration: To control costs and ensure a steady supply of raw materials, Carnegie adopted vertical integration. He acquired iron ore mines, coal fields, and railroads, creating a self-sufficient production chain. This strategy minimized dependency on external suppliers and stabilized production costs.

- Quality and Innovation: Carnegie believed in the importance of quality. He invested in research and development to improve steel production methods and ensure that his products met the highest standards. His mills were constantly updated with the latest technology, and he encouraged innovation at every level of the company.

- Labor Relations: Although Carnegie is often criticized for his harsh labor practices, he believed that well-paid workers were more productive. He introduced profit-sharing plans and other incentives to motivate his employees. However, his methods of dealing with labor disputes were controversial and led to significant conflicts, such as the Homestead Strike.

- Philanthropy and Responsibility: Carnegie's vision extended beyond business success. He believed that those who amassed great wealth had a moral obligation to use it for the greater good. This philosophy, which he articulated in his essay "The Gospel of Wealth," guided his philanthropic endeavors later in life.

Initial Business Challenges

Despite his eventual success, Carnegie faced numerous challenges in the early years of his steel venture. The steel industry was fiercely competitive, with established players resistant to the new methods Carnegie was introducing. Additionally, the economic climate of the late 19th century was volatile, with frequent financial panics and recessions that posed risks to large-scale industrial operations.

One of the significant challenges Carnegie faced was securing a steady supply of raw materials. To address this, he acquired iron ore mines and limestone quarries, ensuring a reliable source of essential inputs for steel production. This move not only stabilized his supply chain but also reduced dependence on external suppliers, a critical factor in maintaining consistent production and cost control.

Labor relations also presented substantial challenges for Carnegie. The steel industry was notorious for its harsh working conditions, and labor unrest was common. Strikes and labor disputes threatened production and profitability. One of the most notable conflicts was the Homestead Strike of 1892, where a violent clash between striking workers and private security agents resulted in multiple deaths and injuries. This incident highlighted the ongoing tensions between labor and management in

Carnegie's mills and tarnished his reputation as a fair employer.

Additionally, Carnegie faced the constant need to invest in new technology and expand production capacity to stay ahead of competitors. His willingness to reinvest profits into the business was crucial for maintaining his competitive edge, but this strategy required significant capital and posed financial risks, particularly during economic downturns.

Despite these challenges, Carnegie's strategic vision, relentless pursuit of efficiency, and ability to adapt to changing market conditions enabled him to overcome obstacles and build a steel empire. His success in the steel industry laid the foundation for his later philanthropic endeavors, which would leave a lasting legacy on society.

Andrew Carnegie's journey from a poor immigrant boy to a steel magnate and philanthropist exemplifies the transformative power of hard work, vision, and strategic thinking. His early life and career were marked by a series of calculated risks and bold decisions that enabled him to rise to the top of the steel industry.

Carnegie's commitment to innovation, efficiency, and integration revolutionized steel production and set new standards for industrial operations. Despite facing significant challenges, including competition, economic volatility, and labor disputes, Carnegie's strategic approach and determination ensured his success.

Carnegie's vision extended beyond his business achievements. He believed in using his wealth to benefit society and made substantial contributions to education, libraries, and scientific research. His philanthropic efforts have left an enduring legacy, reflecting his belief in the responsibility of the wealthy to give back to society.

Andrew Carnegie's life and career offer valuable lessons in leadership, strategic planning, and the potential for business success to drive positive social change. His story continues to inspire and inform the principles of entrepreneurship, industrial management, and philanthropy in the modern era.

Building the Steel Empire

Innovations in Steel Production

Andrew Carnegie's ascent to dominance in the steel industry was fueled by his relentless pursuit of innovation and efficiency in steel production. At the heart of his strategy was the adoption of the Bessemer process, a revolutionary method for mass-producing steel. This process involved blowing air through molten iron to remove impurities, significantly reducing the cost and time required to produce steel. Carnegie was one of the first industrialists in America to adopt and refine this technology, which allowed him to produce steel at a lower cost than his competitors.

Carnegie's commitment to innovation extended beyond the Bessemer process. He continuously invested in the latest technologies and techniques to improve the efficiency and quality of his steel production. One notable example was the use of open-hearth furnaces, which allowed for greater control over the steel-making process and the production of higher-quality steel. He also implemented the use of rail-mounted ladles, which facilitated the efficient handling of molten steel.

To ensure a steady and reliable supply of raw materials, Carnegie integrated backward into mining and transportation. He acquired iron ore mines, limestone quarries, and coal fields, securing the essential ingredients for steel production. This vertical integration minimized costs and reduced reliance on external suppliers. Additionally, Carnegie built a network of railroads and shipping lines to transport raw materials to his mills and finished products to market, further enhancing the efficiency of his operations.

Expansion and Acquisition Strategies

Carnegie's expansion and acquisition strategies were instrumental in building his steel empire. He employed a combination of organic growth and strategic acquisitions to consolidate his position in the industry and eliminate competition.

One of Carnegie's key strategies was the aggressive acquisition of rival steel mills and related businesses. He targeted companies that possessed valuable assets or strategic advantages, such as prime locations or advanced technologies. By acquiring these companies, Carnegie not only expanded his production capacity but also gained control over critical resources and technologies.

In addition to acquiring rival mills, Carnegie focused on expanding his existing facilities. He continually reinvested profits into upgrading and expanding his steel mills, increasing their capacity and efficiency. The Edgar Thomson Steel Works, for example, was expanded multiple times to accommodate new technologies and increased production demands. These expansions allowed Carnegie to produce steel on an unprecedented scale, meeting the growing demand from industries such as railroads, construction, and manufacturing.

Carnegie's strategic vision also included horizontal integration, where he sought to control every stage of the steel production process. He acquired companies involved in the mining, transportation, and processing of raw materials, creating a self-sufficient production network. This approach reduced costs, improved efficiency, and allowed Carnegie to maintain tight control over the quality and supply of his steel.

Labor Relations and the Homestead Strike

While Carnegie's business strategies were highly effective, his approach to labor relations was fraught with controversy and conflict. The most infamous episode in Carnegie's labor relations history was the Homestead Strike of 1892, which highlighted the deep tensions between labor and management in the steel industry.

The Homestead Steel Works, located in Homestead,

Pennsylvania, was one of Carnegie's most important facilities. In 1892, as the existing labor contract was set to expire, negotiations between the Amalgamated Association of Iron and Steel Workers (the union representing the workers) and the management, led by Henry Clay Frick, broke down. Frick, known for his hardline stance on labor issues, refused to negotiate with the union and aimed to break its influence.

Frick's decision to cut wages and lock out the workers led to a bitter and violent conflict. The workers, supported by the local community, seized control of the mill, leading to a standoff with the Pinkerton National Detective Agency, hired by Frick to take back the facility. The ensuing battle resulted in multiple deaths and injuries on both sides. Eventually, the Pennsylvania National Guard intervened, and the strike was broken, but the event left a lasting scar on Carnegie's reputation.

The Homestead Strike underscored the harsh working conditions and low wages faced by steelworkers, and it exposed the deep rift between labor and management. While Carnegie publicly expressed regret over the violence, his reliance on Frick's aggressive tactics damaged his image and highlighted the challenges of maintaining labor relations in an industry characterized by intense competition and demanding work environments.

Competition with Other Steel Magnates

Andrew Carnegie's dominance in the steel industry was not without formidable competition. Other steel magnates, such as John D. Rockefeller (through his investments in iron ore and railroads) and J.P. Morgan, posed significant challenges to Carnegie's empire.

One of Carnegie's most significant competitors was the Illinois Steel Company, led by Elbert H. Gary. The rivalry between Carnegie Steel and Illinois Steel was intense, with both companies vying for control of the burgeoning steel market. However, Carnegie's superior efficiency, innovation, and vertical integration gave him a competitive edge, allowing him to outproduce and outcompete Illinois Steel and other rivals.

The competition reached its peak in the late 1890s, when J.P. Morgan, a powerful financier and industrialist, began consolidating various steel companies to form U.S. Steel Corporation. In 1901, recognizing the growing competition and the potential for a massive industrial consolidation, Carnegie decided to sell Carnegie Steel to Morgan. The sale, valued at $480 million (equivalent to about $15 billion today), made Carnegie one of the richest men in the world and marked the formation of U.S. Steel, the first billion-dollar corporation.

Impact on the American Economy

Andrew Carnegie's steel empire had a profound and lasting impact on the American economy. His innovations and business strategies transformed the steel industry, making steel an affordable and essential material for a wide range of applications. This transformation fueled the growth of key sectors such as railroads, construction, and manufacturing, driving the industrialization of the United States.

Carnegie's emphasis on efficiency and cost reduction set new standards for industrial operations, influencing business practices across various industries. His success demonstrated the importance of vertical integration, technological innovation, and strategic reinvestment in achieving competitive advantage and sustained growth.

The consolidation of the steel industry under Carnegie and, later, U.S. Steel, created a more stable and efficient market. The economies of scale achieved through large-scale production allowed American steel to compete effectively on the global stage, contributing to the country's emergence as an industrial powerhouse.

Moreover, Carnegie's wealth and philanthropy had a significant impact on American society. After selling Carnegie Steel, he dedicated himself to philanthropic endeavors, establishing libraries, educational institutions, and foundations that continue to benefit society today. His belief in the "Gospel of Wealth"—the idea that the rich have a moral obligation to give back to society—left a lasting legacy in the form of numerous charitable institutions and initiatives.

Andrew Carnegie's journey to building a steel empire is a testament to the transformative power of innovation, strategic vision, and relentless pursuit of efficiency. His adoption of cutting-edge technologies, such as the Bessemer process and open-hearth furnaces, revolutionized steel production and set new benchmarks for industrial efficiency.

Carnegie's expansion and acquisition strategies enabled him to consolidate his position in the steel industry, while his commitment to vertical integration ensured a steady supply of raw materials and reduced production costs. Despite facing significant challenges, including intense competition and labor unrest, Carnegie's strategic approach and determination ensured his success.

The Homestead Strike highlighted the complex and often contentious nature of labor relations in the steel industry, underscoring the need for balance between business interests and worker welfare. Carnegie's competition with other steel magnates, such as J.P. Morgan, ultimately led to the formation of U.S. Steel, a monumental consolidation that reshaped the industry.

Carnegie's impact on the American economy extended beyond the steel industry. His innovations and business practices influenced industrial operations across various sectors, contributing to the country's rapid industrialization and economic growth. Moreover, his philanthropic legacy continues to benefit society, reflecting his belief in using wealth for the greater good.

Andrew Carnegie's life and career offer valuable lessons in leadership, innovation, and the potential for business success to drive positive social change. His story continues to inspire and inform the principles of entrepreneurship, industrial management, and philanthropy in the modern era.

Wealth and Philanthropy

Accumulation of Wealth and Business Success

Andrew Carnegie, one of the most influential figures of the late 19th and early 20th centuries, amassed immense wealth through his innovative and strategic approach to the steel industry. Carnegie's journey from a poor Scottish immigrant to one of the wealthiest individuals in history is a testament to his business acumen, hard work, and relentless pursuit of efficiency.

Carnegie's wealth accumulation began in earnest when he entered the steel industry in the 1870s. Through the adoption of the Bessemer process, which allowed for the mass production of high-quality steel at a lower cost, Carnegie revolutionized steel manufacturing. He founded the Carnegie Steel Company in 1892, and under his leadership, it became the largest and most profitable steel company in the world.

Carnegie's business strategies included vertical integration, where he controlled every aspect of production from raw materials to distribution, and horizontal integration, where he acquired competing steel companies to consolidate his market position. His commitment to innovation, efficiency, and cost reduction enabled him to outcompete rivals and dominate the steel industry.

By 1901, Carnegie decided to retire from business and focus on his philanthropic endeavors. He sold Carnegie Steel to J.P. Morgan for $480 million, which led to the formation of U.S. Steel Corporation, the first billion-dollar corporation in the world. The sale made Carnegie one of the richest men of his time, with a fortune equivalent to billions of dollars today.

Transition to Philanthropy

Andrew Carnegie's transition from business mogul to philanthropist was deeply influenced by his personal beliefs and values. He was a firm believer in the "Gospel of Wealth," an essay he published in 1889, which articulated his philosophy that the rich have a moral obligation to use their wealth for the betterment of society. Carnegie argued that the wealthy should live modestly, provide for their dependents, and use the surplus of their wealth to benefit the community.

After retiring from business, Carnegie dedicated the remainder of his life to philanthropy. He believed that the accumulation of wealth was justified only if it was eventually distributed to promote the welfare and happiness of others. Carnegie's approach to philanthropy was strategic and focused on long-term impact rather than immediate relief. He sought to address the root causes of social issues and create lasting institutions that would continue to benefit society long after his death.

Establishment of Libraries, Universities, and Foundations

One of Carnegie's most significant contributions to society was his funding of public libraries. He believed that access to knowledge and education was crucial for personal development and social progress. Between 1883 and 1929, Carnegie funded the construction of over 2,500 libraries worldwide, including 1,689 in the United States. These libraries, often referred to as "Carnegie libraries," provided free access to books and learning resources for millions of people, promoting literacy and education.

In addition to libraries, Carnegie established and supported several universities and educational institutions. One of his most notable contributions was the founding of the Carnegie Institute of Technology in Pittsburgh in 1900, which later became Carnegie Mellon University. This institution focused on providing practical and technical education, preparing students for careers in engineering, science, and the arts.

Carnegie also founded the Carnegie Institution for Science in 1902, which supported scientific research and discovery. He believed that scientific advancement was essential for societal progress and provided significant funding for research in various fields, including astronomy, biology, and physics.

Another major philanthropic endeavor was the establishment of the Carnegie Endowment for International Peace in 1910. Carnegie was a strong advocate for world peace and believed that international cooperation and dialogue were essential for preventing conflicts. The endowment funded research and initiatives aimed at promoting peace and resolving international disputes.

Influence on the Field of Education

Andrew Carnegie's influence on education was profound and far-reaching. His investments in libraries and educational institutions transformed access to knowledge and learning opportunities for people of all backgrounds. Carnegie's belief in the power of education to uplift individuals and communities guided his philanthropic efforts and left a lasting legacy in the field of education.

Carnegie's funding of public libraries democratized access to information, providing millions of people with the resources to educate themselves and improve their lives. These libraries became centers of community life, offering not only books but also programs and services that supported lifelong learning.

In higher education, Carnegie's support for technical and practical education helped shape the development of modern universities and colleges. Institutions like Carnegie Mellon University became leaders in science, engineering, and the arts, producing graduates who contributed to technological advancements and economic growth.

Carnegie's commitment to education extended to his efforts to improve the quality of teaching and learning. He established the Carnegie Foundation for the Advancement of Teaching in 1905, which aimed to promote excellence in education and support teachers. The foundation conducted research, provided grants, and developed initiatives to enhance educational practices and policies.

Legacy in Philanthropic Practices

Andrew Carnegie's philanthropic legacy extends beyond the specific institutions he founded and funded. His approach to giving and his philosophy of the "Gospel of Wealth" have influenced generations of philanthropists and shaped modern philanthropic practices.

Carnegie's emphasis on strategic giving and creating lasting impact has become a guiding principle for many contemporary philanthropists. He believed in addressing the root causes of social issues and investing in solutions that would have a long-term, sustainable impact. This approach is reflected in the work of modern foundations and philanthropic organizations that focus on systemic change and capacity building.

Carnegie's practice of establishing institutions with specific missions and endowments set a precedent for how philanthropy can create enduring legacies. His endowments continue to support education, scientific research, and peace initiatives, demonstrating the lasting power of well-structured philanthropic investments.

Furthermore, Carnegie's belief in the responsibility of the wealthy to give back to society has inspired many of today's leading philanthropists. Figures like Bill Gates and Warren Buffett have echoed Carnegie's sentiments in their own philanthropic endeavors, advocating for the use of wealth to address global challenges and improve human well-being.

Andrew Carnegie's journey from steel magnate to philanthropist is a remarkable story of wealth accumulation and its transformative potential for societal good. His business success in the steel industry provided him with the financial resources to pursue his vision of using wealth to benefit humanity. Carnegie's strategic and impactful philanthropy has left an indelible mark on education, science, and public life.

Carnegie's establishment of libraries, universities, and foundations has expanded access to knowledge and learning opportunities for millions of people. His influence on education, through both direct funding and the promotion of best practices, continues to shape the landscape of higher education and lifelong learning.

The legacy of Andrew Carnegie in philanthropic practices is enduring and influential. His principles of strategic giving, addressing root causes, and creating lasting institutions serve as a model for modern philanthropy. Carnegie's belief in the moral responsibility of the wealthy to give back to society remains a guiding philosophy for many of today's philanthropists.

Andrew Carnegie's life and work offer valuable lessons in the power of wealth to drive positive social change. His story continues to inspire and inform the principles of strategic philanthropy, education, and the pursuit of a better world for all.

The Gospel of Wealth

Carnegie's Philosophy on Wealth Distribution

Andrew Carnegie's philosophy on wealth distribution, famously articulated in his 1889 essay "The Gospel of Wealth," profoundly shaped the philanthropic landscape of his time and beyond. Carnegie believed that the accumulation of wealth by a few was a natural result of capitalism, but he also argued that the wealthy had a moral obligation to redistribute their fortunes in ways that would benefit society. He posited that the rich were merely trustees of their wealth, holding it in trust to improve the world.

Carnegie outlined three modes of distributing surplus wealth: leaving it to family members, bequeathing it to the public upon death, or administering it during one's lifetime for the common good. He staunchly criticized the first two methods, arguing that leaving large inheritances to heirs often resulted in laziness and entitlement, while posthumous philanthropy lacked the opportunity for thoughtful, impactful giving. Instead, Carnegie championed the third method, urging the wealthy to actively engage in philanthropy during their lifetimes to address societal issues directly and effectively.

He believed that wealth should be used to create opportunities for others, particularly in areas like education, science, and cultural institutions, which could empower individuals and promote societal progress. Carnegie's philosophy emphasized that the rich had a responsibility to use their resources to create a "ladder" for those less fortunate to climb, enabling them to improve their circumstances through hard work and perseverance.

Impact on Other Industrialists and Philanthropists
Carnegie's "The Gospel of Wealth" had a significant impact on other industrialists and philanthropists of his era and subsequent generations. His ideas resonated with many of his peers, who began to see philanthropy as a vital component of their legacies. Notable contemporaries like John D. Rockefeller and Henry Ford adopted similar approaches to giving, focusing on initiatives that would have long-term benefits for society.

Rockefeller, for instance, founded the Rockefeller Foundation in 1913, which aimed to "promote the well-being of humanity" by funding medical research, education, and public health initiatives. Ford established the Ford Foundation in 1936, which became one of the largest and most influential philanthropic organizations in the world, supporting various global causes.

Carnegie's approach also influenced the modern philanthropic landscape. Philanthropists like Bill Gates and Warren Buffett have echoed Carnegie's sentiments in their own giving. Gates, through the Bill and Melinda Gates Foundation, focuses on global health, education, and poverty alleviation, while Buffett has pledged the majority of his wealth to philanthropic causes, advocating for responsible and impactful giving.

Carnegie's emphasis on active, thoughtful philanthropy inspired these and many other wealthy individuals to take a strategic approach to their

charitable efforts, focusing on creating lasting change rather than simply donating money.
Criticisms and Controversies

Despite its influence, Carnegie's "The Gospel of Wealth" was not without its criticisms and controversies. Critics argued that Carnegie's philosophy, while noble in intent, glossed over the exploitative practices that enabled industrialists to amass their fortunes in the first place. The harsh labor conditions, low wages, and anti-union tactics employed by Carnegie and his contemporaries were seen as contradictory to the philanthropic ideals he later espoused.

One of the most notable controversies surrounding Carnegie's business practices was the Homestead Strike of 1892. The violent clash between striking steelworkers and private security agents highlighted the brutal realities of labor relations in Carnegie's mills. Critics argued that the vast wealth Carnegie accumulated was built on the backs of exploited workers, making his later philanthropic efforts appear as an attempt to absolve his conscience and repair his public image.

Additionally, some viewed Carnegie's philosophy as paternalistic, suggesting that it placed too much power in the hands of the wealthy to determine what was best for society. This perspective argued that true societal progress required systemic change and the empowerment of all individuals, not just the benevolence of a few wealthy patrons.

Despite these criticisms, Carnegie's ideas have

endured, influencing philanthropic practices and corporate social responsibility initiatives to this day.

Long-term Influence on Corporate Social Responsibility

Carnegie's "The Gospel of Wealth" has had a lasting impact on the concept of corporate social responsibility (CSR). His philosophy underscored the importance of ethical stewardship and the role of businesses in contributing to societal well-being. This idea has evolved into the modern CSR movement, where companies are expected to go beyond profit-making and actively participate in addressing social, environmental, and economic challenges.

Many corporations today integrate CSR into their core business strategies, recognizing that sustainable success requires a commitment to the communities they serve and the environment they operate in. Initiatives such as fair labor practices, environmental sustainability, community engagement, and ethical governance are now seen as essential components of responsible business operations.

Carnegie's emphasis on education and knowledge dissemination is particularly evident in the CSR efforts of technology and information companies. Firms like Google, Microsoft, and IBM invest heavily in educational programs, digital literacy initiatives, and community development projects, reflecting Carnegie's belief in the transformative power of education.

Furthermore, Carnegie's approach to philanthropy has influenced corporate foundations and charitable giving programs. Many companies establish foundations to manage their philanthropic efforts, ensuring that their contributions are strategic, impactful, and aligned with their business values. This structured approach to giving, inspired by Carnegie's model, helps maximize the positive impact of corporate philanthropy.

Lessons for Modern Business Leaders

Carnegie's life and philosophy offer several valuable lessons for modern business leaders:

- Ethical Responsibility: Carnegie's belief in the moral obligation of the wealthy to give back to society underscores the importance of ethical responsibility in business. Modern leaders should recognize that their success is often built on the contributions of others and that they have a duty to use their resources to benefit society.

- Strategic Philanthropy: Carnegie's emphasis on thoughtful and impactful giving highlights the need for strategic philanthropy. Business leaders should approach their charitable efforts with the same rigor and planning that they apply to their business operations, focusing on initiatives that address root causes and create lasting change.

- Education and Empowerment: Carnegie's investments in education demonstrate the transformative power of knowledge and learning. Modern leaders should prioritize initiatives that empower individuals through education, skills development, and access to information, helping to create opportunities for personal and community growth.

- Corporate Social Responsibility: Carnegie's ideas laid the groundwork for modern CSR practices. Business leaders should integrate social and environmental considerations into their core strategies, recognizing that sustainable success requires a commitment to the broader well-being of society and the planet.

- Long-term Vision: Carnegie's legacy of establishing lasting institutions and foundations highlights the importance of a long-term vision in philanthropy and business. Leaders should focus on creating sustainable impact and building institutions that will continue to benefit society for generations to come.

Andrew Carnegie's "The Gospel of Wealth" remains a foundational text in the history of philanthropy and corporate social responsibility. His philosophy on wealth distribution, which emphasized the moral duty of the wealthy to actively engage in philanthropy during their lifetimes, has influenced generations of industrialists, philanthropists, and business leaders.

Carnegie's impact on other industrialists and philanthropists is evident in the continued practice of strategic and impactful giving. His ideas have inspired some of the most significant philanthropic initiatives of the modern era, from the Rockefeller Foundation to the Bill and Melinda Gates Foundation.

While Carnegie's philosophy faced criticisms and controversies, particularly regarding the methods by which he accumulated his wealth, his emphasis on ethical stewardship and the responsible use of wealth for societal benefit remains influential.

The long-term influence of "The Gospel of Wealth" on corporate social responsibility is profound. Companies today recognize the importance of ethical business practices, community engagement, and sustainability, reflecting Carnegie's belief in the role of business in contributing to societal well-being.

Modern business leaders can draw valuable lessons from Carnegie's life and philosophy, emphasizing ethical responsibility, strategic philanthropy, education, corporate social responsibility, and long-term vision. Andrew Carnegie's legacy continues to inspire and inform the principles of philanthropy and responsible business practices, demonstrating the enduring power of using wealth to drive positive social change.

Case Study: Carnegie Steel Company

Growth and Dominance in the Steel Industry

Carnegie Steel Company, founded by Andrew Carnegie in the late 19th century, became the largest and most profitable steel producer in the world, playing a pivotal role in the industrialization of the United States. Carnegie's vision and strategic decisions transformed the company into an industrial giant, dominating the steel industry through innovation, efficiency, and aggressive expansion.

The company's growth began with the establishment of the Edgar Thomson Steel Works in Braddock, Pennsylvania, in 1875. Named after the president of the Pennsylvania Railroad, this mill was among the first in the United States to utilize the Bessemer process, a revolutionary method for mass-producing steel. This process significantly reduced the cost of steel production and increased output, giving Carnegie a competitive edge over other steel producers.

Carnegie Steel's dominance was further cemented through continuous investment in technology and infrastructure. Carnegie reinvested profits into expanding production capacity, acquiring additional mills, and integrating vertically to control every aspect of the production process, from raw materials to distribution. By the 1890s, Carnegie Steel controlled a significant portion of the steel market in the United States, producing more steel than all of Great Britain.

Key Business Decisions and Strategies

Andrew Carnegie's success in building his steel empire was driven by several key business decisions and strategies:

- Vertical Integration: Carnegie believed in controlling every stage of the production process to minimize costs and maximize efficiency. He acquired iron ore mines, coal fields, and limestone quarries, ensuring a steady supply of raw materials. He also built a network of railroads and shipping lines to transport raw materials to his mills and finished products to market, reducing dependency on external suppliers and stabilizing production costs.

- Technological Innovation: Carnegie was a pioneer in adopting and refining new technologies. The Bessemer process was just the beginning; he later introduced the open-hearth furnace, which allowed for greater control over the steel-making process and the production of higher-quality steel. Carnegie also invested in mechanized systems for handling and transporting molten steel, further enhancing efficiency.

- Cost Management: Carnegie's focus on cost control was relentless. He implemented rigorous accounting systems to track expenses and identify areas for improvement. By keeping costs low, Carnegie Steel could offer lower prices than competitors, driving them out of business and consolidating market share.

- Strategic Acquisitions: Carnegie expanded his empire by acquiring rival steel mills and related businesses. These acquisitions allowed him to increase production capacity, eliminate competition, and gain access to valuable assets and technologies. Notable acquisitions included the Homestead Steel Works and the Duquesne Steel Works, which became integral parts of Carnegie Steel's operations.

- Labor Management: While Carnegie publicly advocated for fair labor practices and profit-sharing, his approach to labor management was often harsh and pragmatic. He employed skilled managers like Henry Clay Frick, who were known for their tough stance on labor issues. This approach led to significant conflicts with workers, most notably the Homestead Strike of 1892.

Labor Relations and Management Practices

Labor relations at Carnegie Steel were complex and often contentious. Carnegie's mills were characterized by demanding working conditions, long hours, and low wages. Despite these challenges, Carnegie initially maintained a relatively positive relationship with his workforce, promoting the idea of mutual benefit and profit-sharing.

However, as competition intensified and the need for greater efficiency grew, labor relations deteriorated. Carnegie delegated much of the day-to-day management of his mills to experienced managers like Henry Clay Frick, whose hardline approach to labor disputes led to significant conflicts.

The most infamous labor conflict at Carnegie Steel was the Homestead Strike of 1892. Tensions between the Amalgamated Association of Iron and Steel Workers (the union representing the workers) and management escalated when Frick, acting on Carnegie's directive to reduce costs, proposed wage cuts and refused to negotiate with the union. In response, the workers went on strike and seized control of the Homestead plant.

Frick hired the Pinkerton National Detective Agency to break the strike, leading to a violent confrontation between the Pinkertons and the workers. The conflict resulted in multiple deaths and injuries, drawing national attention and highlighting the brutal realities of labor relations in the steel industry. The Pennsylvania National Guard eventually intervened, and the strike was broken, but the incident left a lasting scar on Carnegie's reputation and underscored the deep rift between labor and management.

Despite the negative publicity, Carnegie continued to emphasize the importance of cost control and efficiency, often at the expense of worker relations. His approach to labor management remained a controversial aspect of his legacy, reflecting the complexities of balancing business interests with social responsibility.

Sale to J.P. Morgan and the Formation of U.S. Steel

By the turn of the 20th century, Carnegie Steel had reached the pinnacle of its success, dominating the steel industry and generating immense profits. However, Carnegie, who had always harbored philanthropic ambitions, began to contemplate retirement and the next phase of his life. He was also aware of the increasing competition and the potential for industrial consolidation in the steel industry.

In 1901, J.P. Morgan, a powerful financier and industrialist, approached Carnegie with a proposal to buy Carnegie Steel and merge it with several other steel companies to form U.S. Steel Corporation. Morgan's vision was to create the first billion-dollar corporation in the world, capable of leveraging economies of scale and dominating the global steel market.

Carnegie agreed to the sale, valuing Carnegie Steel at $480 million. The deal made Carnegie one of the richest men in the world and marked the formation of U.S. Steel, which became the largest steel producer globally. The sale allowed Carnegie to retire from business and focus on his philanthropic endeavors, fulfilling his vision of using his wealth to benefit society.

Carnegie's Lasting Impact on Industry and Philanthropy

Andrew Carnegie's impact on both industry and philanthropy is profound and enduring. His contributions to the steel industry revolutionized manufacturing, setting new standards for efficiency, innovation, and integration. Carnegie's emphasis on cost control, technological advancement, and strategic expansion helped shape the modern industrial landscape, influencing business practices across various sectors.

Carnegie's legacy extends far beyond his industrial achievements. After retiring from business, he dedicated himself to philanthropy, guided by his philosophy of the "Gospel of Wealth." He believed that the wealthy had a moral obligation to use their fortunes for the greater good, and he practiced this belief by donating the majority of his wealth to various causes.

Carnegie's philanthropic contributions include the funding of over 2,500 public libraries worldwide, establishing Carnegie Mellon University, and founding the Carnegie Corporation of New York, the Carnegie Endowment for International Peace, and the Carnegie Foundation for the Advancement of Teaching. These institutions continue to impact education, research, and public policy, reflecting Carnegie's vision of using wealth to create lasting societal benefits.

Carnegie's influence on philanthropy set a precedent for future generations of wealthy individuals, inspiring figures like John D. Rockefeller, Bill Gates, and Warren Buffett to engage in strategic and impactful giving. His emphasis on addressing the root causes of social issues and creating opportunities for others through education and knowledge dissemination remains a guiding principle in modern philanthropy.

The story of Carnegie Steel Company is a testament to Andrew Carnegie's vision, strategic acumen, and relentless pursuit of efficiency. From its humble beginnings to its dominance in the steel industry, Carnegie Steel transformed the landscape of American manufacturing and set new standards for industrial operations.

Carnegie's key business decisions, including vertical integration, technological innovation, and strategic acquisitions, enabled him to build an industrial empire that outcompeted rivals and shaped the future of the steel industry. Despite significant challenges, including labor conflicts and intense competition, Carnegie's strategic approach and determination ensured the success and longevity of his company.

The sale of Carnegie Steel to J.P. Morgan and the formation of U.S. Steel marked the end of an era and the beginning of Carnegie's legacy in philanthropy. Carnegie's lasting impact on industry and philanthropy continues to inspire and inform the principles of entrepreneurship, industrial management, and responsible wealth distribution.

Andrew Carnegie's life and work offer valuable lessons in leadership, innovation, and the potential for business success to drive positive social change. His story serves as a reminder of the transformative power of vision, strategy, and the ethical use of wealth to benefit society.

Chapter 4:

Thomas Edison Innovator and Entrepreneur

Thomas Alva Edison was born on February 11, 1847, in Milan, Ohio, the youngest of seven children. His father, Samuel Edison Jr., was a versatile man who engaged in various businesses, while his mother, Nancy Matthews Elliott, was a former school teacher. Edison's early childhood was marked by frequent illnesses, which delayed his formal education.

Edison attended school for only a few months. His hyperactivity and frequent questioning led his teacher to describe him as "addled." Frustrated with the rigid structure of formal education, Nancy Edison decided to homeschool her son. She nurtured his curiosity, encouraging him to read widely and conduct experiments. This personalized education allowed Edison to explore subjects at his own pace, fostering a lifelong passion for learning and experimentation.

By the age of 12, Edison was already displaying entrepreneurial spirit. He began selling newspapers, snacks, and candy on the Grand Trunk Railroad. This venture not only provided him with an income but also exposed him to the latest news and technological advancements. He even set up a small laboratory in a baggage car, conducting chemical experiments during his free time.

Early Inventions and Experiments

Edison's first foray into invention came during his time as a newsboy. He created a device to print newspapers directly on the train, producing the "Grand Trunk Herald," which he sold to passengers. This innovation marked the beginning of his prolific career as an inventor.

At the age of 15, Edison saved a three-year-old boy from being struck by a runaway train. The boy's grateful father, J.U. MacKenzie, taught Edison telegraphy as a reward. This new skill opened up further opportunities for Edison, who began working as a telegraph operator. His job took him across the Midwest, where he continued to experiment and invent in his spare time.

One of Edison's earliest significant inventions was an improved telegraph device capable of sending multiple messages simultaneously. This invention, known as the quadruplex telegraph, greatly enhanced the efficiency of telegraphic communication and caught the attention of Western Union. The sale of this invention provided Edison with the capital needed to establish his first laboratory in Newark, New Jersey.

Edison's inventive streak continued with the development of the automatic repeater and the stock ticker, both of which automated communication processes and became commercially successful. These early successes validated his approach to invention—focused on practical solutions to real-world problems—and set the stage for his later achievements.

Founding of General Electric

In 1876, Edison moved his laboratory to Menlo Park, New Jersey, which would become the site of some of his most famous inventions. It was here that Edison embarked on his most ambitious project to date: the development of a practical incandescent light bulb. After extensive experimentation with different materials and designs, Edison and his team succeeded in creating a long-lasting, commercially viable light bulb in 1879.

The success of the incandescent light bulb spurred the need for a reliable source of electrical power. Edison responded by developing an entire electrical distribution system, including generators, wiring, and meters. In 1882, he opened the first central power station on Pearl Street in New York City, providing electricity to a small area of lower Manhattan.

Edison's work in electric power led to the founding of the Edison Electric Light Company in 1878, which later merged with several other companies to form General Electric (GE) in 1892. General Electric quickly became a dominant force in the electric industry, expanding its reach into various areas of electrical manufacturing and innovation. GE's formation marked the culmination of Edison's vision to bring electric power and lighting to the masses, fundamentally transforming modern life.

Vision for Technological Innovation

Thomas Edison's vision for technological innovation was grounded in the belief that inventions should be practical, scalable, and beneficial to society. He approached invention with a systematic methodology, combining scientific experimentation with a keen understanding of market needs. Edison believed in the power of technology to improve quality of life and drive economic progress.

Edison's Menlo Park laboratory was the first research and development facility of its kind, designed to foster creativity and collaboration. He assembled a diverse team of skilled workers, including chemists, engineers, and machinists, to work on various projects simultaneously. This collaborative environment allowed for rapid prototyping and testing, accelerating the pace of innovation.

Edison's approach to innovation was also characterized by his perseverance and willingness to embrace failure. He famously conducted thousands of experiments before perfecting the incandescent light bulb, viewing each failure as a step closer to success. This relentless pursuit of improvement exemplified his commitment to technological advancement.

Beyond the light bulb and electrical power, Edison's vision extended to numerous other fields. He made significant contributions to sound recording with the invention of the phonograph in 1877, which revolutionized the music industry. Edison's work in motion pictures, including the kinetoscope and the development of the first motion picture studio, laid the groundwork for the film industry. His patents and inventions spanned various domains, from medical devices to mining equipment, showcasing his diverse interests and innovative spirit.

Initial Business Challenges

Despite his numerous successes, Edison's career was not without challenges. His early ventures faced significant financial and technical hurdles, testing his resilience and ingenuity.

One of the first major challenges Edison encountered was the intense competition in the electric power industry. While Edison was a pioneer in developing the incandescent light bulb and the direct current (DC) power system, he faced stiff competition from George Westinghouse and Nikola Tesla, who advocated for the alternating current (AC) system. The "War of Currents" ensued, with Edison staunchly defending DC as safer and more efficient for residential use, while AC proponents highlighted its advantages for long-distance power transmission.

The competition between DC and AC power systems was fierce, with both sides employing aggressive marketing and public relations tactics. Edison's team even staged public demonstrations to discredit AC by associating it with electrical accidents and animal electrocutions. Despite Edison's efforts, AC ultimately emerged as the dominant standard for electrical distribution, largely due to its efficiency and scalability for long-distance transmission.

Another significant challenge for Edison was

managing his vast portfolio of inventions and business ventures. While his innovative mind constantly generated new ideas, the commercialization and management of these inventions required substantial resources and strategic planning. Edison's businesses often faced financial strain, legal battles over patents, and logistical difficulties in scaling production.

Edison's ambitious project to develop an iron ore milling process in the late 1890s, for instance, was a notable failure. Despite significant investment and extensive experimentation, the project did not yield commercially viable results, leading to considerable financial losses. This setback underscored the risks associated with Edison's relentless pursuit of innovation and his tendency to take on multiple large-scale projects simultaneously.

Moreover, Edison's management style, characterized by hands-on involvement and high expectations, sometimes led to tensions with business partners and employees. His intense focus on innovation occasionally came at the expense of effective business administration, necessitating the involvement of more business-savvy partners to manage the commercial aspects of his ventures.

Thomas Edison's journey from a curious child to a prolific inventor and successful entrepreneur is a remarkable tale of ingenuity, perseverance, and vision. His early life and career were marked by a relentless pursuit of knowledge and a passion for experimentation, which laid the foundation for his numerous groundbreaking inventions.

Edison's key business decisions and strategies, including the founding of General Electric, his systematic approach to innovation, and his ability to commercialize his inventions, played a crucial role in his success. Despite facing significant challenges, such as intense competition and financial setbacks, Edison remained committed to his vision of using technology to improve society.

Edison's lasting impact on industry and technology is profound. His contributions to electric power, sound recording, and motion pictures revolutionized these fields and paved the way for future advancements. His systematic approach to invention, exemplified by the establishment of the Menlo Park laboratory, set the standard for modern research and development practices.

Beyond his technical achievements, Edison's legacy includes his influence on the entrepreneurial spirit and the culture of innovation. His belief in the practical application of science and his willingness to embrace failure as a path to success continue to inspire inventors and entrepreneurs worldwide.

Thomas Edison's life and work offer valuable lessons in creativity, resilience, and the transformative power of technology. His story serves as a testament to the impact that one individual's vision and determination can have on the world, leaving an indelible mark on history and shaping the future of innovation.

Major Inventions and Innovations

Development of the Phonograph

One of Thomas Edison's most remarkable and transformative inventions was the phonograph, developed in 1877. The phonograph was the first device capable of both recording and reproducing sound, making it a groundbreaking innovation in the field of audio technology.

The inspiration for the phonograph came from Edison's work on the telegraph and telephone. He was exploring ways to improve the telegraph's capacity to handle multiple messages simultaneously when he began to think about recording sound. Edison theorized that sound could be captured on a tinfoil-wrapped cylinder through the vibrations of a stylus.

Edison and his team constructed the first working model of the phonograph, which used a hand-cranked cylinder wrapped in tinfoil. When someone spoke into the mouthpiece, the sound vibrations were etched onto the tinfoil by a stylus. By reversing the process, the phonograph could play back the recorded sound. The first successful recording was Edison's own voice reciting the nursery rhyme "Mary Had a Little Lamb."

The phonograph astonished the public and secured Edison's reputation as a leading inventor. It had significant implications for various industries, including music, entertainment, and communication. Initially, the phonograph was envisioned for business uses, such as dictation and letter writing. However, its primary impact was on the music industry, where it revolutionized the way people consumed music, making it possible to record, distribute, and enjoy music in homes across the world.

The development of the phonograph led to the establishment of the recording industry, with record companies producing and selling recorded music. Edison's invention paved the way for future audio technologies, including the gramophone, radio, and digital recording, profoundly influencing the entertainment landscape.

Invention of the Incandescent Light Bulb

Arguably Thomas Edison's most famous invention, the incandescent light bulb, had a profound impact on society and is often credited with ushering in the age of electric light. While Edison did not invent the first electric light bulb, his work significantly improved its practicality, efficiency, and commercial viability.

Prior to Edison's improvements, early electric light bulbs, such as those created by Humphry Davy, Warren de la Rue, and Joseph Swan, faced numerous challenges. They were either too expensive, too short-lived, or too difficult to produce on a large scale. Edison's goal was to develop a light bulb that was affordable, long-lasting, and suitable for widespread use.

In 1878, Edison began his intensive research into electric lighting at his Menlo Park laboratory. He experimented with thousands of materials to find the perfect filament for his light bulb. After extensive testing, Edison discovered that a carbonized bamboo filament could produce light for up to 1,200 hours, making it the most practical and durable option available at the time.

Edison's successful demonstration of his incandescent light bulb in 1879 marked a turning point in the development of electric lighting. He then focused on creating an entire electric lighting system, which included the light bulb, electrical generators, distribution networks, and regulators to ensure a consistent and reliable supply of electricity.

The first public demonstration of Edison's electric lighting system took place on December 31, 1879, in Menlo Park, where he lit up the streets and homes of the area. This event garnered widespread attention and solidified Edison's reputation as the "Wizard of Menlo Park."

The development of the incandescent light bulb and the subsequent creation of a practical electrical lighting system had a transformative impact on society. It extended productive hours beyond daylight, improved safety by reducing the reliance on gas lamps and candles, and paved the way for the electrification of cities and homes around the world.

Creation of the Electric Power Distribution System

The invention of the incandescent light bulb was only one part of Edison's vision for electric lighting. He understood that for electric lighting to be viable on a large scale, there needed to be a reliable and efficient system for generating and distributing electricity. This led to the creation of the electric power distribution system, another of Edison's major innovations.

Edison's work on the power distribution system began in earnest in the early 1880s. He designed and built the first commercial power station, the Pearl Street Station, which began operations in New York City in 1882. This station used direct current (DC) electricity to supply power to a small area of lower Manhattan, serving around 400 lamps for 85 customers.

The Pearl Street Station marked the beginning of the modern electric utility industry. Edison's system included not only the power plant but also the necessary infrastructure for distributing electricity, such as underground cables, junction boxes, and meters. He also developed safety features, such as fuses and circuit breakers, to protect the system from overloads and ensure reliable operation.

While Edison's DC system was initially successful, it faced significant competition from alternating current (AC) systems, which were being developed by other inventors like Nikola Tesla and promoted by industrialists like George Westinghouse. AC systems had the advantage of being able to transmit electricity over longer distances with less loss of power, making them more suitable for widespread distribution.

Despite the competition, Edison's work laid the foundation for the electric power industry. His innovations in power generation, distribution, and electrical safety standards contributed to the widespread adoption of electric lighting and power, transforming everyday life and enabling further technological advancements.

Innovations in Motion Pictures

Thomas Edison's contributions to the motion picture industry are often overshadowed by his work in electric lighting and power, but they were nonetheless significant. Edison played a crucial role in the development of early motion picture technology, including the invention of the kinetoscope and the establishment of the first motion picture studio.

Edison's interest in motion pictures was sparked by the work of his assistant, William Kennedy Laurie Dickson, who was experimenting with photographic technology. Together, they developed the kinetoscope, an early motion picture viewing device. The kinetoscope used a continuous loop of film that passed over a light source, creating the illusion of motion when viewed through a peephole.

The first public demonstration of the kinetoscope took place in 1893 at the Brooklyn Institute of Arts and Sciences. The device quickly gained popularity, leading to the establishment of kinetoscope parlors where people could pay to view short films. While the kinetoscope was limited to individual viewing, it laid the groundwork for the development of the motion picture projector.

Edison's involvement in motion pictures extended beyond the kinetoscope. In 1893, he established the Black Maria, the first motion picture studio, in West Orange, New Jersey. The Black Maria was a purpose-built structure with a retractable roof to allow natural light, and it could rotate to follow the sun. This studio was used to produce some of the earliest motion pictures, featuring simple scenes and vaudeville acts.

Edison's company also developed the Vitascope, an early film projector that allowed for the projection of motion pictures onto a screen for a larger audience. The first commercial exhibition of motion pictures using the Vitascope took place in 1896, marking the beginning of the modern film industry.

Edison's innovations in motion pictures had a profound impact on the entertainment industry. He helped establish the foundations of filmmaking technology and contributed to the development of the film industry, which would go on to become a major cultural and economic force.

Impact on Various Industries

Thomas Edison's inventions and innovations had far-reaching impacts on multiple industries, shaping the modern world in profound ways.

- Electric Lighting and Power Industry: Edison's development of the incandescent light bulb and the electric power distribution system revolutionized the way people lived and worked. Electric lighting extended productive hours, improved safety, and enhanced the quality of life. The establishment of electric power utilities paved the way for the electrification of cities and homes, driving economic growth and technological advancement.

- Music and Entertainment Industry: The invention of the phonograph transformed the music industry by making it possible to record, distribute, and enjoy music in a new way. Edison's phonograph laid the foundation for the recording industry, which has since evolved into a global entertainment powerhouse. His work in motion pictures also contributed to the birth of the film industry, changing the landscape of entertainment forever.

- Communication Industry: Edison's improvements to telegraphy and his development of the stock ticker enhanced communication efficiency and speed, benefiting businesses and individuals alike. His innovations in communication technology paved the way for future advancements, including the telephone and the internet.

- Manufacturing and Industrial Processes: Edison's emphasis on efficiency and his development of new manufacturing techniques influenced industrial processes across various sectors. His approach to invention, characterized by systematic experimentation and prototyping, set new standards for research and development practices.

- Medical and Scientific Research: Edison's work extended to medical devices and scientific instruments, including the fluoroscope, an early X-ray machine. His contributions to medical technology improved diagnostic capabilities and patient care, advancing the field of medicine.

Thomas Edison's legacy as an innovator and entrepreneur is marked by his remarkable contributions to multiple industries through his inventions and technological advancements. From the development of the phonograph and the incandescent light bulb to the creation of the electric power distribution system and innovations in motion pictures, Edison's work transformed society and laid the groundwork for modern technological progress.

Edison's systematic approach to invention, characterized by perseverance, experimentation, and a focus on practical applications, set new standards for innovation and research. His impact on the electric lighting and power industry, the music and entertainment industry, the communication industry, and beyond, continues to be felt today.

Thomas Edison's story serves as a testament to the power of creativity, determination, and vision in driving technological advancement and shaping the future. His enduring legacy as one of history's greatest inventors and entrepreneurs inspires future generations to push the boundaries of what is possible and to use technology to improve the world.

Business Ventures and Strategies

Establishment of Menlo Park Laboratory

In 1876, Thomas Edison established his now-famous laboratory in Menlo Park, New Jersey, which would become a pioneering model for modern research and development. Known as the "invention factory," Menlo Park was the first industrial research lab in the world, dedicated to systematic experimentation and innovation.

Edison's vision for Menlo Park was to create a space where scientific research and practical engineering could intersect, leading to the rapid development of new technologies. He brought together a diverse team of skilled workers, including chemists, engineers, and machinists, to collaborate on various projects. This collaborative environment was designed to foster creativity and facilitate the rapid prototyping and testing of new ideas.

One of the most notable achievements at Menlo Park was the invention of the phonograph in 1877, which established Edison's reputation as a leading inventor. Following this success, Edison and his team embarked on the ambitious project of developing a practical incandescent light bulb. After extensive experimentation with different materials and designs, they succeeded in creating a long-lasting, commercially viable light bulb in 1879.

Menlo Park became a symbol of innovation and a benchmark for future research institutions. Edison's approach of combining theoretical research with practical application set new standards for industrial R&D. The establishment of Menlo Park also marked the beginning of a new era in which systematic, collaborative research would drive technological progress.

Commercialization of Inventions

Thomas Edison was not only a prolific inventor but also a shrewd businessman who understood the importance of commercializing his inventions. He recognized that bringing an invention to market required more than just a good idea; it required strategic planning, effective marketing, and reliable manufacturing processes.

Edison's strategy for commercializing his inventions involved several key steps:

- Market Research: Before fully committing to an invention, Edison conducted market research to assess its potential demand and commercial viability. He identified industries and consumer needs that his inventions could address, ensuring that there was a ready market for his products.

- Patenting: Edison was meticulous about securing patents for his inventions to protect his intellectual property and prevent others from copying his work. Patents provided him with the legal rights to exclusively produce and sell his inventions, giving him a competitive edge in the market.

- Partnerships and Financing: Edison understood the importance of securing financial backing and strategic partnerships to scale his inventions. He often partnered with investors and business leaders who could provide the necessary capital and resources to commercialize his products. For instance, the formation of the Edison Electric Light Company in 1878 brought together financiers like J.P. Morgan and the Vanderbilt family, who provided crucial support for the development and commercialization of electric lighting.

- Manufacturing and Distribution: To ensure the quality and reliability of his products, Edison established manufacturing facilities that adhered to strict standards. He also developed distribution networks to bring his inventions to market efficiently. For example, Edison set up factories to produce light bulbs and electrical equipment and created distribution systems to supply electricity to homes and businesses.

- Marketing and Publicity: Edison was a master of self-promotion and used media coverage to generate public interest in his inventions. He organized public demonstrations, such as the lighting of Menlo Park and the Pearl Street Station, to showcase the effectiveness of his electric lighting system. These events generated significant publicity and helped build consumer trust in his products.

- Continuous Improvement: Edison's commitment to innovation did not end with the commercialization of an invention. He continuously sought ways to improve his products and adapt to changing market needs. This approach ensured that his inventions remained relevant and competitive over time.

Patents and Intellectual Property Strategies

Thomas Edison's success as an inventor was closely tied to his strategic use of patents and intellectual property. Throughout his career, Edison was awarded 1,093 patents in the United States, a testament to his prolific inventiveness and his understanding of the importance of protecting his ideas.

Edison's approach to patents and intellectual property included several key strategies:

- Comprehensive Patenting: Edison was thorough in patenting every aspect of his inventions, from the core technology to ancillary components. This comprehensive approach ensured that competitors could not easily circumvent his patents by making minor modifications to his designs. For example, when developing the incandescent light bulb, Edison patented not only the bulb itself but also the filament materials, the vacuum inside the bulb, and the methods of manufacturing it.

- Defensive Patenting: Edison used patents defensively to protect his market position and prevent others from exploiting his innovations. By securing a broad range of patents related to his inventions, he created a formidable barrier to entry for competitors. This strategy was particularly evident in his work on electric lighting, where he held multiple patents covering different aspects of the technology.

- Patent Litigation: Edison was not hesitant to

engage in legal battles to defend his patents. He frequently took legal action against individuals and companies that infringed on his intellectual property rights. One notable example was the legal dispute with George Westinghouse over the use of alternating current (AC) versus direct current (DC) for electrical distribution. Although Edison ultimately lost the "War of Currents," his aggressive defense of his patents underscored his commitment to protecting his inventions.

- Licensing: Edison also used licensing as a strategy to monetize his patents and expand the reach of his inventions. By licensing his technologies to other manufacturers and businesses, he generated additional revenue streams and facilitated the widespread adoption of his innovations. For instance, Edison licensed the phonograph technology to various companies, allowing them to produce and sell phonographs while paying royalties to him.

- Innovation Ecosystem: Edison's extensive patent portfolio contributed to the creation of an innovation ecosystem around his inventions. By securing patents and licensing them strategically, he encouraged other inventors and businesses to build upon his work, leading to further technological advancements and market growth.

Competition with Other Inventors and Businesses

Thomas Edison's career was marked by intense competition with other inventors and businesses, which drove him to continually innovate and refine his technologies. Some of the most notable competitive rivalries included:

- The War of Currents: One of the most famous rivalries in Edison's career was with George Westinghouse and Nikola Tesla over the use of AC versus DC for electrical power distribution. Edison advocated for DC, which he believed was safer and more efficient for residential use, while Westinghouse and Tesla promoted AC, which was more efficient for long-distance transmission. The competition was fierce, with both sides engaging in public demonstrations and campaigns to discredit the other's technology. Ultimately, AC became the dominant standard for electrical distribution, but the rivalry underscored the competitive nature of the burgeoning electric power industry.

- Phonograph vs. Gramophone: Edison's phonograph faced competition from Emile Berliner's gramophone, which used flat discs instead of cylinders to record sound. The gramophone offered several advantages, including easier storage and mass production of records. Despite the competition, Edison continued to improve his phonograph and adapt to market demands, demonstrating his resilience and commitment to innovation.

- Motion Picture Technology: Edison's work in motion pictures also faced competition from other inventors and companies. The development of motion picture cameras, projectors, and film production techniques involved numerous inventors, including the Lumière brothers and William Kennedy Laurie Dickson, who initially worked for Edison but later contributed to the success of other companies. Edison's competitive nature drove him to continue developing new technologies and business strategies to maintain his position in the emerging film industry.

- Telegraphy and Communication: Edison's innovations in telegraphy, such as the quadruplex telegraph, faced competition from other inventors seeking to improve telegraphic communication. His rivalry with inventors like Alexander Graham Bell, who developed the telephone, highlighted the rapidly evolving nature of communication technology during that era. Edison's persistence in refining his telegraphy inventions and exploring new communication technologies demonstrated his adaptability and competitive spirit.

Despite these rivalries, Edison's ability to navigate competitive landscapes and continuously innovate allowed him to maintain his status as one of the foremost inventors of his time. His competitive drive pushed him to constantly seek new solutions and improve existing technologies, contributing to his lasting legacy in multiple industries.

Expansion of General Electric

The formation and expansion of General Electric (GE) were pivotal in solidifying Thomas Edison's impact on the electric power industry and beyond. GE emerged from the consolidation of several Edison-related businesses and other electric companies, creating a powerful entity capable of driving innovation and market expansion.

- Formation of GE: In 1892, the Edison General Electric Company merged with the Thomson-Houston Electric Company to form General Electric. This merger combined the strengths and resources of both companies, creating a diversified enterprise with extensive capabilities in electric lighting, power generation, and distribution. The merger was driven by the need to compete more effectively in the rapidly growing electric industry and to pool resources for further innovation.

- Diversification and Innovation: Under the GE umbrella, the company expanded its product offerings and continued to innovate across various sectors. GE developed new electrical appliances, industrial equipment, and advanced technologies, reinforcing its position as a leader in the electric industry. The company's commitment to research and development, inspired by Edison's approach, led to numerous technological breakthroughs and patents.

- Global Expansion: GE's growth extended beyond the United States, as the company pursued international markets and established a global presence. GE's technologies and products were exported worldwide, contributing to the electrification of cities and industries across the globe. The company's international expansion reflected Edison's vision of bringing electric power and innovation to a global audience.

- Research and Development: GE continued to prioritize research and development, building on the legacy of Menlo Park. The company established its own research laboratories, attracting top scientists and engineers to work on cutting-edge projects. This focus on R&D ensured that GE remained at the forefront of technological advancements and maintained its competitive edge.

- Corporate Governance and Management: The formation of GE also marked a shift in corporate governance and management practices. The company adopted modern management techniques, focusing on efficiency, strategic planning, and market-driven innovation. This professionalization of management helped GE navigate the complexities of a rapidly evolving industry and adapt to changing market conditions.

GE's expansion and success were a testament to Edison's vision and entrepreneurial spirit. The company's growth and diversification reflected his belief in the transformative power of technology and the importance of continuous innovation. GE's impact on the electric power industry, manufacturing, and global markets underscored Edison's lasting influence on modern industrial practices.

Thomas Edison's business ventures and strategies were characterized by a relentless pursuit of innovation, strategic commercialization of inventions, and a deep understanding of the importance of patents and intellectual property. The establishment of Menlo Park laboratory set new standards for research and development, fostering a collaborative environment that accelerated technological progress.

Edison's ability to commercialize his inventions and navigate competitive landscapes demonstrated his business acumen and adaptability. His strategic use of patents protected his innovations and created a sustainable ecosystem for further technological advancements.

The formation and expansion of General Electric marked the culmination of Edison's vision for the electric power industry. GE's growth, diversification, and global reach reflected his enduring legacy and impact on modern industrial practices.

Thomas Edison's life and work offer valuable lessons in creativity, resilience, and the transformative power of technology. His story serves as a testament to the impact that one individual's vision and determination can have on the world, leaving an indelible mark on history and shaping the future of innovation.

Leadership and Management Style

Edison's Approach to Innovation

Thomas Edison's approach to innovation was characterized by relentless experimentation, a systematic method of problem-solving, and a deep understanding of the practical applications of his inventions. Edison believed that success in invention required not just inspiration but also perspiration. His famous quote, "Genius is one percent inspiration and ninety-nine percent perspiration," encapsulated his belief that hard work, perseverance, and meticulous experimentation were crucial to innovation.

Edison's innovative process began with identifying a problem or a need in society that technology could address. He would then brainstorm potential solutions, often generating hundreds of ideas before zeroing in on the most promising ones. Edison's approach was hands-on, and he was deeply involved in the experimentation phase, constantly tinkering and adjusting until he achieved the desired outcome.

Edison's systematic approach to experimentation involved meticulous documentation. He maintained detailed notes on every experiment, recording both successes and failures. This methodical documentation allowed him to learn from each attempt and refine his approach continuously. It also facilitated collaboration within his team, as the records could be referenced and built upon by other researchers.

One of the defining features of Edison's approach to

innovation was his focus on practical application. He was not content with theoretical discoveries; he aimed to create marketable products that could improve people's lives. This pragmatic approach drove his work on the phonograph, incandescent light bulb, and numerous other inventions. Edison's insistence on practicality ensured that his innovations had a tangible impact on society and found commercial success.

Management Practices and Team Building

Thomas Edison's management practices and team-building strategies were integral to his success as an inventor and entrepreneur. He understood that innovation was a collaborative effort and that building a strong, diverse team was essential for sustained creativity and productivity.

- Collaborative Environment: Edison fostered a collaborative environment at his Menlo Park and later West Orange laboratories. He brought together individuals with diverse skills and expertise, including chemists, engineers, machinists, and physicists. This multidisciplinary approach allowed for a cross-pollination of ideas and accelerated the pace of innovation. Edison's laboratories were buzzing with activity, as team members worked together to solve complex problems and develop new technologies.

- Hands-on Leadership: Edison was a hands-on leader who worked alongside his team members, offering guidance, feedback, and encouragement. He believed in leading by example and was often found working late into the night on experiments. Edison's active involvement in the day-to-day operations of his laboratories inspired his team and demonstrated his commitment to their shared goals.

- Incentives and Rewards: Edison recognized the importance of incentivizing his team to maintain high levels of motivation and productivity. He offered financial rewards and recognition for successful inventions and breakthroughs. This practice not only motivated his team but also fostered a sense of ownership and pride in their work.

- Tolerance for Failure: Edison's management style included a high tolerance for failure. He viewed failures as valuable learning experiences that brought his team closer to finding the right solution. This acceptance of failure created a safe environment for experimentation, encouraging team members to take risks and explore bold ideas without fear of repercussions.

- Structured Processes: While Edison encouraged creativity and experimentation, he also implemented structured processes to ensure efficiency and productivity. His laboratories operated with a clear workflow, from ideation and experimentation to prototyping and testing. This structured approach helped manage the chaos of continuous innovation and ensured that projects progressed steadily toward completion.

Dealing with Failures and Setbacks

Thomas Edison's career was marked by numerous failures and setbacks, yet his ability to persevere and learn from these experiences was a key factor in his success. Edison's approach to dealing with failures was rooted in resilience, adaptability, and an unwavering belief in his vision.

- Resilience: Edison's resilience in the face of failure was legendary. He famously conducted thousands of experiments before perfecting the incandescent light bulb, encountering countless setbacks along the way. Instead of being discouraged, Edison viewed each failure as a step closer to success. His determination and refusal to give up were essential to overcoming the many obstacles he faced.

- Adaptability: Edison's ability to adapt to changing circumstances and new information was crucial in navigating failures. When an experiment did not yield the desired results, Edison was quick to adjust his approach, try new materials, or modify his designs. This adaptability allowed him to remain flexible and responsive to the challenges that arose during the innovation process.

- Learning from Failure: Edison approached failures as valuable learning opportunities. He meticulously documented every experiment, noting what worked and what didn't. This systematic approach enabled him to identify patterns, refine his methods, and build on previous attempts. By learning from his failures, Edison continuously improved his inventions and increased his chances of eventual success.

- Maintaining a Positive Attitude: Edison's positive attitude and optimism were critical in dealing with setbacks. He maintained a forward-looking perspective, always believing that a solution was within reach. This optimism not only fueled his perseverance but also inspired his team to stay motivated and focused on their goals.

- Balancing Risk and Reward: Edison understood the importance of balancing risk and reward in his ventures. While he was willing to take significant risks to achieve breakthroughs, he also managed his resources carefully to mitigate potential losses. This strategic approach allowed him to pursue ambitious projects while maintaining the financial stability needed to sustain his operations.

Balancing Creativity and Business Acumen

Thomas Edison's success as both an inventor and an entrepreneur was due in large part to his ability to balance creativity with business acumen. He recognized that innovation alone was not enough;

bringing inventions to market required strategic planning, effective management, and a keen understanding of the business landscape.

- Market-Oriented Innovation: Edison's approach to invention was driven by a clear understanding of market needs and consumer demand. He focused on developing practical solutions to real-world problems, ensuring that his inventions had commercial viability. This market-oriented approach helped him create products that were not only innovative but also in high demand.

- Strategic Commercialization: Edison was adept at commercializing his inventions, turning them into profitable business ventures. He established manufacturing facilities, distribution networks, and sales channels to bring his products to market efficiently. Edison's ability to commercialize his inventions ensured that they reached a wide audience and generated significant revenue.

- Building a Brand: Edison understood the importance of building a strong brand to support his business ventures. He actively promoted his inventions through public demonstrations, media coverage, and strategic partnerships. Edison's reputation as a leading inventor and his brand's association with innovation and quality helped build consumer trust and loyalty.

- Financial Management: Edison's financial

acumen played a critical role in his success. He secured funding from investors, managed costs carefully, and reinvested profits into his ventures. Edison's ability to attract investment and manage financial resources ensured that his projects had the necessary support to succeed.

- Adaptation to Market Changes: Edison's business acumen included the ability to adapt to changing market conditions and technological advancements. He kept a close eye on industry trends and competitive developments, adjusting his strategies as needed to stay ahead of the curve. This adaptability helped him navigate the competitive landscape and maintain his leadership position in multiple industries.

Legacy in Modern Business Practices

Thomas Edison's leadership and management style have left a lasting legacy in modern business practices. His systematic approach to innovation, emphasis on collaboration, and ability to balance creativity with business acumen have influenced generations of entrepreneurs and business leaders.

- Research and Development: Edison's establishment of the Menlo Park laboratory set a precedent for modern R&D practices. His model of systematic experimentation, interdisciplinary collaboration, and continuous improvement has become the standard for innovation in industries ranging from technology to pharmaceuticals.

- Corporate Innovation: Edison's approach to innovation, which combined creativity with practical application, has shaped corporate innovation strategies. Companies today invest heavily in R&D, encourage cross-functional collaboration, and focus on developing market-driven solutions to stay competitive.

- Intellectual Property Management: Edison's strategic use of patents and intellectual property protection has influenced how businesses approach IP management. Modern companies prioritize securing patents, defending their IP rights, and leveraging their IP portfolios to gain a competitive edge and drive revenue.

- Entrepreneurial Mindset: Edison's resilience, adaptability, and willingness to embrace failure are key components of the entrepreneurial mindset. His belief in learning from setbacks and maintaining a positive attitude in the face of challenges continues to inspire entrepreneurs to pursue bold ideas and persevere through difficulties.

- Balancing Innovation and Business Strategy: Edison's ability to balance innovation with sound business strategy has become a guiding principle for successful companies. Modern business leaders recognize the importance of aligning their innovative efforts with market needs, financial goals, and long-term strategic objectives.

Thomas Edison's leadership and management style were instrumental in his success as an inventor and entrepreneur. His systematic approach to innovation, collaborative team-building practices, resilience in the face of failure, and ability to balance creativity with business acumen set him apart as a visionary leader.

Edison's legacy extends far beyond his numerous inventions. His influence on modern business practices, from R&D and corporate innovation to IP management and entrepreneurial resilience, continues to shape how companies operate and innovate. Edison's life and work offer valuable lessons for business leaders, emphasizing the importance of perseverance, strategic thinking, and a commitment to continuous improvement.

Thomas Edison's story serves as a testament to the transformative power of innovation and the enduring impact of effective leadership. His contributions to technology, industry, and business practices have left an indelible mark on the world, inspiring future generations to push the boundaries of what is possible and drive positive change through innovation.

Case Study: The Electric Light and Power Industry

Development and Commercialization of Electric Lighting

The development and commercialization of electric lighting are perhaps Thomas Edison's most famous and impactful contributions to modern technology. Before Edison's innovations, lighting was primarily provided by gas lamps and candles, which were not only inefficient but also posed significant safety hazards. Edison's work on electric lighting transformed the way people lived and worked, paving the way for the modern electric power industry.

Edison's journey to develop a practical electric light bulb began in the late 1870s. His goal was to create a light source that was both long-lasting and energy-efficient, making it a viable alternative to gas lighting. After experimenting with thousands of materials, Edison and his team discovered that a carbonized bamboo filament provided the best combination of longevity and durability. In 1879, Edison successfully demonstrated his incandescent light bulb, which could burn for up to 1,200 hours.

The next challenge was to create an entire system to generate and distribute electricity. Edison understood that the light bulb alone would not revolutionize lighting; it needed to be part of a comprehensive electric lighting system. In 1882, Edison opened the Pearl Street Station in New York City, the world's first central power station. The station used direct current (DC) electricity to supply power to a small area of lower Manhattan, providing electricity to about 400 lamps for 85 customers.

Edison's Pearl Street Station was a monumental achievement, demonstrating the feasibility and benefits of electric lighting and power distribution. The success of this project laid the foundation for the widespread adoption of electric lighting and the growth of the electric power industry.

Impact on Urban Development and Industry

The introduction of electric lighting had a profound impact on urban development and industry, transforming cities and revolutionizing the way businesses operated.

- Urban Development: Electric lighting fundamentally changed the urban landscape. Streets, homes, and public spaces illuminated by electric lights became safer and more accessible at night, extending the hours during which people could work, shop, and socialize. This transformation contributed to the growth of nightlife and the development of vibrant urban centers. Electric lighting also enabled cities to expand, as new neighborhoods and commercial areas could be developed without the limitations imposed by gas lighting infrastructure.

- Industrial Operations: The impact of electric lighting on industry was equally significant. Factories and workplaces could operate around the clock, increasing productivity and efficiency. Electric lighting improved working conditions, reducing the risk of accidents and enabling more precise and detailed work. This shift was particularly important in industries such as manufacturing, textiles, and mining, where adequate lighting was crucial for safety and productivity.

- Economic Growth: The widespread adoption of electric lighting stimulated economic growth by creating new markets and industries. The demand for electrical equipment, such as light bulbs, wiring, and generators, led to the rapid expansion of the electrical manufacturing industry. Additionally, the increased productivity and extended operating hours facilitated by electric lighting contributed to economic development and urban prosperity.

- Public Health and Safety: Electric lighting also had positive implications for public health and safety. It reduced the reliance on gas lamps, which emitted harmful fumes and posed fire hazards. The cleaner, safer environment created by electric lighting contributed to improved public health outcomes and enhanced quality of life in urban areas.

Competition with Gas Lighting and Other Technologies

The commercialization of electric lighting was not without its challenges. Edison faced significant competition from established gas lighting companies and other emerging technologies.

- Gas Lighting: At the time Edison introduced electric lighting, gas lighting was the dominant technology for street and indoor lighting. Gas lighting companies had substantial infrastructure and a large customer base, making it difficult for electric lighting to gain a foothold. Gas lighting was well-entrenched, with extensive networks of gas lines and a strong market presence.

To compete with gas lighting, Edison had to demonstrate the superiority of electric lighting in terms of efficiency, safety, and cost-effectiveness. He conducted public demonstrations, such as the lighting of Menlo Park and the Pearl Street Station, to showcase the benefits of electric lighting. These events generated public interest and built consumer confidence in the new technology.

- Arc Lighting: Another competing technology was arc lighting, which was used for street lighting and large public spaces. Arc lights were bright and effective but unsuitable for indoor use due to their intense light and high heat output. Edison's incandescent light bulb offered a more versatile and practical solution for both indoor and outdoor lighting, making it a more attractive option for widespread adoption.

- Direct Current (DC) vs. Alternating Current (AC): Edison's use of direct current (DC) electricity faced competition from alternating current (AC) systems developed by Nikola Tesla and promoted by George Westinghouse. AC systems had significant advantages for long-distance power transmission, as they could be easily transformed to different voltage levels and transmitted over greater distances with less power loss.

The rivalry between DC and AC systems, known as the "War of Currents," was intense. Edison staunchly defended DC, arguing that it was safer for residential use, while Westinghouse and Tesla highlighted the efficiency and scalability of AC. Despite Edison's efforts, AC ultimately became the dominant standard for electrical distribution, but the competition drove significant advancements in electrical technology and infrastructure.

Formation of Electric Utility Companies

The development and commercialization of electric lighting and power distribution led to the formation of electric utility companies, which played a crucial role in expanding access to electricity and driving the growth of the industry.

- Edison Electric Light Company: In 1878, Edison founded the Edison Electric Light Company to finance and develop his electric lighting system. The company attracted significant investment from prominent financiers, including J.P. Morgan and the Vanderbilt family. This financial backing provided the resources needed to build the Pearl Street Station and other early power plants.

- Consolidation and Expansion: As the electric power industry grew, numerous electric utility companies were established to build and operate power plants and distribution networks. Many of these companies were initially small, local operations, but they soon began to consolidate and expand. Edison's companies, including Edison General Electric, played a central role in this consolidation process.

- Formation of General Electric: In 1892, Edison General Electric merged with the Thomson-Houston Electric Company to form General Electric (GE). This merger created a powerful entity with extensive capabilities in electric lighting, power generation, and distribution. GE's formation marked a significant milestone in the evolution of the electric power industry, bringing together leading technologies and resources to drive further innovation and growth.

- Regulation and Standardization: The rapid growth of electric utility companies necessitated the development of regulatory frameworks and standards to ensure reliable and safe electricity supply. Governments and industry organizations established guidelines for electrical infrastructure, safety standards, and pricing. These regulations helped stabilize the industry and build consumer trust in electric utilities.

- Rural Electrification: While urban areas quickly adopted electric lighting and power, rural electrification lagged behind due to the high costs of building infrastructure in sparsely populated areas. In the 1930s, government initiatives, such as the Rural Electrification Administration (REA) in the United States, provided funding and support to extend electrical grids to rural communities. This effort significantly increased access to electricity, improving the quality of life and economic opportunities for rural populations.

Edison's Enduring Influence on Modern Technology

Thomas Edison's contributions to the development and commercialization of electric lighting and power distribution have left an enduring legacy on modern technology and society.

- Foundation of the Electric Power Industry: Edison's work laid the groundwork for the modern electric power industry. His innovations in electric lighting and power distribution systems set the stage for the widespread adoption of electricity, transforming how people live and work. The establishment of central power stations and distribution networks revolutionized urban development and industrial operations.

- Technological Advancements: Edison's approach to systematic experimentation and practical application of technology has influenced countless innovations. His emphasis on developing marketable products that address real-world needs continues to inspire modern inventors and engineers. Edison's legacy is evident in the ongoing advancements in electrical engineering, from smart grids to renewable energy technologies.

- Research and Development Practices: The model of industrial research and development pioneered by Edison at Menlo Park has become a standard practice in modern technology companies. The collaborative, interdisciplinary approach to innovation that Edison championed is now a cornerstone of R&D efforts in industries ranging from pharmaceuticals to information technology.

- Corporate Innovation: Edison's ability to balance creativity with business acumen has shaped corporate innovation strategies. Companies today prioritize aligning their innovative efforts with market demands and strategic goals, ensuring that new technologies are both groundbreaking and commercially viable.

- Global Electrification: Edison's vision of widespread electrification has become a reality, with electricity now being a fundamental utility across the globe. The impact of electric lighting and power on economic development, public health, and quality of life cannot be overstated. Edison's work has enabled the growth of global industries and the modernization of societies worldwide.

- Sustainability and Energy Efficiency: Edison's legacy also informs contemporary efforts to develop sustainable and energy-efficient technologies. The ongoing pursuit of improved lighting technologies, such as LED and smart lighting systems, reflects Edison's commitment to innovation and efficiency. His pioneering work continues to inspire efforts to create environmentally friendly and sustainable solutions in the energy sector.

Thomas Edison's contributions to the electric light and power industry revolutionized the way people live and work, laying the foundation for the modern electric power industry. His development and commercialization of electric lighting transformed urban development, industrial operations, and public health. Despite significant competition from gas lighting and other technologies, Edison's innovations proved superior in efficiency, safety, and practicality.

The formation of electric utility companies and the establishment of central power stations were crucial steps in expanding access to electricity and driving economic growth. Edison's enduring influence on modern technology is evident in the ongoing advancements in electrical engineering, research and development practices, and corporate innovation strategies.

Edison's legacy serves as a testament to the transformative power of innovation and the lasting impact of visionary leadership. His work continues to inspire future generations of inventors and entrepreneurs to push the boundaries of what is possible and to harness technology for the betterment of society.

Chapter 5:

Sam Walton Revolutionizing Retail

Sam Walton, born on March 29, 1918, in Kingfisher, Oklahoma, grew up during the Great Depression, an era that significantly shaped his values and work ethic. Walton's parents, Thomas Gibson Walton and Nancy Lee Walton, were farmers, but the economic hardships of the 1920s and 1930s forced the family to move frequently in search of better opportunities.

From a young age, Walton demonstrated a strong work ethic and entrepreneurial spirit. He took on various jobs to help support his family, such as delivering newspapers, selling magazine subscriptions, and milking cows. These early experiences instilled in him the importance of hard work, frugality, and customer service, values that would later become the foundation of his business philosophy.

Walton was also an active and determined student. He excelled in academics and athletics, serving as student body president and an accomplished football player in high school. His leadership skills and competitive nature were evident early on and would prove essential in his future business endeavors.

After graduating from high school in 1936, Walton attended the University of Missouri, where he studied economics. He worked various jobs throughout college, including waiting tables and lifeguarding, to finance his education. Walton's academic background in economics provided him with a solid understanding of business principles, which he would later apply in his retail ventures.

Entry into the Retail Industry

Sam Walton's entry into the retail industry began after his graduation from the University of Missouri in 1940. He initially joined the management training program at J.C. Penney, a leading retailer at the time. This experience gave Walton invaluable insights into the retail business, including store management, merchandising, and customer service.

Walton's time at J.C. Penney was short-lived due to his enlistment in the U.S. Army during World War II. After serving as an Army intelligence officer, Walton returned to civilian life in 1945 with a determination to start his own business. He used his savings, along with a loan from his father-in-law, to purchase a Ben Franklin variety store in Newport, Arkansas. This store was part of a chain of franchise stores managed by Butler Brothers.

Running the Ben Franklin store provided Walton with hands-on experience in retail management. He experimented with various strategies to attract customers and increase sales, such as offering a wider range of products, improving store layout, and emphasizing customer service. Walton's innovative approach led to significant increases in sales and profits, laying the groundwork for his future success.

Founding of Walmart

Despite his success with the Ben Franklin store, Walton faced a setback in 1950 when the lease on his Newport store was not renewed. Undeterred, he moved to Bentonville, Arkansas, where he opened a new Ben Franklin franchise store. This store also flourished, reinforcing Walton's belief in his retail strategies.

In 1962, Sam Walton took a bold step by founding the first Walmart store in Rogers, Arkansas. Walton's vision for Walmart was based on the idea of providing customers with low prices and great value, which he believed could be achieved through efficient operations, high volume sales, and leveraging economies of scale.

The first Walmart store was a discount center, offering a wide variety of products at lower prices than traditional department stores. Walton's approach was revolutionary at the time, as it focused on rural and small-town markets that were often overlooked by large retailers. He believed that by serving these communities, Walmart could fill a significant gap in the retail market and build a loyal customer base.

Walton's emphasis on low prices and customer satisfaction resonated with consumers, leading to rapid growth and expansion. By the end of the 1960s, Walmart had opened 24 stores across Arkansas, achieving impressive sales and establishing a strong presence in the discount retail market.

Vision for Discount Retailing

Sam Walton's vision for discount retailing was driven by his commitment to offering the lowest prices and best value to customers. He believed that by keeping prices low, Walmart could attract more customers and drive higher sales volumes, which in turn would lower costs through economies of scale. This vision became the cornerstone of Walmart's business strategy and revolutionized the retail industry.

Walton's approach to discount retailing involved several key principles:

- Everyday Low Prices (EDLP): Walton introduced the concept of everyday low prices, which meant that Walmart consistently offered products at the lowest possible prices rather than relying on periodic sales or promotions. This strategy built customer trust and encouraged repeat business, as customers knew they could always find good deals at Walmart.

- Efficient Supply Chain Management: Walton understood the importance of an efficient supply chain in maintaining low prices. He invested in advanced logistics and inventory management systems, such as computerized tracking and distribution centers, to streamline operations and reduce costs. Walmart's ability to quickly replenish stock and maintain optimal inventory levels became a significant competitive advantage.

- High Volume Sales: By focusing on high volume sales, Walmart could negotiate better terms with suppliers, leading to lower procurement costs. Walton's philosophy was to sell more units at lower margins, which would result in higher overall profits. This volume-driven approach allowed Walmart to offer competitive prices while maintaining profitability.

- Rural and Small-Town Focus: Walton's strategy of targeting rural and small-town markets was a departure from the traditional retail focus on urban centers. He recognized that these areas had underserved consumers who were looking for affordable products. By catering to these markets, Walmart built a loyal customer base and faced less competition from established retailers.

- Customer-Centric Culture: Walton emphasized the importance of customer service and satisfaction. He believed that happy customers were the key to Walmart's success. This customer-centric culture was ingrained in Walmart's operations, with employees encouraged to go above and beyond to meet customer needs.

Initial Business Challenges

Despite his innovative approach and early successes, Sam Walton faced several challenges in the initial stages of building Walmart. These challenges tested his resilience and determination, ultimately shaping the strategies that would lead to Walmart's dominance in the retail industry.

- Skepticism from Suppliers: In the early days, Walton struggled to convince suppliers to provide products at the low prices he needed to maintain his discount strategy. Many suppliers were hesitant to do business with a new and unproven retailer, especially one based in rural areas. Walton had to work hard to build relationships with suppliers and demonstrate the potential for high sales volumes and long-term partnerships.

- Competition from Established Retailers: Established retailers viewed Walmart's low-price strategy with skepticism and saw it as a threat to their business models. Walton faced significant competition from these retailers, who often had more resources and established customer bases. To overcome this, Walton focused on differentiating Walmart through superior customer service, efficient operations, and relentless cost control.

- Financial Constraints: Financing the rapid expansion of Walmart was a constant challenge. Walton had to be resourceful in securing the necessary capital to open new stores and invest in technology and infrastructure. He reinvested profits back into the business and used creative financing methods, such as stock options for employees, to align their interests with the company's growth.

- Operational Efficiency: Maintaining operational efficiency across a growing number of stores was a complex task. Walton had to ensure that each store adhered to Walmart's standards for pricing, inventory management, and customer service. He invested in technology and developed standardized processes to maintain consistency and efficiency across the entire organization.

- Building a Corporate Culture: As Walmart expanded, maintaining a cohesive corporate culture became increasingly important. Walton's leadership style emphasized humility, hard work, and a focus on customer satisfaction. He made efforts to instill these values in all employees, fostering a culture of teamwork and dedication to the company's mission.

Sam Walton's journey from his early life to the founding of Walmart is a testament to his vision, innovation, and relentless drive to revolutionize the retail industry. His childhood and early influences instilled in him a strong work ethic and entrepreneurial spirit, which he carried into his career in retail. Walton's experiences at J.C. Penney and his success with Ben Franklin stores provided him with the foundational knowledge and skills to launch Walmart.

The founding of Walmart in 1962 marked the

beginning of a retail revolution. Walton's vision for discount retailing, based on everyday low prices, efficient supply chain management, high volume sales, and a focus on rural markets, set Walmart apart from its competitors. Despite facing numerous challenges, Walton's strategic approach and commitment to customer satisfaction drove Walmart's rapid growth and success.

Walton's innovative strategies transformed the retail landscape, making Walmart one of the largest and most influential retail chains in the world. His legacy continues to impact the industry, as Walmart remains a leader in retail innovation and customer service.

Sam Walton's story offers valuable lessons in leadership, resilience, and the power of a clear vision. His ability to balance creativity with business acumen, adapt to challenges, and build a strong corporate culture has left an enduring mark on the retail industry. Walton's dedication to providing value to customers and his pioneering approach to discount retailing continue to inspire entrepreneurs and business leaders worldwide.

Growth and Expansion of Walmart

Strategies for Rapid Expansion

The rapid expansion of Walmart is a defining characteristic of the company's rise to retail dominance. Sam Walton's vision for Walmart was built on the principles of offering low prices, exceptional customer service, and extensive product variety. This vision was executed through a series of strategic decisions and innovations that fueled Walmart's growth.

- Aggressive Store Expansion: From the beginning, Walton pursued an aggressive store expansion strategy. By the end of the 1960s, Walmart had grown to 24 stores. This expansion continued throughout the 1970s and 1980s, with Walmart opening hundreds of new stores each year. Walton focused on rural and suburban areas that were underserved by other retailers, allowing Walmart to build a strong customer base with less direct competition.

- Frugality and Cost Control: Walton's emphasis on frugality and cost control was a cornerstone of Walmart's expansion strategy. The company's headquarters were famously modest, reflecting Walton's belief that saving money on operational expenses allowed Walmart to pass on savings to customers. This focus on cost efficiency permeated every aspect of Walmart's operations, from store design to inventory management.

- Recruiting and Training: Walton understood that the success of his expansion strategy depended on having competent and motivated employees. Walmart invested heavily in recruiting and training programs to ensure that new stores were staffed with capable managers and associates who were aligned with the company's culture and goals. Walton believed in promoting from within, which helped to cultivate loyalty and a deep understanding of

Walmart's values among employees.

- Technology Investment: Early on, Walton recognized the importance of technology in supporting Walmart's growth. The company invested in advanced computer systems for inventory management and sales tracking. This technological edge allowed Walmart to operate more efficiently and respond quickly to market changes. By the 1980s, Walmart had one of the most sophisticated retail computer systems in the world.

- Hub-and-Spoke Distribution: Walton implemented a hub-and-spoke distribution model to support Walmart's rapid expansion. Distribution centers were strategically located to serve clusters of stores within a specific radius. This model minimized transportation costs and ensured that stores were consistently stocked with the products customers wanted. The efficiency of Walmart's distribution network was a significant factor in its ability to expand quickly and maintain low prices.

Innovations in Supply Chain Management

Walmart's success is closely tied to its innovative approach to supply chain management. The company's ability to move products efficiently from suppliers to stores and ultimately to customers has been a critical factor in maintaining its low-cost leadership.

- Centralized Distribution Centers: Walmart

pioneered the use of centralized distribution centers to streamline its supply chain. By consolidating inventory in regional warehouses, Walmart could reduce shipping times and costs, ensuring that stores were always well-stocked. These distribution centers were equipped with advanced technology to manage inventory and coordinate shipments to stores.

- Cross-Docking: One of Walmart's most significant supply chain innovations was the implementation of cross-docking. In this system, products are unloaded from incoming trucks and immediately loaded onto outbound trucks for delivery to stores, without being stored in the warehouse. This practice reduces storage costs, minimizes handling, and speeds up the movement of goods through the supply chain, ensuring fresh inventory at stores.

- Vendor Partnerships: Walmart developed strong partnerships with its suppliers to enhance supply chain efficiency. The company worked closely with vendors to implement just-in-time inventory practices, which reduced excess stock and minimized waste. Walmart also shared sales data with suppliers to help them anticipate demand and adjust production schedules accordingly.

- Technology Integration: Walmart invested heavily in technology to improve supply chain visibility and efficiency. The company's proprietary Retail Link system allowed suppliers to access real-time sales data and inventory levels, enabling better coordination and planning. Walmart also adopted radio frequency identification (RFID) technology to track products throughout the supply chain, further enhancing inventory accuracy and reducing losses.

- Sustainability Initiatives: In recent years, Walmart has focused on making its supply chain more sustainable. The company has implemented initiatives to reduce energy consumption, minimize waste, and source products responsibly. Walmart's sustainability efforts include working with suppliers to reduce packaging, improve energy efficiency in transportation, and promote sustainable agriculture practices.

Development of the Big-Box Store Format

The development of the big-box store format was a key factor in Walmart's expansion and success. This format, characterized by large, warehouse-style stores offering a wide range of products at low prices, became synonymous with Walmart and revolutionized the retail industry.

- One-Stop Shopping: Walton's vision for Walmart was to create a one-stop shopping destination where customers could find everything they needed under one roof. The big-box store format allowed Walmart to offer a vast selection of products, from groceries and clothing to electronics and home goods. This convenience attracted customers and encouraged them to do more of their shopping at Walmart.

- Economies of Scale: The large size of Walmart's stores enabled the company to achieve economies of scale in purchasing and operations. By buying in bulk, Walmart could negotiate lower prices with suppliers, which translated into lower prices for customers. The spacious layout of the stores also allowed for efficient stocking and display of products, reducing labor costs.

- Store Layout and Design: Walmart's big-box stores were designed with the customer in mind. Wide aisles, clear signage, and logical product placement made shopping easy and enjoyable. The stores were organized to maximize sales, with high-traffic items placed strategically to encourage impulse purchases. The layout also facilitated efficient stocking and replenishment, ensuring that popular products were always available.

- Expansion into Supercenters: Building on the success of its big-box stores, Walmart introduced the supercenter concept in the late 1980s. Supercenters combined a traditional Walmart store with a full-service grocery store, providing customers with an even more comprehensive shopping experience. The addition of groceries drove increased foot traffic and higher sales, further cementing Walmart's dominance in the retail market.

- Adaptation to Local Markets: While the big-box format was standardized, Walmart also adapted its stores to meet the needs of local markets. This included adjusting product assortments to reflect local preferences, offering region-specific services, and participating in community events. This local customization helped Walmart build strong connections with customers and communities.

Impact on Small Businesses and Local Economies

Walmart's rapid expansion and dominance in the retail industry have had significant impacts on small businesses and local economies, both positive and negative.

- Displacement of Small Businesses: One of the most contentious aspects of Walmart's growth has been its impact on small, local businesses. Many small retailers have struggled to compete with Walmart's low prices and extensive product selection. The arrival of a Walmart store in a community often leads to the closure of local shops, which can have a ripple effect on the local economy and reduce the diversity of retail options.

- Job Creation and Economic Development: Despite the challenges faced by small businesses, Walmart's expansion has also brought economic benefits to many communities. The opening of a Walmart store often creates hundreds of jobs, providing employment opportunities for local residents. Additionally, Walmart's presence can attract other businesses and drive economic development in the surrounding area.

- Lower Prices for Consumers: Walmart's commitment to low prices has benefited consumers by making a wide range of products more affordable. This has been particularly important for low-income families, who can stretch their budgets further by shopping at Walmart. The increased purchasing power of consumers can stimulate local economies by freeing up income for other spending.

- Philanthropic Initiatives: Walmart has also contributed to local communities through its philanthropic initiatives. The company donates millions of dollars each year to various causes, including education, healthcare, disaster relief, and hunger programs. Walmart's charitable efforts have supported community development and provided resources to address local challenges.

- Supply Chain and Local Producers: Walmart's influence extends to local producers and suppliers. The company's focus on efficiency and cost control has pushed suppliers to improve their operations and adopt best practices. While this has led to greater competitiveness, some small producers have struggled to meet Walmart's demands for large volumes and low prices, leading to consolidation in the supplier base.

Competition with Other Retailers

Walmart's rise to prominence has been marked by intense competition with other retailers. The company's strategies for managing and overcoming this competition have been critical to its success.

- Competing with Discount Retailers: In its early years, Walmart faced competition from established discount retailers such as Kmart and Target. Walton's focus on rural and suburban markets, combined with his relentless emphasis on low prices and customer service, allowed Walmart to carve out a unique market position. Over time, Walmart's efficient operations and aggressive expansion helped it outpace these competitors.

- Battling Supermarket Chains: With the introduction of Walmart Supercenters, the company entered the grocery market, challenging established supermarket chains like Kroger and Safeway. Walmart leveraged its supply chain efficiencies and buying power to offer groceries at lower prices, quickly gaining market share. The convenience of combining grocery shopping with other retail purchases made Walmart Supercenters a popular choice for consumers.

- Responding to Specialty Retailers: Walmart has also faced competition from specialty retailers that focus on specific product categories, such as electronics, apparel, and home goods. To compete, Walmart has expanded and improved its product offerings in these categories, often through strategic partnerships and acquisitions. For example, Walmart's acquisition of Jet.com in 2016 enhanced its e-commerce capabilities and allowed it to better compete with online retailers like Amazon.

- Embracing E-Commerce: The rise of e-commerce presented a significant challenge to traditional brick-and-mortar retailers, including Walmart. In response, Walmart has made substantial investments in its online platform and digital infrastructure. The company has developed a robust e-commerce presence, offering a wide range of products online and implementing services like free two-day shipping and in-store pickup. Walmart's acquisition of e-commerce startups and investments in technology have helped it compete with online giants like Amazon.

- Global Expansion: To further expand its market reach, Walmart has pursued international growth, entering markets in Latin America, Asia, and Europe. The company has faced varying degrees of success abroad, adapting its strategies to meet local market conditions and preferences. Walmart's international expansion has diversified its revenue streams and provided new opportunities for growth, but it has also presented challenges in navigating different regulatory environments and cultural differences.

Sam Walton's vision and strategies for Walmart transformed the retail industry and established Walmart as a global retail powerhouse. Through aggressive expansion, innovations in supply chain management, and the development of the big-box store format, Walmart revolutionized how products are sold and delivered to consumers.

Walmart's impact on small businesses and local economies has been profound, creating both challenges and opportunities. While the company's expansion has displaced some small retailers, it has also brought economic benefits, including job creation and lower prices for consumers. Walmart's philanthropic efforts and contributions to community development have further shaped its legacy.

The intense competition with other retailers has driven Walmart to continuously innovate and adapt. From discount retailers to online giants, Walmart has faced numerous challenges but has remained resilient through strategic investments and a focus on customer value.

Sam Walton's legacy lives on through Walmart's enduring influence on modern retailing. The principles he established—such as frugality, customer focus, and operational efficiency—continue to guide the company and inspire retailers worldwide. Walmart's story is a testament to the transformative power of vision, innovation, and relentless pursuit of excellence.

Corporate Culture and Employee Relations

Walton's Approach to Employee Management

Sam Walton's approach to employee management was rooted in his belief that employees, or "associates" as he preferred to call them, were the key to Walmart's success. Walton viewed his employees as partners in the business, and his management style emphasized respect, empowerment, and open communication.

- Respect and Empowerment: Walton believed that every associate should be treated with respect and valued for their contributions. He encouraged managers to empower their employees by involving them in decision-making processes and seeking their input on ways to improve operations. Walton's philosophy was that those closest to the day-to-day activities often had the best insights into how to make things better.

- Open Communication: Walton fostered a culture of open communication within Walmart. He implemented an open-door policy, encouraging associates at all levels to share their ideas, concerns, and feedback directly with management. Walton himself was known for walking the aisles of Walmart stores, talking to employees and customers to understand their needs and perspectives.

- Visibility and Accessibility: Walton made it a point to be visible and accessible to his employees. He traveled extensively to visit

Walmart stores across the country, often arriving unannounced to get a genuine sense of the store operations and employee morale. This hands-on approach helped Walton stay connected with the workforce and reinforce the company's core values.

- Training and Development: Walton placed a strong emphasis on training and development, recognizing that well-trained employees were essential to providing excellent customer service and driving the company's growth. Walmart invested in comprehensive training programs to equip associates with the skills and knowledge needed to excel in their roles.

- Recognition and Appreciation: Walton believed in recognizing and appreciating the hard work of his associates. He implemented various programs to celebrate employee achievements and milestones, from simple gestures like handwritten notes of thanks to more formal recognition events. This focus on recognition helped build a positive and motivating work environment.

Development of Walmart's Corporate Culture

Walmart's corporate culture, shaped by Sam Walton's values and principles, has been a significant factor in the company's success. The culture is characterized by a strong emphasis on customer service, efficiency, teamwork, and a shared commitment to the company's mission of saving people money so they can live better.

- Customer Focus: At the heart of Walmart's corporate culture is an unwavering focus on the customer. Associates are trained to prioritize customer needs and provide exceptional service. This customer-centric approach has been a driving force behind Walmart's efforts to maintain low prices and high levels of customer satisfaction.

- Efficiency and Cost-Consciousness: Walton's frugality and focus on cost control are deeply ingrained in Walmart's culture. Associates are encouraged to find ways to operate more efficiently and reduce costs without compromising quality or service. This emphasis on efficiency helps Walmart maintain its competitive pricing and profitability.

- Teamwork and Collaboration: Walmart promotes a culture of teamwork and collaboration, recognizing that collective effort is essential to achieving the company's goals. Associates work together across departments and levels to solve problems, improve processes, and enhance the customer experience. This collaborative spirit fosters a sense of unity and shared purpose.

- Innovation and Continuous Improvement: Walmart's culture encourages innovation and continuous improvement. Associates are empowered to suggest new ideas and approaches to enhance operations and drive growth. This culture of innovation has helped

Walmart adapt to changing market conditions and stay ahead of the competition.

- Integrity and Ethics: Integrity and ethical conduct are core values at Walmart. Associates are expected to uphold high standards of honesty and transparency in their dealings with customers, colleagues, and suppliers. Walmart's commitment to ethical business practices is reinforced through training programs and a robust code of conduct.

Employee Incentives and Profit-Sharing Programs

To motivate and reward its workforce, Walmart has implemented various employee incentives and profit-sharing programs. These initiatives reflect Walton's belief that employees should share in the company's success and be rewarded for their hard work and dedication.

- Profit Sharing: One of Walton's most notable initiatives was the profit-sharing program, introduced in 1971. Under this program, a portion of Walmart's pre-tax profits was distributed to employees, allowing them to benefit directly from the company's financial success. The profit-sharing program helped align the interests of associates with those of the company, fostering a sense of ownership and commitment.

- Stock Ownership: Walton also encouraged employee stock ownership, believing that associates who had a stake in the company would be more motivated and engaged. Walmart offered stock purchase plans that allowed employees to buy company shares at a discount, providing an opportunity to build wealth and participate in Walmart's growth.

- Bonuses and Incentives: Walmart has implemented various bonus and incentive programs to reward employees for exceptional performance. These programs include performance-based bonuses, sales incentives, and recognition awards. By tying rewards to individual and team achievements, Walmart incentivizes employees to strive for excellence and contribute to the company's success.

- Benefits and Compensation: Walmart offers a comprehensive benefits package that includes health insurance, retirement plans, and paid time off. The company continually evaluates and updates its benefits to ensure they meet the needs of its diverse workforce. Competitive compensation and benefits help Walmart attract and retain talented employees.

- Training and Career Development: Investing in employee training and career development is another key aspect of Walmart's approach to employee incentives. The company offers various training programs, leadership development initiatives, and opportunities for career advancement. By supporting employee growth and development, Walmart helps associates build long-term careers within the company.

Labor Relations and Controversies

Despite its efforts to create a positive work environment, Walmart has faced significant labor relations challenges and controversies over the years. These issues have centered around employee wages, working conditions, and efforts to unionize the workforce.

- Wages and Compensation: Walmart has been criticized for paying low wages, particularly for entry-level positions. Critics argue that the company's compensation practices do not provide a living wage for many employees, leading to financial insecurity and reliance on public assistance programs. Walmart has responded by gradually increasing its minimum wage and offering additional benefits, but the issue of fair compensation remains a contentious topic.

- Working Conditions: Concerns about working conditions at Walmart have also been raised, including allegations of long hours, inadequate breaks, and demanding workloads. Some employees have reported issues related to workplace safety and the physical demands of the job. Walmart has implemented measures to address these concerns, such as enhancing safety protocols and providing training on ergonomic practices, but challenges persist.

- Unionization Efforts: Walmart has faced

numerous efforts by employees and labor organizations to unionize its workforce. The company has historically opposed unionization, arguing that it prefers to address employee concerns directly rather than through third parties. This stance has led to legal battles and accusations of anti-union tactics, including allegations of retaliation against pro-union employees.

- Class-Action Lawsuits: Walmart has been involved in several high-profile class-action lawsuits related to labor practices. One notable case was the Dukes v. Walmart Stores, Inc. lawsuit, which alleged gender discrimination in pay and promotions. Although the U.S. Supreme Court ultimately ruled in favor of Walmart, the case highlighted ongoing concerns about equitable treatment and diversity within the company.

- Global Labor Practices: As a global retailer, Walmart's labor practices in international markets have also come under scrutiny. The company has faced criticism for labor conditions in supplier factories, particularly in countries with weak labor protections. Walmart has taken steps to improve labor standards in its supply chain, including implementing stricter supplier guidelines and conducting regular audits, but challenges remain in ensuring compliance.

Long-Term Impact on Corporate Culture

Despite the controversies and challenges, Walmart's corporate culture and employee relations practices have had a lasting impact on the company and the broader retail industry. Walmart's approach to employee management, shaped by Sam Walton's principles, continues to influence its operations and reputation.

- Employee Engagement and Loyalty: Walmart's focus on respect, empowerment, and recognition has helped build a culture of engagement and loyalty among its associates. Many employees have long tenures with the company, reflecting a sense of commitment and connection to Walmart's mission. This engagement contributes to a stable and motivated workforce.

- Adaptability and Resilience: Walmart's corporate culture has enabled the company to adapt to changing market conditions and overcome challenges. The emphasis on innovation, continuous improvement, and collaboration fosters resilience and agility, allowing Walmart to respond effectively to new opportunities and threats.

- Industry Influence: Walmart's employee management practices have influenced the broader retail industry. Other companies have adopted similar approaches to employee incentives, profit-sharing, and open communication, recognizing the value of these practices in driving employee satisfaction and business success.

- Corporate Social Responsibility: Walmart's commitment to ethical conduct and community involvement has shaped its corporate social responsibility (CSR) initiatives. The company's philanthropic efforts, sustainability programs, and focus on diversity and inclusion reflect a broader understanding of its role and responsibilities as a global retailer. Walmart's CSR initiatives have set benchmarks for other companies in the industry.

- Evolving Employee Relations: Walmart continues to evolve its employee relations practices in response to feedback and changing expectations. The company has made strides in improving wages, benefits, and working conditions, demonstrating a commitment to addressing employee concerns. Walmart's ongoing efforts to enhance its corporate culture and employee relations are critical to maintaining its competitive edge and reputation.

Sam Walton's approach to employee management and the development of Walmart's corporate culture have been fundamental to the company's growth and success. Walton's emphasis on respect, empowerment, and open communication laid the foundation for a positive and productive work environment. Walmart's employee incentives and profit-sharing programs aligned the interests of associates with the company's goals, fostering a sense of ownership and commitment.

Despite facing significant labor relations challenges and controversies, Walmart has made efforts to improve wages, working conditions, and employee engagement. The company's corporate culture has had a lasting impact on its operations and reputation, influencing the broader retail industry and setting benchmarks for corporate social responsibility.

Walmart's story offers valuable lessons in leadership, employee management, and the importance of fostering a strong corporate culture. Sam Walton's legacy continues to shape Walmart's approach to business and inspire future generations of leaders to prioritize respect, empowerment, and innovation in their organizations.

Customer Focus and Service

Emphasis on Customer Satisfaction

From its inception, Walmart has been deeply committed to customer satisfaction, a principle instilled by its founder, Sam Walton. Walton believed that the customer was the key to the company's success, and he made it a priority to understand and meet their needs. This customer-centric approach has been a driving force behind Walmart's business strategies and innovations.

- Customer-First Philosophy: Walton's mantra, "The customer is the boss," encapsulates the company's approach to customer satisfaction. He emphasized that Walmart's primary goal was to make customers happy, and this philosophy has guided every aspect of the business, from product selection to store layout and customer service.

- Listening to Customers: Walton was known for his practice of walking through Walmart stores and talking to customers to get their feedback. He believed that listening to customers was crucial for understanding their needs and improving the shopping experience. This practice of gathering customer insights continues to be an integral part of Walmart's operations.

- Empowering Employees: Walmart empowers its associates to go above and beyond to satisfy customers. Associates are encouraged to take initiative in resolving customer issues and providing personalized service. This empowerment helps create a positive shopping experience and builds customer loyalty.

- Customer Satisfaction Guarantee: Walmart's commitment to customer satisfaction is reflected in its generous return policy. The company offers a customer satisfaction guarantee, allowing customers to return or exchange products with ease. This policy helps build trust and confidence in the Walmart brand.

Strategies for Maintaining Low Prices

One of Walmart's core strategies for achieving

customer satisfaction is its commitment to maintaining low prices. Sam Walton's vision of offering everyday low prices (EDLP) has been a cornerstone of Walmart's success and a key differentiator in the competitive retail market.

- Everyday Low Prices (EDLP): Walmart's EDLP strategy means that the company consistently offers products at lower prices than its competitors. This strategy eliminates the need for frequent sales and promotions, ensuring that customers can always find good deals at Walmart. EDLP builds customer trust and encourages repeat business.

- Efficient Supply Chain Management: Walmart's ability to maintain low prices is largely due to its highly efficient supply chain. The company has invested heavily in logistics and technology to streamline operations and reduce costs. Techniques such as cross-docking, centralized distribution centers, and real-time inventory management enable Walmart to minimize expenses and pass on savings to customers.

- Economies of Scale: Walmart leverages its massive buying power to negotiate favorable terms with suppliers. By purchasing products in large quantities, the company can secure lower prices and better deals. These economies of scale allow Walmart to offer lower prices to customers while maintaining profitability.

- Cost Control: Walmart's culture of frugality

extends to all aspects of the business, from store operations to corporate headquarters. The company is known for its cost-conscious approach, which includes minimizing waste, optimizing labor productivity, and implementing energy-efficient practices. By controlling costs, Walmart can keep prices low without compromising quality.

- Private Label Brands: Walmart has developed a range of private label brands that offer quality products at lower prices than national brands. These private labels, such as Great Value and Equate, provide customers with affordable alternatives and help Walmart differentiate itself in the market.

Innovations in Customer Service

Walmart has consistently sought to innovate in customer service to enhance the shopping experience and meet evolving customer expectations. The company's efforts to improve service have included the adoption of new technologies, the introduction of convenient shopping options, and the development of customer-centric programs.

- Self-Checkout: Walmart was an early adopter of self-checkout technology, allowing customers to scan and pay for their purchases without the assistance of a cashier. Self-checkout lanes provide a faster and more convenient option for customers, reducing wait times and improving the overall shopping experience.

- Online Shopping and E-Commerce: Recognizing the growing importance of e-commerce, Walmart has made significant investments in its online platform. The company's website and mobile app offer a seamless shopping experience, with features such as easy navigation, personalized recommendations, and a wide selection of products. Walmart's e-commerce capabilities have been further enhanced by acquisitions of online retailers like Jet.com.

- Grocery Pickup and Delivery: To meet the needs of busy customers, Walmart has introduced grocery pickup and delivery services. Customers can place orders online and choose to either pick up their groceries at a nearby store or have them delivered to their doorstep. These services provide convenience and flexibility, making it easier for customers to shop for groceries.

- Customer Service Desks: Walmart stores feature customer service desks where associates assist with returns, exchanges, and other inquiries. These desks are staffed by knowledgeable associates who are trained to resolve issues quickly and efficiently, ensuring that customers leave satisfied.

- Walmart Pay: Walmart Pay is a mobile payment solution integrated into the Walmart app. It allows customers to pay for their purchases using their smartphones, streamlining the checkout process. Walmart Pay also integrates with the company's savings programs, such as the Savings Catcher, which automatically compares prices and provides refunds for price differences.

Development of the Walmart Brand

The development of the Walmart brand has been instrumental in the company's growth and success. Walmart's brand is built on the principles of affordability, convenience, and trust, and the company has worked diligently to reinforce these values through its marketing, store experience, and corporate practices.

- Brand Positioning: Walmart's brand positioning as a provider of everyday low prices and one-stop shopping has resonated with a broad customer base. The company's marketing campaigns emphasize its commitment to helping customers save money and live better. Slogans such as "Save Money. Live Better." encapsulate Walmart's value proposition.

- Consistent Store Experience: Walmart has maintained a consistent store experience across its locations, ensuring that customers know what to expect when they shop at Walmart. This consistency extends to store layout, product assortment, and customer service, creating a reliable and familiar shopping environment.

- Community Involvement: Walmart has actively engaged with the communities it serves, contributing to its positive brand image. The company supports local initiatives through donations, volunteerism, and partnerships with nonprofit organizations. Walmart's community involvement reinforces its commitment to being a good corporate citizen and building strong community ties.

- Sustainability and Corporate Responsibility: Walmart has made significant strides in sustainability and corporate responsibility, enhancing its brand reputation. The company has set ambitious goals to reduce its environmental impact, promote sustainable sourcing, and support social initiatives. These efforts demonstrate Walmart's dedication to responsible business practices and resonate with socially conscious consumers.

- Customer Loyalty Programs: Walmart has developed loyalty programs to reward and retain customers. Programs like Walmart+ offer members benefits such as free delivery, fuel discounts, and exclusive deals. These programs enhance customer loyalty and encourage repeat business, strengthening the Walmart brand.

Lessons for Modern Retail Businesses

Walmart's approach to customer focus and service offers valuable lessons for modern retail businesses. The company's strategies and innovations provide insights into how retailers can achieve sustained growth and success in a competitive market.

- Prioritize Customer Satisfaction: Walmart's customer-centric approach underscores the importance of prioritizing customer satisfaction. Retailers should actively seek customer feedback, empower employees to provide exceptional service, and implement policies that build trust and loyalty. Satisfied customers are more likely to become repeat buyers and brand advocates.

- Implement Cost-Efficiency Measures: Walmart's focus on cost control and efficiency has been a key driver of its ability to offer low prices. Retailers should identify opportunities to streamline operations, reduce waste, and optimize supply chain processes. Efficient operations can lead to cost savings that can be passed on to customers in the form of lower prices.

- Embrace Technology and Innovation: Walmart's adoption of technology has been critical to its success. Retailers should invest in technologies that enhance the shopping experience, improve operational efficiency, and enable data-driven decision-making. Innovations such as e-commerce platforms, mobile payment solutions, and automated inventory management can provide a competitive edge.

- Adapt to Changing Consumer Preferences:

Walmart's ability to adapt to changing consumer preferences has been a key factor in its continued growth. Retailers should stay attuned to market trends and customer needs, offering convenient shopping options such as online ordering, curbside pickup, and home delivery. Flexibility and responsiveness are essential in meeting evolving customer expectations.

- Build a Strong Brand: Walmart's development of a strong brand has been central to its success. Retailers should focus on building a brand that resonates with customers, emphasizing core values such as affordability, convenience, and trust. Consistent branding, community engagement, and corporate responsibility initiatives can enhance brand reputation and customer loyalty.

- Foster a Positive Corporate Culture: Walmart's corporate culture, centered on respect, empowerment, and teamwork, has contributed to its success. Retailers should cultivate a positive work environment that values employee contributions and encourages collaboration. A motivated and engaged workforce is better equipped to deliver excellent customer service and drive business success.

Walmart's emphasis on customer focus and service has been a cornerstone of its growth and success. From prioritizing customer satisfaction to implementing cost-efficiency measures and embracing technological innovations, Walmart has consistently sought to enhance the shopping experience and meet the needs of its customers.

The development of the Walmart brand, built on principles of affordability, convenience, and trust, has further solidified the company's position as a leader in the retail industry. Walmart's strategies and innovations offer valuable lessons for modern retail businesses, highlighting the importance of customer-centricity, operational efficiency, adaptability, and brand strength.

Sam Walton's vision and principles continue to guide Walmart's approach to customer service and business operations, ensuring that the company remains focused on its mission of saving people money so they can live better. Walmart's enduring success serves as a testament to the power of a customer-first philosophy and the impact of innovative, efficient retail practices.

Case Study: Walmart's Supply Chain Innovations

Evolution of Walmart's Supply Chain Management

Walmart's supply chain management has undergone significant evolution since the company's inception, transforming from a regional retailer to a global powerhouse. The company's ability to innovate and adapt its supply chain strategies has been a key factor in its success, enabling it to maintain low prices and meet customer demands efficiently.

- Early Years: In the early years, Sam Walton focused on building a regional supply chain network that could support Walmart's rapid expansion across rural America. Walton emphasized the importance of minimizing costs and maximizing efficiency, principles that would guide Walmart's supply chain strategy for decades. The early supply chain relied on a combination of direct store deliveries and regional warehouses to ensure product availability.

- Centralized Distribution: A major shift in Walmart's supply chain came with the introduction of centralized distribution centers. By consolidating inventory in strategically located regional distribution centers, Walmart could reduce transportation costs and improve inventory management. This centralized approach allowed for more consistent product availability across stores and laid the foundation for further innovations.

- Hub-and-Spoke Model: Walmart adopted the hub-and-spoke distribution model, where distribution centers served as hubs, and individual stores were the spokes. This model enabled efficient transportation of goods, reduced lead times, and ensured that stores were consistently stocked with high-demand items. The hub-and-spoke system became a critical component of Walmart's supply chain efficiency.

- Cross-Docking: One of the most significant

innovations in Walmart's supply chain was the implementation of cross-docking. In cross-docking, products are unloaded from inbound trucks and immediately loaded onto outbound trucks for delivery to stores, without being stored in the warehouse. This practice reduces handling, storage costs, and time in transit, significantly improving supply chain efficiency.

- Global Expansion: As Walmart expanded internationally, the company adapted its supply chain strategies to meet the challenges of operating in diverse markets. Walmart's global supply chain incorporates local sourcing, regional distribution centers, and global logistics networks to ensure product availability and cost efficiency in different regions.

Use of Technology and Data Analytics

Walmart's use of technology and data analytics has been instrumental in revolutionizing its supply chain management. By leveraging advanced technologies, Walmart has enhanced its ability to forecast demand, manage inventory, and optimize operations.

- Retail Link: One of Walmart's pioneering technology initiatives was the development of Retail Link, a proprietary information system that connects Walmart with its suppliers. Retail Link provides suppliers with real-time access to sales data, inventory levels, and forecasts, enabling better coordination and planning. This system enhances collaboration and helps suppliers respond quickly to changing demand patterns.

- Barcode Scanning: Walmart was an early adopter of barcode scanning technology, which enabled accurate and efficient tracking of inventory. Barcode scanning facilitates real-time data collection at the point of sale, improving inventory accuracy and enabling better replenishment decisions. This technology also streamlines the checkout process and enhances the customer experience.

- Radio Frequency Identification (RFID): Walmart has invested in RFID technology to further improve inventory visibility and accuracy. RFID tags, which are attached to products, allow for automated tracking throughout the supply chain. This technology reduces shrinkage, improves stock accuracy, and enables more efficient inventory management.

- Data Analytics: Walmart's extensive use of data analytics allows the company to gain insights into customer behavior, demand trends, and supply chain performance. Advanced analytics tools help Walmart optimize inventory levels, forecast demand, and identify opportunities for cost reduction. Data-driven decision-making is a cornerstone of Walmart's supply chain strategy.

- Internet of Things (IoT): Walmart has explored the use of IoT devices to enhance supply chain operations. IoT sensors can monitor conditions such as temperature and humidity during transportation and storage, ensuring product quality and compliance with safety standards. IoT technology also enables real-time tracking of shipments, providing greater visibility and control over the supply chain.

Impact on Inventory Management and Cost Reduction

Walmart's innovations in supply chain management have had a profound impact on inventory management and cost reduction, contributing to the company's ability to offer everyday low prices to customers.

- Just-In-Time Inventory: Walmart's adoption of just-in-time (JIT) inventory practices allows the company to minimize excess stock and reduce carrying costs. By receiving goods only as they are needed, Walmart can operate with leaner inventory levels while still meeting customer demand. This practice reduces the risk of overstocking and obsolescence, leading to significant cost savings.

- Automated Replenishment: The integration of technology and data analytics enables Walmart to automate the replenishment process. Automated replenishment systems use real-time sales data to trigger orders when inventory levels reach predetermined thresholds. This ensures that stores are consistently stocked with high-demand items while minimizing stockouts and excess inventory.

- Demand Forecasting: Walmart's use of advanced analytics for demand forecasting allows the company to anticipate customer needs more accurately. By analyzing historical sales data, seasonal trends, and external factors, Walmart can make informed decisions about inventory levels and procurement. Accurate demand forecasting reduces the likelihood of stockouts and overstock situations, optimizing inventory management.

- Cost-Efficient Transportation: Walmart's centralized distribution centers and cross-docking practices streamline transportation and reduce logistics costs. By optimizing routes and minimizing handling, Walmart can lower transportation expenses and pass the savings on to customers. Efficient transportation also reduces lead times, ensuring timely delivery of products to stores.

- Supplier Collaboration: Walmart's close collaboration with suppliers enhances inventory management and cost efficiency. Through initiatives such as vendor-managed inventory (VMI), suppliers take responsibility for monitoring and replenishing stock levels at Walmart's distribution centers. This collaborative approach reduces lead times, improves inventory accuracy, and lowers overall supply chain costs.

Collaboration with Suppliers and Logistics Partners

Collaboration with suppliers and logistics partners has been a key element of Walmart's supply chain success. By fostering strong relationships and working closely with its partners, Walmart has created a more responsive and efficient supply chain.

- Vendor Partnerships: Walmart's Retail Link system exemplifies the company's commitment to transparency and collaboration with suppliers. By providing suppliers with access to real-time sales and inventory data, Walmart enables better coordination and planning. Suppliers can adjust production schedules, manage inventory levels, and respond quickly to changes in demand.

- Supplier Development: Walmart invests in supplier development programs to enhance the capabilities of its vendors. These programs provide training and support to help suppliers improve their processes, quality, and efficiency. By building stronger supplier relationships, Walmart ensures a reliable supply of high-quality products at competitive prices.

- Logistics Partnerships: Walmart collaborates with logistics partners to optimize transportation and distribution. The company works with third-party logistics providers (3PLs) to manage warehousing, transportation, and delivery services. These partnerships allow Walmart to leverage specialized expertise and resources, enhancing supply chain efficiency.

- Sustainability Initiatives: Walmart's collaboration with suppliers extends to sustainability efforts. The company works with suppliers to reduce environmental impact through initiatives such as sustainable sourcing, waste reduction, and energy efficiency. Walmart's Project Gigaton, for example, aims to eliminate one billion metric tons of greenhouse gases from its supply chain by 2030, encouraging suppliers to adopt sustainable practices.

- Innovation and Technology: Walmart encourages suppliers and logistics partners to adopt innovative technologies that enhance supply chain performance. This includes the use of RFID, IoT, and data analytics to improve inventory visibility, track shipments, and optimize operations. Collaborative innovation helps Walmart and its partners stay ahead of industry trends and meet evolving customer expectations.

Walmart's Enduring Influence on Global Supply Chains

Walmart's supply chain innovations have had a lasting impact on global supply chains, setting new standards for efficiency, collaboration, and technology adoption. The company's practices have influenced the broader retail industry and beyond, shaping the way businesses approach supply chain management.

- Benchmark for Efficiency: Walmart's supply chain efficiency has become a benchmark for other companies. Retailers and manufacturers worldwide look to Walmart's practices as a model for reducing costs, improving inventory management, and enhancing operational performance. Walmart's success demonstrates the importance of lean supply chain strategies and continuous improvement.

- Technology Adoption: Walmart's use of technology and data analytics has accelerated the adoption of these tools across industries. Companies recognize the value of real-time data, advanced analytics, and automated processes in optimizing supply chain operations. Walmart's pioneering efforts have paved the way for widespread use of technologies such as RFID, IoT, and predictive analytics.

- Collaboration and Transparency: Walmart's collaborative approach with suppliers and logistics partners has highlighted the benefits of transparency and cooperation. Businesses are increasingly adopting collaborative supply chain models that emphasize data sharing, joint planning, and mutual accountability. These practices enhance supply chain resilience and responsiveness.

- Sustainability Leadership: Walmart's sustainability initiatives have set a precedent for integrating environmental and social considerations into supply chain management.

Companies across sectors are following Walmart's lead in implementing sustainable sourcing, reducing carbon footprints, and promoting ethical practices. Walmart's leadership in sustainability underscores the importance of responsible supply chain management.

- Global Supply Chain Networks: Walmart's global supply chain networks exemplify the complexity and interconnectedness of modern supply chains. The company's ability to manage diverse suppliers, navigate regulatory environments, and adapt to local market conditions provides valuable insights for businesses operating in a globalized economy. Walmart's experience underscores the need for agility, cultural understanding, and strategic partnerships in global supply chain management.

Walmart's supply chain innovations have been instrumental in the company's growth and success, enabling it to maintain low prices, meet customer demands, and drive operational efficiency. The evolution of Walmart's supply chain management, from centralized distribution and cross-docking to the adoption of advanced technologies and data analytics, has set new standards for the industry.

Walmart's impact on inventory management and cost reduction, achieved through just-in-time inventory practices, automated replenishment, and efficient transportation, highlights the importance of optimizing supply chain processes. The company's collaboration with suppliers and logistics partners, exemplified by initiatives such as Retail Link and vendor-managed inventory, underscores the value of transparency and cooperation in supply chain management.

Walmart's enduring influence on global supply chains extends beyond the retail industry, shaping practices and setting benchmarks for efficiency, technology adoption, collaboration, and sustainability. The company's leadership in supply chain innovation continues to inspire businesses worldwide, demonstrating the transformative power of strategic supply chain management.

Sam Walton's vision and principles, combined with Walmart's commitment to innovation and continuous improvement, have created a supply chain that is agile, efficient, and responsive to the needs of customers. Walmart's supply chain story offers valuable lessons for modern businesses, emphasizing the importance of technology, collaboration, and sustainability in achieving supply chain excellence.

Chapter 6:

Walt Disney Creating a Media Empire

Walter Elias Disney was born on December 5, 1901, in Chicago, Illinois, to Elias and Flora Disney. Walt was one of five children and spent much of his early childhood on a farm in Marceline, Missouri, where his love for drawing and storytelling began to blossom. Marceline had a profound impact on Walt, and many of his later works were inspired by his experiences in this idyllic small town.

The Disney family moved frequently due to Elias's varying business ventures, but it was in Kansas City where Walt's artistic talents were first formally recognized. He attended the Kansas City Art Institute and later took classes at the Chicago Academy of Fine Arts. These early educational experiences laid the foundation for his skills in drawing and animation.

Walt's early influences included his love for the stories his mother read to him and the vaudeville shows his father took him to see. These experiences sparked his imagination and ignited a passion for storytelling and entertainment that would define his career.
Entry into the Animation Industry

Walt Disney's entry into the animation industry began in earnest when he returned to Kansas City after serving briefly in the Red Cross during World War I. There, he started working as a commercial artist and later joined the Kansas City Film Ad Company, where he first experimented with animation. This job involved creating animated advertisements for local businesses, and it was here that Walt honed his skills and developed a keen interest in the burgeoning field of animation.

In 1922, Walt and his colleague, Ub Iwerks, founded their first company, Laugh-O-Gram Studio, where they produced a series of short films based on fairy tales. Despite their creative efforts, the studio faced financial difficulties and eventually went bankrupt. Undeterred, Walt decided to move to Hollywood, where he believed there would be more opportunities to succeed in the entertainment industry.

Founding of The Walt Disney Company

In 1923, Walt Disney and his brother Roy O. Disney co-founded the Disney Brothers Studio, which would later become The Walt Disney Company. With a loan from Roy and other family members, they set up a small studio in their uncle's garage in Los Angeles. Their first major project was a series of live-action/animated films featuring a character named Alice, which became known as the "Alice Comedies."

The success of the Alice Comedies allowed the Disney brothers to establish a foothold in the industry. Walt's innovative approach to blending live-action and animation captivated audiences and set the stage for future successes. During this time, they hired talented animators, including Ub Iwerks, whose technical skills were instrumental in bringing Walt's creative visions to life.

In 1928, Walt created Mickey Mouse, a character that would become synonymous with The Walt Disney Company. The first Mickey Mouse cartoon with synchronized sound, "Steamboat Willie," premiered in 1928 and was an instant hit. This success propelled Disney to the forefront of the animation industry and marked the beginning of a new era in entertainment.

Vision for Family Entertainment

Walt Disney's vision for family entertainment was rooted in his desire to create content that would appeal to audiences of all ages and bring families together. He believed in the power of storytelling to inspire, educate, and entertain, and he was committed to producing high-quality, wholesome entertainment.

- Innovative Animation: Walt was a pioneer in the field of animation, constantly pushing the boundaries of what was possible. He introduced new techniques and technologies, such as synchronized sound, Technicolor, and multi-plane cameras, to create more immersive and visually stunning animated films. His dedication to innovation set new standards in the industry and ensured that Disney films were always at the cutting edge.

- Character Development: Walt understood the importance of strong characters in storytelling. He created memorable characters like Mickey Mouse, Donald Duck, and Goofy, who became beloved icons around the world. These characters were designed to be relatable and endearing, with personalities and traits that resonated with audiences.

- Feature-Length Animation: Walt's vision extended beyond short cartoons. He dreamed of creating feature-length animated films that could tell more complex and emotionally engaging stories. This dream was realized with the release of "Snow White and the Seven Dwarfs" in 1937, the first full-length animated feature film. The film's success proved that animated features could be both commercially viable and artistically significant.

- Theme Parks: Walt's vision for family entertainment also led to the creation of Disneyland, a theme park where families could experience the magic of Disney's stories and characters in a real-world setting. Disneyland, which opened in 1955, was a revolutionary concept that combined entertainment, innovation, and storytelling to create a unique and immersive experience for visitors.

Initial Business Challenges

Despite his groundbreaking ideas and creative talent, Walt Disney faced numerous business challenges in the early years of his career. These challenges tested his resilience and determination, ultimately shaping the future of The Walt Disney Company.

- Financial Struggles: One of the most significant

challenges Walt faced was securing adequate funding for his projects. The early years of The Walt Disney Company were marked by financial instability, with the studio often operating on a shoestring budget. The production of "Snow White and the Seven Dwarfs" was particularly risky, as it required a substantial investment and was dubbed "Disney's Folly" by skeptics who doubted its success. However, the film's unprecedented success not only recouped the investment but also provided the financial foundation for future projects.

- Competition and Imitation: Walt's innovative work in animation attracted competition and imitation from other studios. One notable challenge was the loss of his character Oswald the Lucky Rabbit, which was taken over by Universal Pictures. This experience taught Walt the importance of retaining control over his creations, leading to the birth of Mickey Mouse, a character wholly owned by Disney.

- Labor Disputes: The 1941 Disney animators' strike was a significant challenge for the studio. Dissatisfaction with working conditions, wages, and lack of recognition led to a strike that lasted for several weeks. The strike had a profound impact on Walt personally and professionally, leading to changes in the studio's labor practices and management style.

- Technological and Artistic Risks: Walt's commitment to innovation often involved significant technological and artistic risks. The production of "Fantasia" (1940) and "Pinocchio" (1940) pushed the boundaries of animation but faced initial commercial challenges. While these films are now considered classics, their initial reception tested the company's financial stability and resilience.

- World War II: The outbreak of World War II brought additional challenges, as the European market for Disney films was significantly disrupted. The studio also contributed to the war effort by producing training and propaganda films for the U.S. government, which diverted resources away from commercial projects. Despite these challenges, Walt and his team continued to innovate and create, laying the groundwork for post-war successes.

Walt Disney's early life and career were marked by a passion for storytelling, innovation, and resilience in the face of numerous challenges. From his humble beginnings in Marceline, Missouri, to his pioneering work in animation and the founding of The Walt Disney Company, Walt's journey is a testament to his visionary approach to family entertainment.

Walt's emphasis on creating high-quality, wholesome entertainment that appealed to audiences of all ages revolutionized the entertainment industry. His innovative techniques in animation, character development, and feature-length films set new standards and captivated audiences worldwide.

Despite facing significant financial, competitive, and labor challenges, Walt's determination and creativity enabled him to overcome obstacles and establish The Walt Disney Company as a leading force in the industry.

Walt Disney's vision extended beyond films to include theme parks, creating immersive experiences that brought his stories and characters to life. The opening of Disneyland in 1955 was a groundbreaking achievement that further solidified Disney's legacy in family entertainment.

The early years of Walt Disney's career laid the foundation for the creation of a media empire that continues to thrive and inspire. His legacy lives on through the enduring success of The Walt Disney Company, which remains at the forefront of entertainment innovation and storytelling. Walt Disney's story serves as an inspiration to creators and entrepreneurs, demonstrating the power of vision, perseverance, and a relentless pursuit of excellence.

Innovations in Animation and Entertainment

Development of Synchronized Sound and Color in Animation

One of Walt Disney's most significant contributions to the field of animation was the development of synchronized sound and color, which transformed the medium and set new standards for animated films.

- Synchronized Sound: The release of "Steamboat Willie" in 1928 marked a milestone in animation history as the first cartoon to feature synchronized sound. This innovation was groundbreaking, as it synchronized the movements of the characters with a musical score and sound effects, creating a more immersive and engaging experience for audiences. The success of "Steamboat Willie" not only propelled Mickey Mouse to stardom but also demonstrated the potential of sound in animation, leading other studios to adopt this technology.

- Technicolor: Disney was also a pioneer in the use of color in animation. In 1932, the company secured an exclusive contract with Technicolor, allowing Disney to produce the first full-color animated short film, "Flowers and Trees." The use of Technicolor brought a new level of vibrancy and visual appeal to animation, making the characters and settings more vivid and captivating. The success of "Flowers and Trees" led to the widespread adoption of color in animated films, and Disney continued to innovate with the use of color in subsequent productions.

- Multi-Plane Camera: Another significant technological innovation introduced by Disney was the multi-plane camera, developed in the 1930s. This device allowed animators to create a sense of depth and dimensionality in their films by layering different elements of a scene on separate planes and moving them at varying speeds. The multi-plane camera was first used in the 1937 short "The Old Mill" and later in

"Snow White and the Seven Dwarfs," enhancing the visual richness and complexity of Disney's animated features.

- These technological advancements in synchronized sound and color established Disney as a leader in animation and set the stage for the creation of iconic characters and stories that would define the company's legacy.
- Creation of Iconic Characters and Stories

- Walt Disney's genius lay in his ability to create timeless characters and stories that resonated with audiences of all ages. These characters and narratives became the foundation of the Disney brand and continue to be beloved worldwide.

- Mickey Mouse: Mickey Mouse, created in 1928, became the symbol of The Walt Disney Company and an icon of popular culture. With his cheerful personality, optimistic outlook, and distinctive voice (initially provided by Walt Disney himself), Mickey captured the hearts of audiences. Mickey's enduring popularity paved the way for a host of other memorable characters and solidified Disney's reputation as a master storyteller.

- Snow White and the Seven Dwarfs: In 1937, Disney released "Snow White and the Seven Dwarfs," the first full-length animated feature film. This groundbreaking film showcased Disney's commitment to high-quality animation and compelling storytelling. The success of "Snow White" demonstrated the commercial viability of feature-length animated films and established a template for future Disney classics.

- Classic Characters: Disney continued to introduce a cast of iconic characters, including Donald Duck, Goofy, and Pluto, each with unique personalities and charm. These characters starred in numerous shorts and feature films, becoming integral parts of the Disney brand. The creation of these characters showcased Disney's talent for developing relatable and enduring figures that audiences loved.

- Storytelling Excellence: Disney's approach to storytelling was characterized by its emphasis on universal themes, emotional depth, and meticulous attention to detail. Films like "Pinocchio," "Fantasia," "Dumbo," and "Bambi" not only showcased advanced animation techniques but also explored complex narratives and emotional experiences, appealing to both children and adults.

- Adaptations of Fairy Tales and Folklore: Disney's success was also built on the adaptation of classic fairy tales and folklore. By reimagining these timeless stories with memorable characters and captivating animation, Disney brought these tales to new generations. Films like "Cinderella," "Sleeping Beauty," and "Peter Pan" became defining works in the Disney canon, blending traditional narratives with innovative animation.

- Expansion into Theme Parks and Resorts

- Walt Disney's vision extended beyond animation to creating immersive experiences that brought his characters and stories to life. This vision led to the creation of Disneyland and the subsequent expansion into theme parks and resorts worldwide.

- Disneyland: Disneyland, which opened in 1955 in Anaheim, California, was the first-ever theme park of its kind. Walt Disney envisioned a place where families could experience the magic of Disney's stories in a real-world setting. Disneyland featured themed lands, such as Adventureland, Fantasyland, and Tomorrowland, each offering unique attractions and experiences. The park's innovative design, attention to detail, and commitment to guest experience set new standards for the entertainment industry and established a new model for family entertainment.

- Walt Disney World: Following the success of Disneyland, Walt Disney began planning an even more ambitious project in Florida. Walt Disney World, which opened in 1971, included the Magic Kingdom, EPCOT, Disney's Hollywood Studios, and Disney's Animal Kingdom. This sprawling resort complex offered a diverse array of experiences, from theme parks and hotels to shopping and dining, solidifying Disney's position as a leader in the tourism and entertainment industries.

- International Expansion: Disney's theme park empire expanded globally with the opening of Tokyo Disneyland in 1983, Disneyland Paris in 1992, Hong Kong Disneyland in 2005, and Shanghai Disney Resort in 2016. Each international park incorporated elements of Disney's classic attractions while adapting to local cultures and preferences. This global expansion introduced Disney's magic to millions of people worldwide and reinforced the company's international appeal.

- Innovation and Immersion: Disney continually innovated within its theme parks, introducing advanced technologies and immersive experiences. Attractions like "Pirates of the Caribbean," "The Haunted Mansion," and "Space Mountain" pushed the boundaries of ride design and storytelling. More recent innovations, such as the interactive experiences in "Star Wars: Galaxy's Edge," showcase Disney's ongoing commitment to creating cutting-edge attractions that captivate and delight visitors.

- Innovations in Television and Film Production

- Walt Disney's influence extended to television and film production, where he pioneered new formats and storytelling techniques that shaped the entertainment industry.

- Disneyland TV Show: In 1954, Disney launched the "Disneyland" television show on ABC, which served as both an entertainment program and a promotional tool for the upcoming Disneyland park. The show featured a mix of original content, classic Disney cartoons, and behind-the-scenes looks at the park's development. This innovative use of television helped build anticipation for Disneyland and established Disney as a major player in the burgeoning medium of television.

- The Mickey Mouse Club: Another significant television innovation was "The Mickey Mouse Club," which premiered in 1955. This variety show featured a cast of young performers known as Mouseketeers and included music, dance, cartoons, and educational segments. "The Mickey Mouse Club" became a cultural phenomenon, influencing generations of children and cementing Disney's presence in the television landscape.

- Walt Disney's Wonderful World of Color: In 1961, Disney introduced "Walt Disney's Wonderful World of Color," a television anthology series that showcased Disney films, nature documentaries, and original programming. The show was one of the first to be broadcast in color, highlighting Disney's commitment to innovation and pushing the boundaries of television technology.

- Live-Action Films: In addition to animation, Disney ventured into live-action film production with movies like "20,000 Leagues Under the Sea" (1954), "Old Yeller" (1957), and "Mary Poppins" (1964). "Mary Poppins," which combined live-action with animation, was a critical and commercial success, earning multiple Academy Awards and demonstrating Disney's versatility as a filmmaker.

- Disney Channel: The launch of the Disney Channel in 1983 marked a significant expansion of Disney's television presence. The network provided a platform for Disney's vast library of animated and live-action content, as well as original programming tailored to children and families. The Disney Channel's success contributed to Disney's dominance in the family entertainment market and expanded the company's reach into households around the world.

Impact on the Entertainment Industry

Walt Disney's innovations in animation, storytelling, and entertainment had a profound and lasting impact on the entertainment industry, influencing generations of creators and shaping the landscape of modern media.

- Setting Industry Standards: Disney's commitment to quality and innovation set new standards for the entertainment industry. From pioneering synchronized sound and color in animation to creating immersive theme park experiences, Disney continually pushed the boundaries of what was possible. The company's dedication to excellence inspired other studios and creators to strive for higher standards in their work.

- Expansion of the Animation Genre: Disney's success with feature-length animated films demonstrated the commercial and artistic viability of the genre. The company's influence paved the way for other animation studios, such as Warner Bros., Pixar, and DreamWorks, to produce their own animated features. Disney's legacy is evident in the continued popularity and evolution of animated films, which remain a staple of family entertainment.

- Integration of Technology and Storytelling: Disney's innovative use of technology to enhance storytelling has had a lasting impact on the entertainment industry. The integration of cutting-edge techniques, such as CGI and motion capture, has become standard practice in film and television production. Disney's willingness to embrace new technologies and incorporate them into its narratives has set a precedent for other creators.

- Diversification of Entertainment Offerings: Walt Disney's vision extended beyond traditional media, encompassing theme parks, resorts, television networks, and consumer products. This diversification strategy has been emulated by other entertainment companies, leading to the creation of multimedia conglomerates that offer a wide range of entertainment experiences. Disney's approach to building a comprehensive entertainment ecosystem has become a model for the industry.

- Cultural Impact and Legacy: Disney's characters and stories have become integral parts of global popular culture. Iconic figures like Mickey Mouse, Cinderella, and Simba are recognized and beloved worldwide, transcending generations. Disney's impact on culture is reflected in the enduring popularity of its films, the success of its theme parks, and the influence of its storytelling techniques on other media.

Walt Disney's innovations in animation and entertainment have left an indelible mark on the industry, shaping the way stories are told and experienced. From pioneering synchronized sound and color to creating iconic characters and expanding into theme parks and television, Disney's visionary approach revolutionized entertainment and set new standards for quality and creativity.

Disney's ability to innovate and adapt, combined with his commitment to storytelling and family entertainment, has ensured the enduring success and influence of The Walt Disney Company. The company's impact on the entertainment industry is evident in the continued popularity of its films, the success of its theme parks, and the widespread adoption of its technological and storytelling innovations.

Walt Disney's legacy as a pioneer and innovator

continues to inspire creators and entertain audiences around the world. His contributions to the entertainment industry have created a lasting cultural legacy that will continue to shape the future of media and entertainment for generations to come.

Business Strategies and Expansion

Diversification of Revenue Streams

One of the hallmarks of The Walt Disney Company's success has been its ability to diversify its revenue streams. From its beginnings as an animation studio, Disney has expanded into multiple sectors of the entertainment industry, ensuring a stable and growing income by leveraging various business opportunities.

- Theme Parks and Resorts: The opening of Disneyland in 1955 marked Disney's first significant venture beyond film and animation. Disneyland's success demonstrated the potential of theme parks as a major revenue stream. Following Disneyland, Disney opened Walt Disney World in Florida, which included multiple theme parks, resorts, and entertainment complexes. These parks not only generate substantial ticket sales but also bring in revenue from hotel stays, dining, and merchandise sales. The global expansion of Disney theme parks in Tokyo, Paris, Hong Kong, and Shanghai further diversified Disney's income sources.

- Consumer Products: Disney's entry into

consumer products involved licensing its characters and franchises for toys, clothing, and other merchandise. The success of Mickey Mouse and other Disney characters led to a wide range of products that contributed significantly to the company's revenue. The establishment of Disney Stores around the world allowed the company to directly sell its merchandise, further boosting its consumer products division.

- Media Networks: The acquisition of ABC in 1996 expanded Disney's footprint in the media industry. ABC's television network, along with cable channels like ESPN, became key revenue drivers. Disney's media networks generate income through advertising, subscription fees, and syndication of content. The launch of the Disney Channel in 1983 further capitalized on the growing cable television market, providing a dedicated platform for Disney's extensive library of family-friendly programming.

- Studio Entertainment: Disney continued to dominate the film industry with its animation studios, live-action films, and the acquisition of other successful studios. The studio entertainment division includes Pixar, Marvel, Lucasfilm, and 20th Century Fox, which have produced blockbuster franchises like "Toy Story," "The Avengers," "Star Wars," and "Avatar." These films generate significant box office revenue, as well as income from home video sales, digital downloads, and licensing deals.

- Interactive Media and Digital Platforms: Recognizing the importance of digital media, Disney has invested in interactive entertainment and digital platforms. This includes video games, mobile apps, and online content. The acquisition of companies like Maker Studios has expanded Disney's reach in the digital content space, allowing it to engage with younger audiences on platforms like YouTube.

Acquisition of Other Entertainment Companies

Strategic acquisitions have played a crucial role in Disney's growth and diversification. By acquiring other entertainment companies, Disney has expanded its portfolio, gained access to new intellectual properties, and strengthened its position in the global market.

- Pixar Animation Studios: In 2006, Disney acquired Pixar for $7.4 billion. This acquisition brought together two of the most successful animation studios and revitalized Disney's animation division. Pixar's innovative approach to storytelling and cutting-edge technology complemented Disney's traditional animation style. The collaboration resulted in critically acclaimed and commercially successful films like "Finding Nemo," "The Incredibles," and "Toy Story 3."

- Marvel Entertainment: Disney's acquisition of

Marvel Entertainment in 2009 for $4 billion was a game-changer. Marvel's vast library of characters and stories provided Disney with a treasure trove of content. The Marvel Cinematic Universe (MCU) has since become one of the most successful film franchises in history, with blockbuster hits like "The Avengers," "Black Panther," and "Guardians of the Galaxy." This acquisition also expanded Disney's presence in the comic book industry and related merchandise.

- Lucasfilm: In 2012, Disney acquired Lucasfilm for $4.05 billion, bringing the iconic "Star Wars" franchise into its portfolio. This acquisition allowed Disney to produce new "Star Wars" films, television series, and merchandise. The success of films like "Star Wars: The Force Awakens" and the expansion of the franchise into theme parks with "Star Wars: Galaxy's Edge" further solidified Disney's dominance in the entertainment industry.

- 21st Century Fox: In 2019, Disney completed its acquisition of 21st Century Fox for $71.3 billion. This monumental deal expanded Disney's content library with valuable assets like "Avatar," "The Simpsons," and "X-Men." The acquisition also included Fox's television production and distribution businesses, enhancing Disney's capabilities in both film and TV. This deal significantly increased Disney's content offerings for its streaming service, Disney+.

- BAMTech: Disney's acquisition of a majority stake in BAMTech in 2017 for $1.58 billion was a strategic move to bolster its digital streaming capabilities. BAMTech's technology platform became the backbone for Disney+, ESPN+, and Hulu. This acquisition positioned Disney to compete effectively in the rapidly growing streaming market.

Development of Global Brand and Franchises

Disney's strategic focus on building a global brand and developing strong franchises has been central to its success. By leveraging its iconic characters and stories, Disney has created a cohesive and recognizable brand that resonates with audiences worldwide.

- Iconic Characters: Characters like Mickey Mouse, Minnie Mouse, Donald Duck, and Goofy have become symbols of the Disney brand. These characters are not only central to Disney's animated content but also feature prominently in merchandise, theme parks, and marketing campaigns. Their timeless appeal and global recognition have made them valuable assets for the company.

- Expanding Franchises: Disney has successfully expanded its franchises across multiple platforms and media. Franchises like "The Lion King," "Frozen," and "Toy Story" have extended beyond films to include sequels, television series, stage productions, theme park attractions, and merchandise. This multi-platform approach ensures that Disney's franchises remain relevant and continue to generate revenue long after their initial release.

- Global Theme Parks: Disney's theme parks play a crucial role in building the global brand. Each park is meticulously designed to provide an immersive experience that reflects Disney's storytelling and characters. The international parks, including Tokyo Disneyland, Disneyland Paris, Hong Kong Disneyland, and Shanghai Disney Resort, cater to regional audiences while maintaining the core elements of the Disney brand. These parks attract millions of visitors annually, reinforcing Disney's global presence.

- International Markets: Disney has made significant efforts to tailor its content and products to international markets. Localization strategies, such as dubbing films in multiple languages and creating region-specific marketing campaigns, have helped Disney connect with diverse audiences. The company also collaborates with local talent and production companies to create content that resonates with regional cultures.

- Streaming Services: The launch of Disney+ in 2019 marked a significant step in Disney's global brand strategy. Disney+ offers a vast library of content, including Disney classics, Pixar films, Marvel and Star Wars franchises, and original programming. The service's global rollout has been instrumental in reaching new audiences and reinforcing Disney's brand as a leader in family entertainment.

Strategic Partnerships and Collaborations

Strategic partnerships and collaborations have been key to Disney's ability to innovate and expand its reach. By working with other companies and leveraging their strengths, Disney has enhanced its capabilities and accessed new markets.

- ABC and Capital Cities: Disney's acquisition of ABC and its parent company, Capital Cities, in 1996 was a significant strategic move. This partnership provided Disney with a major television network and a range of cable channels, including ESPN. The acquisition expanded Disney's distribution capabilities and content offerings, strengthening its position in the media industry.

- Apple and Pixar: Disney's relationship with Apple and Pixar co-founder Steve Jobs was instrumental in the company's digital transformation. The acquisition of Pixar brought Steve Jobs onto Disney's board of directors, fostering a close collaboration between Disney and Apple. This partnership led to innovations in digital content distribution and the development of Disney's digital strategy.

- Joint Ventures: Disney has entered into numerous joint ventures to expand its global reach. For example, Disney partnered with Oriental Land Company to develop Tokyo Disneyland, its first international theme park. This collaboration allowed Disney to enter the Japanese market while leveraging the local partner's expertise and resources.

- Media Collaborations: Disney has collaborated with other media companies to create and distribute content. Partnerships with companies like Comcast (Hulu) and AT&T (ESPN+) have enabled Disney to expand its streaming offerings and reach new audiences. These collaborations have also facilitated the sharing of technology and resources, enhancing Disney's competitive edge.

- Merchandising and Licensing: Disney's partnerships with retailers and manufacturers have been crucial in expanding its consumer products division. Collaborations with companies like Mattel, Hasbro, and LEGO have resulted in successful merchandise lines based on Disney's characters and franchises. Licensing agreements with retailers like Target and Walmart ensure that Disney products are widely available, driving consumer engagement and sales.

Long-Term Growth and Sustainability

Disney's focus on long-term growth and sustainability has been integral to its business strategy. By investing in sustainable practices and planning for the future, Disney aims to ensure its continued success and positive impact on the world.

- Environmental Sustainability: Disney has made significant commitments to environmental sustainability. The company's initiatives include reducing greenhouse gas emissions, conserving water, and minimizing waste. Disney's theme parks have implemented energy-efficient technologies, such as solar power and LED lighting, to reduce their environmental footprint. The company also promotes sustainable practices in its supply chain, including responsible sourcing of materials and reducing plastic waste.

- Corporate Social Responsibility: Disney's corporate social responsibility efforts focus on making a positive impact on communities. The company supports various philanthropic initiatives, including educational programs, disaster relief, and conservation efforts. Disney's VoluntEARS program encourages employees to volunteer in their communities, furthering the company's commitment to social responsibility.

- Innovation and Technology: Disney's investment in innovation and technology is central to its long-term growth strategy. The company continually explores new technologies to enhance its content, improve operational efficiency, and create new entertainment experiences. Innovations like virtual reality, augmented reality, and artificial intelligence are being integrated into Disney's offerings to stay ahead of industry trends.

- Content Creation and Distribution: Disney's focus on creating high-quality content and expanding its distribution channels is key to its long-term success. The company continues to invest in original programming for Disney+, as well as new films and series for its various franchises. By expanding its streaming services and leveraging its extensive content library, Disney aims to reach new audiences and generate sustainable revenue.

- Talent Development: Disney's commitment to talent development ensures that the company remains a leader in creativity and innovation. The Disney Creative Talent Development and Inclusion program provides opportunities for underrepresented talent to succeed in the entertainment industry. By fostering a diverse and inclusive workforce, Disney aims to drive creativity and ensure long-term growth.

Walt Disney's vision and strategic business decisions have transformed The Walt Disney Company into a global entertainment powerhouse. Through diversification of revenue streams, strategic acquisitions, development of a global brand, and innovative partnerships, Disney has built a resilient and dynamic business model.

The company's focus on long-term growth and sustainability, combined with its commitment to creating high-quality content and experiences, ensures that Disney will continue to captivate audiences and lead the entertainment industry for generations to come. Disney's legacy as a pioneer in animation and entertainment, and its ongoing dedication to innovation and excellence, remain at the heart of its enduring success.

Leadership and Corporate Culture

Disney's Approach to Creative Leadership

Walt Disney's approach to creative leadership was instrumental in shaping The Walt Disney Company's success and establishing its enduring legacy. His leadership style emphasized innovation, storytelling, and a relentless pursuit of excellence.

- Visionary Leadership: Walt Disney was a visionary leader who always looked to the future. He had an uncanny ability to see potential where others did not, whether it was in the development of synchronized sound and color in animation, the creation of iconic characters, or the conception of Disneyland. His vision extended beyond mere entertainment; he sought to create immersive experiences that would captivate audiences and leave a lasting impact.

- Empowering Creativity: Disney believed in empowering his team to explore their creative potential. He assembled a talented group of animators, writers, and designers, whom he called "Imagineers." He encouraged them to take risks, experiment, and push the boundaries of what was possible. Disney's leadership created an environment where creativity thrived, and innovation was celebrated.

- Attention to Detail: Walt Disney's meticulous attention to detail set him apart as a leader. He was involved in every aspect of his projects, from story development to final production. This hands-on approach ensured that the quality of Disney's work was consistently high and that every product reflected his exacting standards. Disney's insistence on perfection helped establish the company's reputation for excellence.

- Adaptability and Innovation: Walt Disney was not afraid to embrace new technologies and adapt to changing market conditions. His willingness to invest in pioneering technologies, such as Technicolor and the multi-plane camera, demonstrated his commitment to innovation. Disney's adaptability allowed the company to stay ahead of the competition and continuously reinvent itself.

- Storytelling Mastery: Central to Disney's approach was his belief in the power of storytelling. He understood that great stories could transcend generations and cultures. By focusing on universal themes and emotional resonance, Disney created timeless tales that continue to resonate with audiences worldwide. His leadership ensured that storytelling remained at the heart of the company's creative endeavors.

Building a Strong Corporate Culture

Walt Disney's leadership also played a crucial role in building a strong corporate culture that has been integral to the company's success. The principles and values he established continue to guide The Walt Disney Company and shape its identity.

- Shared Mission and Values: Disney instilled a strong sense of mission and values within the company. The core mission was to create happiness and provide high-quality entertainment for people of all ages. Values such as creativity, innovation, integrity, and excellence were embedded into the company's culture. This shared mission and these values have united employees and provided a clear direction for the company.

- Collaborative Environment: Disney fostered a collaborative work environment where teamwork was highly valued. He believed that the best ideas often came from collaboration and that everyone, regardless of their role, could contribute to the creative process. This inclusive approach encouraged open communication and idea sharing, leading to innovative solutions and successful projects.

- Recognition and Rewards: Recognizing and rewarding employees for their contributions was a key aspect of Disney's corporate culture. Disney implemented various recognition programs and awards to celebrate achievements and acknowledge hard work. This practice helped motivate employees and reinforced the importance of their contributions to the company's success.

- Commitment to Quality: A commitment to quality was at the heart of Disney's corporate culture. From animation and theme parks to merchandise and customer service, the company consistently strived to exceed expectations. This dedication to quality helped build trust and loyalty among customers and set Disney apart from its competitors.

- Continuous Learning and Development: Disney valued continuous learning and development, providing opportunities for employees to enhance their skills and advance their careers. The company invested in training programs, workshops, and mentorship to support employee growth. This focus on development ensured that Disney's workforce remained highly skilled and capable of driving the company's success.

Employee Engagement and Motivation

Employee engagement and motivation have been central to Disney's ability to maintain a high-performing and dedicated workforce. The company's strategies for engaging and motivating employees have contributed to its sustained success.

- Inclusive Leadership: Disney's inclusive

leadership style has been pivotal in fostering employee engagement. Leaders at Disney are encouraged to be approachable, supportive, and inclusive. This leadership style creates an environment where employees feel valued and heard, which enhances their commitment to the company.

- Empowerment and Autonomy: Empowering employees to take ownership of their work and make decisions has been a key factor in motivating Disney's workforce. By giving employees autonomy and trusting their expertise, Disney fosters a sense of responsibility and pride in their contributions. This empowerment drives innovation and performance.

- Purpose-Driven Work: Aligning employees' work with the company's mission and values provides a sense of purpose and meaning. Disney's mission to create happiness and entertain people worldwide resonates with employees, making their work feel impactful and fulfilling. This purpose-driven approach enhances motivation and job satisfaction.

- Engagement Programs: Disney implements various engagement programs to foster a positive work environment and build strong relationships among employees. Programs such as team-building activities, social events, and employee resource groups provide opportunities for employees to connect, collaborate, and build a sense of community.

- Recognition and Appreciation: Regular recognition and appreciation of employees' efforts are crucial to maintaining high levels of motivation. Disney's recognition programs, including awards, shout-outs, and performance bonuses, highlight the value of employees' contributions. This recognition reinforces positive behaviors and encourages continued excellence.

Dealing with Competition and Market Changes

The Walt Disney Company has faced significant competition and market changes throughout its history. Disney's strategies for navigating these challenges have been instrumental in maintaining its leadership position in the entertainment industry.

- Innovation and Adaptation: Disney's commitment to innovation and adaptation has been a critical factor in dealing with competition and market changes. The company continually invests in new technologies, creative content, and innovative experiences to stay ahead of industry trends. By embracing change and anticipating market shifts, Disney has remained relevant and competitive.

- Strategic Acquisitions: Disney's strategic acquisitions of companies like Pixar, Marvel, Lucasfilm, and 21st Century Fox have strengthened its competitive position. These acquisitions have expanded Disney's content library, diversified its offerings, and enhanced its market reach. By integrating these companies, Disney has leveraged their strengths to create synergies and drive growth.

- Diversification: Disney's diversification strategy has enabled the company to mitigate risks and capitalize on new opportunities. By expanding into various sectors, including film, television, theme parks, consumer products, and digital media, Disney has created multiple revenue streams. This diversification provides stability and allows the company to adapt to changing market conditions.

- Global Expansion: Disney's focus on global expansion has been instrumental in navigating competition and market changes. The company has successfully entered international markets through theme parks, media networks, and localized content. This global presence has diversified Disney's audience base and opened new growth opportunities.

- Customer-Centric Approach: Disney's customer-centric approach has been a key factor in dealing with competition. By prioritizing customer satisfaction and creating exceptional experiences, Disney has built a loyal customer base. The company continually seeks feedback and adapts its offerings to meet customer needs and preferences, ensuring sustained relevance and competitiveness.

Legacy in Modern Entertainment and Business Practices

Walt Disney's legacy extends beyond the success of The Walt Disney Company. His influence on modern entertainment and business practices has left a lasting impact on the industry and continues to inspire leaders and creators worldwide.

- Innovation in Entertainment: Disney's commitment to innovation has revolutionized the entertainment industry. His pioneering work in animation, theme parks, and storytelling set new standards and opened new possibilities. Disney's legacy of innovation continues to drive advancements in entertainment technology, from CGI and virtual reality to immersive experiences.

- Creative Leadership: Walt Disney's leadership style, characterized by vision, creativity, and empowerment, has influenced generations of leaders. His approach to fostering a collaborative and innovative environment has become a model for creative leadership in various industries. Disney's legacy demonstrates the importance of balancing creative freedom with strategic direction.

- Brand Building: Disney's mastery of brand building has had a profound impact on modern business practices. The Disney brand, synonymous with quality, creativity, and family-friendly entertainment, has become a global icon. Disney's strategies for brand development, including character creation, storytelling, and multi-platform expansion, continue to inform best practices in brand management.

- Corporate Culture: The corporate culture that Walt Disney established, centered on creativity, collaboration, and excellence, has influenced organizational practices beyond the entertainment industry. Disney's emphasis on employee engagement, continuous learning, and quality has become a benchmark for building strong corporate cultures.

- Sustainability and Social Responsibility: Disney's focus on sustainability and social responsibility has set a precedent for corporate citizenship. The company's initiatives in environmental conservation, community support, and ethical business practices demonstrate the importance of integrating social responsibility into business strategies. Disney's legacy highlights the role of companies in contributing positively to society and the environment.

Walt Disney's leadership and the corporate culture he built have been fundamental to the success and enduring legacy of The Walt Disney Company. Disney's visionary approach to creative leadership, commitment to innovation, and emphasis on storytelling have shaped the company's identity and guided its growth.

Building a strong corporate culture based on shared

values, collaboration, and continuous improvement has been instrumental in fostering employee engagement and motivation. Disney's strategies for navigating competition and market changes, including innovation, strategic acquisitions, and diversification, have ensured the company's sustained relevance and leadership in the entertainment industry.

Disney's legacy extends beyond the company's achievements, influencing modern entertainment and business practices. His impact on creative leadership, brand building, corporate culture, and social responsibility continues to inspire leaders and organizations worldwide. The principles and values that Walt Disney instilled in his company remain at the heart of The Walt Disney Company, driving its success and shaping its future.

Case Study: The Creation of Disneyland

Vision and Planning for Disneyland

Walt Disney's vision for Disneyland was rooted in his desire to create a place where families could experience joy and wonder together. Unlike the amusement parks of his time, which were often dirty and uninspired, Disney envisioned a clean, immersive, and meticulously themed environment that would transport visitors to different worlds.

- Inspiration: Walt Disney's inspiration for Disneyland came from his experiences visiting amusement parks with his daughters in the 1930s and 1940s. He felt that there was a need for a family-friendly destination that both children and adults could enjoy. His trips to Tivoli Gardens in Denmark and the World's Fair further influenced his vision, demonstrating the potential of well-designed and themed environments.

- Conceptualization: Disney began conceptualizing Disneyland in the early 1950s. He imagined a park divided into distinct themed lands, each offering unique attractions and experiences. These lands would include Main Street, U.S.A., Adventureland, Frontierland, Fantasyland, and Tomorrowland. Each area would be meticulously designed to immerse visitors in a different narrative, from the charm of a turn-of-the-century American town to the futuristic world of tomorrow.

- Design and Layout: Disney worked closely with a team of designers, engineers, and architects, whom he called "Imagineers," to develop the design and layout of the park. The design process involved extensive research, planning, and creative brainstorming. Disney's attention to detail was evident in every aspect of the park, from the architectural styles and landscaping to the costumes and storytelling elements.

- Location Selection: Finding the right location for Disneyland was crucial. After considering several sites, Disney selected a 160-acre orange grove in Anaheim, California. The location was strategically chosen for its proximity to major highways and the growing population of

Southern California. The mild climate also made it an ideal setting for an outdoor theme park.

- Planning and Development: The planning and development phase of Disneyland involved numerous challenges and meticulous attention to detail. Disney and his team created detailed blueprints, models, and prototypes to visualize and refine their ideas. They also conducted surveys and gathered feedback to ensure that the park would meet the expectations of visitors. The planning process was iterative, with continuous adjustments and improvements to the design.

Overcoming Financial and Logistical Challenges

The creation of Disneyland was a monumental undertaking that involved overcoming significant financial and logistical challenges. Walt Disney's determination and innovative problem-solving were key to navigating these obstacles.

- Securing Funding: Financing Disneyland was one of the biggest challenges Walt Disney faced. The estimated cost of the project was $17 million, a substantial sum at the time. To secure the necessary funding, Disney leveraged his personal assets and negotiated deals with investors and sponsors. One of the key partnerships was with ABC, which provided a significant portion of the funding in exchange for a television show that promoted the park.

This partnership not only secured the necessary capital but also generated public interest and excitement for Disneyland.

- Construction Challenges: The construction of Disneyland was a massive logistical challenge. The project involved transforming an orange grove into a fully functional theme park within a tight timeframe. The construction site was bustling with activity as workers built the infrastructure, attractions, and themed environments. Managing the construction process required meticulous coordination, problem-solving, and adaptability. Disney's hands-on approach and constant presence on the construction site helped ensure that the project stayed on track.

- Innovative Solutions: To overcome financial and logistical challenges, Disney and his team developed innovative solutions. For example, they used advanced construction techniques and materials to create the park's attractions and structures. The development of the monorail system, which was the first daily operating monorail in the Western Hemisphere, demonstrated Disney's commitment to innovation. Additionally, the use of forced perspective in the park's architecture created the illusion of greater height and scale, enhancing the immersive experience.

- Opening Day Hurdles: Disneyland's opening day on July 17, 1955, was fraught with challenges. The event, which was broadcast live on television, was attended by 28,000 guests, far more than the anticipated 15,000. The park faced issues such as unfinished attractions, long lines, and a shortage of food and beverages. Despite these hurdles, the opening day generated immense public interest and marked the beginning of Disneyland's success. Disney and his team quickly addressed the initial issues, and the park's popularity continued to grow.

Impact on the Theme Park Industry

The creation of Disneyland had a profound impact on the theme park industry, setting new standards for design, operation, and guest experience. Disneyland's success revolutionized the concept of amusement parks and inspired the development of themed entertainment worldwide.

- Themed Environments: Disneyland introduced the concept of immersive themed environments, where every aspect of the park contributed to a cohesive narrative. This approach set a new standard for theme park design, emphasizing the importance of storytelling, theming, and attention to detail. Other parks adopted similar strategies, creating themed lands and attractions that transported visitors to different worlds.

- Guest Experience: Disneyland's focus on guest experience transformed the theme park industry. Disney prioritized cleanliness, safety, and customer service, creating an environment where visitors felt welcome and valued. The emphasis on guest experience extended to every aspect of the park, from attraction design to employee training. This approach influenced other parks to prioritize guest satisfaction and create memorable experiences.

- Innovation and Technology: Disneyland's use of innovative technologies and construction techniques set a precedent for the industry. The park introduced advanced ride systems, animatronics, and special effects that enhanced the guest experience. Disney's commitment to innovation inspired other parks to adopt new technologies and push the boundaries of what was possible in themed entertainment.

- Economic Impact: Disneyland's success had a significant economic impact on the region, attracting millions of visitors and generating substantial revenue. The park's popularity led to the development of hotels, restaurants, and other businesses in the surrounding area. The economic success of Disneyland demonstrated the potential of theme parks as major drivers of tourism and economic development.

- Global Influence: Disneyland's impact extended beyond the United States, influencing the development of theme parks worldwide. Parks such as Tokyo Disneyland, Disneyland Paris, and Hong Kong Disneyland were modeled after the original Disneyland, incorporating similar design principles and theming. Disney's approach to themed entertainment became a global standard, shaping the development of parks in different cultural contexts.

Expansion and Development of Additional Parks

The success of Disneyland in Anaheim led to the expansion and development of additional Disney parks around the world. Each park built on the legacy of Disneyland, incorporating unique elements while maintaining the core principles of Disney's vision.

- Walt Disney World: Walt Disney World, located in Orlando, Florida, opened in 1971 and represented a significant expansion of Disney's theme park concept. The resort included the Magic Kingdom, EPCOT, Disney's Hollywood Studios, and Disney's Animal Kingdom, along with hotels, restaurants, and recreational facilities. Walt Disney World became a comprehensive vacation destination, attracting millions of visitors each year and solidifying Disney's dominance in the theme park industry.

- Tokyo Disneyland: Tokyo Disneyland, which opened in 1983, was Disney's first international park. The park was developed in partnership with the Oriental Land Company and incorporated many of the design elements and attractions from Disneyland and Walt Disney World. Tokyo Disneyland's success demonstrated the global appeal of Disney's brand and storytelling, leading to further international expansion.

- Disneyland Paris: Disneyland Paris, originally known as Euro Disney, opened in 1992 in Marne-la-Vallée, France. The park faced initial challenges, including cultural differences and financial difficulties, but eventually became a popular destination. Disneyland Paris features unique attractions and theming that reflect European culture, while still maintaining the core Disney experience.

- Hong Kong Disneyland and Shanghai Disney Resort: Hong Kong Disneyland, which opened in 2005, and Shanghai Disney Resort, which opened in 2016, further expanded Disney's presence in Asia. Both parks incorporated elements of Chinese culture and design, creating a unique and culturally relevant experience for visitors. Shanghai Disney Resort, in particular, featured innovative attractions and technologies that set new standards for the industry.

- Disney California Adventure and Other Expansions: In addition to new parks, Disney expanded its existing properties with new attractions and themed lands. Disney California Adventure, adjacent to Disneyland in Anaheim, opened in 2001 and offered new experiences based on California's history and culture. Other expansions, such as the addition of Star Wars: Galaxy's Edge and Marvel-themed lands, continued to innovate and attract visitors.

Disney's Enduring Influence on Family Entertainment

Walt Disney's vision for Disneyland and the subsequent development of Disney parks have had a lasting impact on family entertainment. Disney's influence extends beyond theme parks, shaping the broader entertainment industry and setting standards for quality and innovation.

- Family-Friendly Entertainment: Disney's commitment to creating family-friendly entertainment has set a benchmark for the industry. The emphasis on wholesome, high-quality experiences that appeal to all ages has become a defining characteristic of Disney's brand. This focus on family entertainment has influenced other companies to prioritize similar values in their offerings.

- Innovative Storytelling: Disney's approach to storytelling, which emphasizes immersive environments and emotional resonance, has become a model for the entertainment industry. The integration of storytelling into theme park design, attractions, and experiences has set new standards for creating engaging and memorable entertainment. This approach has been adopted by other theme parks, attractions, and entertainment venues worldwide.

- Technological Advancements: Disney's

commitment to innovation and technology has driven advancements in the entertainment industry. From animatronics and special effects to advanced ride systems and interactive experiences, Disney has consistently pushed the boundaries of what is possible. These technological advancements have inspired other companies to invest in innovation and enhance their offerings.

- Global Reach and Cultural Impact: Disney's theme parks have become cultural icons, attracting millions of visitors from around the world. The global reach of Disney's parks has created a shared cultural experience that transcends borders and languages. Disney's influence on popular culture, through its parks, films, and merchandise, is unparalleled and continues to shape the entertainment landscape.

- Industry Standards: Disney's commitment to quality, customer service, and guest experience has set industry standards that others strive to meet. The company's focus on cleanliness, safety, and attention to detail has become a benchmark for theme parks and entertainment venues. Disney's success has demonstrated the importance of creating immersive, high-quality experiences that leave a lasting impact on guests.

The creation of Disneyland was a groundbreaking achievement that revolutionized the theme park industry and established Walt Disney's enduring legacy. From Walt Disney's visionary planning and innovative design to overcoming financial and logistical challenges, Disneyland set new standards for themed entertainment and guest experience.

The impact of Disneyland extended beyond the original park, inspiring the development of additional Disney parks around the world and influencing the broader entertainment industry. Disney's commitment to storytelling, innovation, and family-friendly entertainment has shaped the way experiences are designed and delivered, creating a lasting influence on popular culture.

Walt Disney's vision for Disneyland continues to resonate with audiences worldwide, and the principles he established remain at the heart of The Walt Disney Company's success. Disneyland's legacy as a place of joy, wonder, and imagination endures, inspiring future generations to dream big and create magic.

Chapter 7:

Steve Jobs Transforming Technology

Steve Jobs was born on February 24, 1955, in San Francisco, California. He was adopted by Paul and Clara Jobs, who provided him with a stable and nurturing home in the Silicon Valley area. Growing up in this region, which was becoming the epicenter of technology and innovation, had a profound influence on Jobs. His father, Paul, a machinist and handyman, introduced young Steve to the world of electronics by teaching him how to work on mechanical objects. This hands-on experience fostered a curiosity and passion for technology that would shape Jobs's future.

Jobs was an intelligent but often rebellious student. He struggled with the rigid structures of formal education, but his exceptional intellect and creativity were apparent to those who knew him. One of his early influences was his friendship with Steve Wozniak, a fellow electronics enthusiast who shared Jobs's interest in technology. This friendship would later prove pivotal in the founding of Apple Inc.

Jobs's exposure to diverse ideas also shaped his thinking. During his high school years, he attended lectures at the Hewlett-Packard Explorers Club, where he met engineers and saw cutting-edge technology firsthand. These experiences deepened his interest in electronics and engineering.

After graduating from high school in 1972, Jobs briefly attended Reed College in Portland, Oregon. Although he dropped out after just one semester, Jobs continued to audit classes that interested him, such as a calligraphy course that would later influence the design of Apple's typography and user interfaces. His time at Reed College also exposed him to the countercultural and philosophical ideas that would influence his thinking and approach to business.

Entry into the Technology Industry

Steve Jobs's entry into the technology industry began with his involvement in the burgeoning personal computer movement in the early 1970s. After dropping out of Reed College, Jobs returned to California and joined the Homebrew Computer Club, a group of electronics hobbyists who shared ideas and projects. It was here that Jobs reconnected with Steve Wozniak, who had developed a prototype for a simple, build-it-yourself computer.

In 1974, Jobs took a job at Atari, a leading video game company. While at Atari, Jobs honed his technical skills and learned about the nascent computer industry. He also saved money to fund a trip to India, where he sought spiritual enlightenment and explored Eastern philosophies. This journey deepened his appreciation for simplicity and design, concepts that would later influence Apple's products.

Jobs's big break came when Wozniak showed him the Apple I, a computer he had designed and built. Recognizing its potential, Jobs convinced Wozniak that they should sell the computer to the public. Together, they began assembling the computers in Jobs's garage, marking the humble beginnings of what would become one of the most influential technology companies in the world.

Founding of Apple Inc.

In 1976, Steve Jobs and Steve Wozniak co-founded Apple Computer, Inc., along with Ronald Wayne, who soon sold his shares and left the company. The Apple I, their first product, was a single-board computer kit sold primarily to hobbyists. While the Apple I was not a commercial success, it provided the foundation for their next venture.

In 1977, Apple released the Apple II, a groundbreaking product that was one of the first highly successful mass-produced personal computers. The Apple II featured a color display, an integrated keyboard, and expansion slots, making it user-friendly and versatile. It quickly became popular in homes and schools, helping to establish Apple as a significant player in the emerging personal computer market.

The success of the Apple II attracted investors, and Apple went public in 1980, raising significant capital. This financial boost enabled the company to expand and innovate further. Jobs's vision for Apple extended beyond just creating computers; he wanted to build a company that combined cutting-edge technology with exceptional design and user experience.

Vision for Personal Computing

Steve Jobs's vision for personal computing was revolutionary. He believed that computers should not only be powerful tools for professionals but also accessible to everyday people. This vision was driven by several key principles:

- User-Friendly Design: Jobs was adamant that computers should be easy to use and aesthetically pleasing. He prioritized simplicity and intuitive design, ensuring that Apple products were accessible to non-technical users. This philosophy was evident in the Apple II and later in the Macintosh, which featured a graphical user interface (GUI) and a mouse, making it far more user-friendly than the text-based interfaces of the time.

- Integration of Hardware and Software: Jobs believed in tightly integrating hardware and software to create a seamless user experience. This approach allowed Apple to optimize performance and ensure that all components worked harmoniously. The synergy between hardware and software became a hallmark of Apple products.

- Innovation and Quality: Jobs was committed to pushing the boundaries of what was possible with technology. He encouraged his team to think differently and pursue bold ideas. This drive for innovation led to numerous breakthroughs, such as the development of the GUI and the introduction of the first affordable laser printer with the Apple LaserWriter.

- Creating a Lifestyle: Jobs envisioned Apple as more than just a technology company; he saw it as a brand that represented creativity, innovation, and quality. He wanted Apple products to enhance people's lives and become an integral part of their daily routines. This vision was reflected in Apple's marketing campaigns, which often highlighted the personal and transformative impact of their products.

Initial Business Challenges

Despite the early success of the Apple II, the company faced significant challenges during its formative years. These challenges tested Jobs's leadership and ultimately shaped the future direction of Apple.

- Management Conflicts: As Apple grew, tensions arose between Jobs and other executives. Jobs's intense and often demanding leadership style led to conflicts, particularly with Mike Markkula, an early investor, and John Sculley, a former PepsiCo executive who was brought in as CEO in 1983. Jobs's visionary approach sometimes clashed with the pragmatic business strategies of his colleagues.

- The Lisa Project: The Apple Lisa, introduced in 1983, was one of Apple's first attempts at creating a computer with a graphical user interface. However, the Lisa was plagued by delays, high costs, and technical issues. Its commercial failure highlighted the challenges of balancing innovation with market viability. Despite its shortcomings, the Lisa project provided valuable lessons that influenced the development of future products.

- Macintosh Launch: The launch of the Macintosh in 1984 was a pivotal moment for Apple. The Macintosh was revolutionary, featuring a user-friendly GUI, a mouse, and an innovative design. However, its high price and limited software compatibility initially hindered its market acceptance. Additionally, the marketing costs associated with the Macintosh's iconic "1984" Super Bowl commercial strained Apple's finances.

- Internal Struggles and Departure: By 1985, internal struggles reached a tipping point. Conflicts between Jobs and Sculley escalated, leading to a power struggle within the company. Ultimately, the board sided with Sculley, and Jobs was removed from his managerial role. Feeling marginalized, Jobs resigned from Apple later that year. His departure marked the end of an era, but it also set the stage for his eventual return and Apple's resurgence.

Steve Jobs's early life and career were marked by a unique blend of creativity, technical prowess, and visionary thinking. His childhood and early influences, particularly his exposure to electronics and his experiences in Silicon Valley, laid the groundwork for his entry into the technology industry. Jobs's partnership with Steve Wozniak and the founding of Apple Inc. marked the beginning of a transformative journey that would revolutionize personal computing.

Jobs's vision for personal computing, characterized by user-friendly design, hardware-software integration, innovation, and quality, set Apple apart from its competitors. Despite facing significant business challenges, including management conflicts, product failures, and internal struggles, Jobs's relentless pursuit of excellence and his commitment to his vision ultimately shaped Apple's trajectory.

Steve Jobs's story is a testament to the power of visionary leadership and the impact of perseverance in the face of adversity. His early experiences and the lessons learned from initial challenges laid the foundation for his later successes and his enduring legacy in the technology industry. The principles and values that Jobs instilled in Apple continue to guide the company, driving innovation and shaping the future of technology.

Innovations and Product Development

Development of the Apple I and II

The development of the Apple I and Apple II marked the beginning of a new era in personal computing and set the stage for Apple Inc.'s future success. Steve Jobs and Steve Wozniak's collaboration on these early computers combined technical ingenuity with a visionary approach to product development.

- Apple I: The Apple I was introduced in 1976 as

a single-board computer kit designed by Wozniak and marketed by Jobs. Unlike other hobbyist computers of the time, which required extensive assembly, the Apple I came fully assembled and included a pre-installed BASIC interpreter. It featured a relatively affordable price of $666.66 and was aimed at hobbyists and tech enthusiasts. The Apple I's simplicity and ease of use made it an attractive option, and it sold approximately 200 units through small computer stores, notably the Byte Shop.

- Apple II: Building on the success of the Apple I, Jobs and Wozniak developed the Apple II, which was introduced in 1977. The Apple II was a significant leap forward in terms of design, functionality, and market appeal. It featured a plastic case, integrated keyboard, color graphics, and eight expansion slots, making it highly versatile. The Apple II was one of the first computers to come with a built-in programming language, AppleSoft BASIC, and it supported a wide range of third-party software. The inclusion of a floppy disk drive, the Disk II, further enhanced its capabilities.

- The Apple II's user-friendly design and powerful features made it a hit in both the consumer and education markets. It became one of the best-selling personal computers of its time, with millions of units sold. The success of the Apple II established Apple as a major player in the emerging personal computer industry and provided the financial foundation for future innovations.

Introduction of the Macintosh

The introduction of the Macintosh in 1984 was a pivotal moment in the history of personal computing. The Macintosh was designed to be a revolutionary product that would make computing accessible to the masses through its intuitive graphical user interface (GUI).

- Development and Design: The Macintosh project, initially conceived as an affordable and user-friendly computer, underwent several iterations before its release. Jef Raskin, an Apple employee, originally envisioned the Macintosh as a low-cost appliance computer. However, after Raskin left the project, Jobs took over and shifted the focus towards creating a more powerful and visually appealing machine.

- The Macintosh featured a compact design with an all-in-one case that housed the computer, monitor, and disk drive. It introduced the concept of the GUI, which allowed users to interact with the computer using a mouse and graphical icons instead of text-based commands. The interface included windows, menus, and icons, making it much easier for non-technical users to navigate and operate the computer.

- Iconic Launch: The launch of the Macintosh was accompanied by one of the most famous commercials in advertising history, the "1984" Super Bowl ad directed by Ridley Scott. The commercial positioned the Macintosh as a revolutionary product that would challenge the dominance of IBM and liberate users from conformity. The bold and memorable ad generated significant buzz and anticipation for the product.

- Initial Reception and Challenges: Despite its innovative design and user-friendly interface, the Macintosh faced several challenges upon its release. The high price of $2,495 limited its accessibility to many consumers. Additionally, the limited software available for the Macintosh at launch hindered its adoption. However, over time, the development of applications like Microsoft Word and Excel, along with graphic design software like Adobe Photoshop, helped the Macintosh gain traction.

- Long-Term Impact: The Macintosh's introduction of the GUI set a new standard for personal computing and influenced the design of future operating systems, including Microsoft Windows. The focus on user experience and design aesthetics became hallmarks of Apple's product philosophy. The Macintosh's legacy can be seen in the continued evolution of Apple's desktop and laptop computers, which prioritize ease of use, elegant design, and seamless integration of hardware and software.

Innovations in Software and User Interfaces

Apple's commitment to innovation extended beyond

hardware to include significant advancements in software and user interfaces. These innovations transformed how users interacted with computers and set new benchmarks for the industry.

- Mac OS: The Macintosh Operating System (Mac OS) was one of the first operating systems to feature a GUI. Its design principles, such as the desktop metaphor, drag-and-drop functionality, and intuitive navigation, made computing more accessible to a broader audience. Mac OS's focus on simplicity and user experience influenced the development of subsequent operating systems.

- QuickTime: Introduced in 1991, QuickTime was a multimedia framework developed by Apple that allowed users to play, create, and stream digital video and audio files. QuickTime's versatility and performance made it a popular choice for multimedia applications and contributed to the growth of digital media.

- Final Cut Pro: In 1999, Apple released Final Cut Pro, a professional video editing software that became a favorite among filmmakers and video editors. Its powerful features, user-friendly interface, and affordability revolutionized the video editing industry and cemented Apple's reputation as a leader in creative software.

- iLife Suite: Apple introduced the iLife suite of applications, which included iPhoto, iMovie, iDVD, GarageBand, and iWeb. These applications were designed to help users manage and create digital content, such as photos, videos, music, and websites. The iLife suite made multimedia creation accessible to non-professional users and highlighted Apple's focus on creativity and user empowerment.

- iOS: With the introduction of the iPhone in 2007, Apple launched iOS, a mobile operating system that redefined the smartphone experience. iOS's touch-based interface, intuitive gestures, and App Store ecosystem revolutionized mobile computing and set new standards for smartphone design and functionality. The success of iOS paved the way for the development of the iPad and other mobile devices.

Development of the iPod, iPhone, and iPad

Steve Jobs's return to Apple in 1997 marked the beginning of a new era of innovation, leading to the development of iconic products that transformed the technology landscape: the iPod, iPhone, and iPad.

- iPod: Introduced in 2001, the iPod was a portable digital music player that revolutionized how people listened to music. Its sleek design, intuitive click wheel interface, and ability to store thousands of songs made it a game-changer in the music industry. The iTunes Store, launched in 2003, complemented the iPod by providing a convenient platform for purchasing and downloading music. The iPod's success helped revive Apple's fortunes and established the company as a major player in consumer electronics.

- iPhone: The launch of the iPhone in 2007 was a watershed moment in the history of technology. The iPhone combined a mobile phone, iPod, and internet communication device into a single, elegantly designed product. Its multi-touch interface, App Store ecosystem, and seamless integration of hardware and software set new standards for smartphones. The iPhone's success redefined the mobile phone market, making Apple one of the most valuable companies in the world and influencing the design of future smartphones.

- iPad: In 2010, Apple introduced the iPad, a tablet computer that bridged the gap between smartphones and laptops. The iPad's large multi-touch display, powerful hardware, and extensive library of apps made it a versatile device for work, entertainment, and education. The iPad's success demonstrated the potential of tablet computing and established a new product category in the technology market.

- Ecosystem Integration: One of the key factors behind the success of the iPod, iPhone, and iPad was Apple's emphasis on ecosystem integration. Products were designed to work seamlessly together, creating a cohesive user experience. The introduction of services like iCloud further enhanced this integration by allowing users to sync and access their data across multiple devices effortlessly.

- Continuous Innovation: Apple's commitment to continuous innovation ensured that the iPod, iPhone, and iPad remained at the forefront of technology. Regular updates and new features kept the products relevant and competitive. Innovations such as the App Store, Siri, Touch ID, and Face ID continued to push the boundaries of what was possible with mobile devices.

Impact on the Technology Industry

Steve Jobs's innovations and product developments had a profound and lasting impact on the technology industry, influencing how technology is designed, marketed, and experienced.

- Design Excellence: Jobs's insistence on design excellence set a new standard for the technology industry. Apple's products were not only functional but also beautifully designed, with a focus on simplicity, elegance, and user experience. This emphasis on design has influenced countless other companies and elevated consumer expectations for product aesthetics and usability.

- User-Centric Approach: Apple's user-centric approach, prioritizing ease of use and intuitive interfaces, revolutionized the way people interact with technology. The success of the Macintosh, iPhone, and iPad demonstrated the importance of designing technology that is accessible and enjoyable for all users, not just technical experts.

- Innovation Culture: Jobs fostered a culture of innovation at Apple, encouraging his teams to think creatively and challenge the status quo. This culture led to groundbreaking products and technologies that transformed industries. Apple's commitment to innovation inspired other companies to invest in research and development and pursue bold ideas.

- Ecosystem and Integration: The concept of creating an integrated ecosystem of devices and services became a defining characteristic of Apple's strategy. This approach enhanced the user experience and created a loyal customer base. The success of Apple's ecosystem has influenced other technology companies to develop integrated solutions that provide seamless experiences across multiple devices and platforms.

- Market Leadership: Apple's ability to anticipate and shape market trends has solidified its position as a leader in the technology industry. The introduction of the iPod, iPhone, and iPad redefined their respective markets and forced competitors to adapt. Apple's market leadership has driven innovation and competition, benefiting consumers and advancing the industry as a whole.

- App Economy: The launch of the App Store with the iPhone created a thriving app economy, providing opportunities for developers and transforming how software is distributed and consumed. The success of the

App Store has influenced other platforms and led to the proliferation of app-based ecosystems across various devices and operating systems.

Steve Jobs's innovations and product developments revolutionized the technology industry and reshaped the way people interact with technology. The development of the Apple I and II, the introduction of the Macintosh, and the groundbreaking advancements in software and user interfaces set new standards for personal computing. The launch of the iPod, iPhone, and iPad marked a new era of mobile computing and established Apple as a global leader in consumer electronics.

Jobs's commitment to design excellence, user-centricity, and continuous innovation has left an indelible mark on the technology industry. His vision for integrated ecosystems and seamless user experiences has influenced countless companies and set new benchmarks for product development. Steve Jobs's legacy continues to inspire and drive innovation, ensuring that his impact on technology and society will be felt for generations to come.

Business Strategies and Market Disruption

Focus on Design and User Experience

One of the cornerstones of Steve Jobs's business strategy was his unwavering focus on design and user experience. Jobs believed that the aesthetic appeal and functionality of a product were equally important, and he infused this philosophy into every aspect of

Apple's operations.

- Aesthetic Excellence: Jobs had a deep appreciation for beauty and simplicity in design. He worked closely with industrial designer Jony Ive to create products that were not only functional but also visually stunning. This collaboration resulted in iconic designs like the iMac, with its translucent colored casing, and the sleek, minimalist iPhone. Apple's products stood out in a market saturated with utilitarian devices, capturing the imagination of consumers and setting new standards for design in technology.

- User-Centric Design: Jobs's approach to design was always user-centric. He insisted that Apple products be intuitive and easy to use, even for those without technical expertise. This philosophy was evident in the graphical user interface of the Macintosh, the touch-based interface of the iPhone, and the simple, streamlined design of the iPod. Apple's focus on user experience ensured that its products were accessible and enjoyable for a wide audience.

- Attention to Detail: Jobs was known for his obsessive attention to detail. He scrutinized every aspect of product design, from the layout of circuit boards to the curvature of device edges. This meticulous approach ensured that Apple products were not only beautiful but also highly functional and reliable. Jobs's insistence on perfection often led to delays and higher costs, but the result was a level of quality that distinguished Apple from its competitors.

- Integrated Ecosystem: Apple's design philosophy extended beyond individual products to encompass a seamless ecosystem of devices and services. The integration of hardware, software, and services created a cohesive user experience, allowing customers to easily transition between devices and access their content from anywhere. This ecosystem approach enhanced user satisfaction and loyalty, making it difficult for competitors to replicate the seamless experience that Apple offered.

Strategies for Entering and Dominating New Markets

Steve Jobs was a master strategist when it came to entering and dominating new markets. He leveraged Apple's strengths in design, innovation, and user experience to disrupt established markets and create new opportunities for growth.

- Identifying Market Opportunities: Jobs had a keen sense for identifying market opportunities and unmet consumer needs. He recognized the potential for personal computing, digital music, smartphones, and tablets before these markets fully matured. By entering these markets early and setting high standards for product quality and innovation, Apple established itself as a leader and set the pace for competitors.

- Creating Disruptive Products: Apple's strategy for entering new markets often involved creating disruptive products that redefined consumer expectations. The iPod revolutionized digital music by offering a portable, user-friendly device with an extensive library of songs available through the iTunes Store. The iPhone reimagined the smartphone with its touch interface, app ecosystem, and integration of multiple functions into one device. The iPad introduced a new category of portable computing with its large touch screen and versatile capabilities. These products disrupted existing markets and attracted millions of new customers to Apple's ecosystem.

- Marketing and Branding: Jobs understood the power of marketing and branding in creating consumer desire and loyalty. Apple's marketing campaigns, such as the iconic "Think Different" ads and the "1984" Super Bowl commercial, effectively communicated the company's values of innovation, creativity, and rebellion against the status quo. Apple's branding emphasized simplicity, elegance, and premium quality, positioning its products as desirable and aspirational.

- Pricing Strategy: Apple's pricing strategy was often premium, reflecting the high quality and innovative features of its products. While this approach limited initial accessibility, it created a perception of exclusivity and desirability. Over time, Apple introduced more affordable models and versions of its products, broadening its market reach while maintaining its premium brand image.

- Leveraging Distribution Channels: Apple's strategic use of distribution channels also played a key role in its market dominance. The company initially partnered with established retailers to reach a wide audience. Later, Apple revolutionized its distribution strategy with the introduction of Apple Stores, which offered a direct and controlled retail experience.

Innovation in Retail with Apple Stores

The introduction of Apple Stores was a groundbreaking move that transformed retail in the technology sector. Steve Jobs envisioned Apple Stores as more than just places to buy products; he saw them as destinations for experiencing the Apple brand and receiving unparalleled customer service.

- Design and Experience: Apple Stores were designed with the same meticulous attention to detail as Apple's products. The sleek, minimalist aesthetic, open floor plans, and innovative use of glass and natural materials created a unique and inviting atmosphere. This design philosophy extended to every aspect of the store, from the layout of products to the presentation of accessories. The stores were intended to be experiential spaces where customers could interact with Apple products in a hands-on, immersive environment.

- Customer Service: The Apple Store experience was defined by its exceptional customer service. The introduction of the Genius Bar, where customers could receive technical support and repairs, set a new standard for in-store service. Apple's emphasis on knowledgeable and friendly staff ensured that customers received personalized assistance and guidance. This focus on service fostered customer loyalty and trust.

- Retail Innovation: Apple Stores introduced several retail innovations, such as the use of mobile point-of-sale systems and interactive product displays. The stores also hosted educational workshops and events, providing value-added services that enhanced the customer experience. These innovations set Apple Stores apart from traditional electronics retailers and created a new model for technology retail.

- Global Expansion: Apple strategically expanded its retail presence globally, opening flagship stores in major cities around the world. Each store was designed to reflect its location while maintaining the core principles of Apple's retail philosophy. The global presence of Apple Stores strengthened the company's brand and provided a consistent and high-quality experience for customers worldwide.

- Integration with Online Retail: Apple seamlessly integrated its physical retail stores with its online store, providing a unified shopping experience. Customers could order products online and pick them up in-store, or receive assistance with online purchases at the Apple Store. This omnichannel approach ensured that customers had flexible and convenient options for purchasing and receiving support for their Apple products.

Competition with Other Tech Giants

Steve Jobs's leadership saw Apple face fierce competition from other tech giants. Apple's strategies for competing with and often outmaneuvering its rivals were critical to its success.

- Innovation and Differentiation: Apple's primary strategy for competing with other tech giants was innovation and differentiation. The company continually introduced groundbreaking products and features that set it apart from competitors. Whether it was the introduction of the iPod's seamless integration with iTunes, the iPhone's revolutionary touch interface, or the iPad's versatility, Apple's focus on innovation ensured that its products were often the first and best in their categories.

- Ecosystem Lock-In: Apple created a tightly integrated ecosystem of devices and services that encouraged customer loyalty and made it difficult for users to switch to competing products. The seamless integration of iOS devices with services like iCloud, Apple Music, and the App Store created a cohesive user experience that competitors struggled to replicate. This ecosystem lock-in not only drove repeat purchases but also attracted new customers seeking a unified technology experience.

- Intellectual Property and Patents: Apple aggressively protected its intellectual property and patents to maintain its competitive edge. The company engaged in numerous legal battles with competitors, particularly over design and technology patents. Notable conflicts included lawsuits against Samsung over smartphone design and functionality. These legal efforts helped Apple safeguard its innovations and assert its leadership in the market.

- Strategic Acquisitions: Apple strategically acquired companies that could enhance its technological capabilities and competitive position. Acquisitions such as NeXT (which brought Jobs back to Apple and provided the foundation for macOS), Beats Electronics (which bolstered Apple's music streaming and headphone offerings), and several AI and machine learning startups helped Apple stay ahead of industry trends and incorporate new technologies into its products.

- Brand Loyalty and Marketing: Apple's powerful brand and effective marketing campaigns created a strong sense of loyalty among its customers. The company's marketing emphasized the unique features and superior design of its products, creating a perception of exclusivity and desirability. Apple's ability to build an emotional connection with its customers through its brand was a significant competitive advantage.

Long-Term Impact on Consumer Electronics

Steve Jobs's business strategies and market disruptions had a profound and lasting impact on the consumer electronics industry. Apple's influence extended beyond its own product lines, shaping industry trends and setting new standards for technology companies worldwide.

- Raising Design Standards: Apple's emphasis on design excellence raised the bar for the entire consumer electronics industry. Competing companies were compelled to improve the aesthetics and user experience of their products to keep up with Apple. This shift led to a greater focus on design and usability across the industry, benefiting consumers with better-designed and more intuitive devices.

- Advancing User Interfaces: The introduction of the graphical user interface with the Macintosh and the touch interface with the iPhone revolutionized how people interacted with technology. These innovations set new benchmarks for user interfaces, leading to widespread adoption of similar concepts by other companies. The intuitive and user-friendly design of Apple's interfaces made technology more accessible to a broader audience.

- Creating New Product Categories: Apple's development of the iPod, iPhone, and iPad created entirely new product categories and transformed existing ones. The success of these products demonstrated the potential for innovation in consumer electronics and encouraged other companies to explore new ideas and product formats. Apple's ability to create and dominate new markets inspired a wave of innovation and competition.

- Ecosystem Integration: Apple's strategy of creating a seamless ecosystem of devices and services influenced other technology companies to pursue similar approaches. The integration of hardware, software, and services became a key competitive strategy, with companies like Google, Microsoft, and Amazon developing their own ecosystems to compete with Apple. This trend has led to more cohesive and connected technology experiences for consumers.

- Redefining Retail: The success of Apple Stores redefined the retail experience for technology products. Apple's emphasis on design, customer service, and experiential retail set new standards for the industry. Other technology companies and retailers adopted elements of Apple's retail strategy, leading to a transformation in how technology products are sold and supported.

- Innovation Culture: Steve Jobs's legacy of fostering a culture of innovation continues to influence the technology industry. Apple's relentless pursuit of new ideas and willingness to take risks has become a model for other companies. The focus on continuous innovation, even at the risk of disrupting one's own products, has driven technological advancements and shaped the future of consumer electronics.

Steve Jobs's business strategies and market disruptions transformed Apple Inc. into one of the most influential technology companies in the world. His focus on design and user experience set new standards for the industry, while his strategies for entering and dominating new markets demonstrated the power of innovation and vision.

The introduction of Apple Stores revolutionized retail in the technology sector, creating a unique and immersive customer experience. Jobs's ability to compete with other tech giants through innovation, ecosystem integration, and strategic acquisitions ensured Apple's leadership position in the market.

The long-term impact of Jobs's strategies on the consumer electronics industry is profound. Apple's influence can be seen in the design, functionality, and integration of technology products worldwide. Steve Jobs's legacy continues to inspire and drive innovation, shaping the future of technology and transforming how people interact with and experience their devices.

Leadership and Management Style

Jobs' Approach to Visionary Leadership

Steve Jobs was renowned for his visionary leadership, which combined a clear and compelling vision with an ability to inspire and drive innovation. His approach to leadership was defined by several key characteristics:

- **Clear Vision:** Jobs had an extraordinary ability to envision the future of technology and see potential where others did not. He articulated a clear vision for Apple and consistently communicated this vision to his team. His vision was not just about creating products but about transforming industries and improving the lives of consumers. This clarity of purpose helped align the efforts of everyone at Apple towards common goals.

- **Inspiring Innovation:** Jobs fostered a culture of innovation at Apple. He encouraged his team to think differently, challenge the status quo, and push the boundaries of what was possible. Jobs believed in the power of innovation to create breakthroughs and was relentless in his pursuit of excellence. His willingness to take risks and embrace bold ideas inspired his team to strive for groundbreaking achievements.

- **Attention to Detail:** Jobs was known for his meticulous attention to detail. He was involved in every aspect of product development, from design and engineering to marketing and customer experience. His hands-on approach ensured that every product met his high standards of quality and aesthetics. This focus on detail helped create products that were not only functional but also beautiful and user-friendly.

- Persistence and Determination: Jobs's visionary leadership was characterized by persistence and determination. He faced numerous setbacks and challenges throughout his career but never wavered in his commitment to his vision. Whether it was overcoming financial difficulties, management conflicts, or product failures, Jobs's resilience and tenacity were instrumental in driving Apple's success.

- Storytelling and Marketing: Jobs was a master storyteller who understood the power of narrative in marketing and leadership. He used storytelling to communicate Apple's mission, values, and vision in a way that resonated with both employees and customers. His keynote presentations, product launches, and marketing campaigns were compelling narratives that captured the imagination and loyalty of millions.

Building and Managing High-Performing Teams

Steve Jobs's ability to build and manage high-performing teams was a critical component of his leadership success. He recognized that achieving his ambitious goals required assembling a team of talented and dedicated individuals.

- Recruiting Top Talent: Jobs was highly selective in recruiting talent. He sought out individuals who were not only highly skilled but also shared his passion for innovation and excellence. Jobs believed that A-players attract other A-players, creating a culture of high performance and mutual respect. He was willing to invest in hiring the best, knowing that top talent would drive the company's success.

- Creating a Collaborative Environment: Jobs fostered a collaborative environment at Apple. He encouraged open communication and idea-sharing across different teams and departments. This cross-functional collaboration enabled Apple to integrate diverse perspectives and expertise, leading to more innovative solutions. Jobs believed that great ideas could come from anyone, and he created an environment where creativity could flourish.

- Empowering Teams: While Jobs was deeply involved in the details of product development, he also empowered his teams to take ownership of their work. He trusted his team members to make decisions and encouraged them to take risks. This empowerment fostered a sense of responsibility and accountability, motivating team members to perform at their best.

- Setting High Standards: Jobs set exceptionally high standards for his team. He challenged them to achieve more than they thought possible and to strive for perfection in everything they did. This relentless pursuit of excellence pushed Apple's employees to innovate and deliver outstanding products. While Jobs's demanding nature could be challenging, it also brought out the best in his team.

- Recognizing and Rewarding Excellence: Jobs understood the importance of recognizing and rewarding excellence. He celebrated the achievements of his team and provided public recognition for their contributions. This acknowledgment helped build morale and reinforced the value of hard work and dedication.

Dealing with Failures and Setbacks

Steve Jobs's career was marked by numerous failures and setbacks. However, his ability to learn from these experiences and turn them into opportunities for growth was a testament to his resilience and leadership.

- Learning from Failure: Jobs viewed failures as learning opportunities. He analyzed what went wrong, identified the lessons, and used that knowledge to improve future endeavors. For example, the commercial failure of the Apple Lisa taught Jobs valuable lessons about product positioning, pricing, and market readiness, which he applied to the development of the Macintosh.

- Adaptability and Flexibility: Jobs demonstrated adaptability and flexibility in the face of setbacks. He was willing to pivot and change direction when necessary. After being ousted from Apple in 1985, Jobs founded NeXT, a computer platform development company. While NeXT was not commercially successful, the technology and software developed there became the foundation for macOS when Jobs returned to Apple.

- Maintaining Vision and Focus: Despite setbacks, Jobs never lost sight of his vision. He remained focused on his long-term goals and continued to pursue his passion for creating innovative technology. This unwavering focus helped him stay motivated and inspired his team to persevere through challenges.

- Resilience and Persistence: Jobs's resilience and persistence were crucial in overcoming failures. He faced numerous obstacles, including financial struggles, management conflicts, and product flops, but he never gave up. His determination and perseverance were key to Apple's eventual turnaround and success.

- Turning Adversity into Opportunity: Jobs had a unique ability to turn adversity into opportunity. His experience at NeXT and Pixar during his time away from Apple provided him with new insights and perspectives that he brought back to Apple. These experiences enriched his leadership and helped him lead Apple to new heights upon his return.

Balancing Creativity and Business Strategy

Steve Jobs's success was rooted in his ability to balance creativity with business strategy. He understood that innovation alone was not enough; it needed to be paired with sound business practices to achieve sustained success.

- Visionary Creativity: Jobs's creativity was a driving force behind Apple's innovative products. He had a unique ability to foresee trends and imagine products that would shape the future. Jobs encouraged his team to think outside the box and explore new ideas, fostering a culture of creativity and innovation.

- Strategic Decision-Making: While Jobs valued creativity, he also made strategic decisions to ensure Apple's growth and profitability. He focused on key areas where Apple could differentiate itself and create competitive advantages. For example, Jobs's decision to develop the iTunes Store alongside the iPod created a seamless ecosystem that transformed the music industry and drove sales of both hardware and digital content.

- Customer-Centric Approach: Jobs balanced creativity with a customer-centric approach.

He believed in understanding and anticipating customer needs and designing products that exceeded their expectations. This focus on the customer ensured that Apple's innovations were not just technologically advanced but also highly relevant and appealing to consumers.

- Product Focus: Jobs emphasized a product-focused strategy, concentrating on a few key products and ensuring they were the best in their categories. This approach allowed Apple to allocate resources effectively and maintain high standards of quality and innovation. Jobs famously cut many underperforming products upon his return to Apple, refocusing the company's efforts on core products like the iMac, iPod, and iPhone.

- Financial Discipline: Despite his emphasis on creativity, Jobs maintained financial discipline. He understood the importance of managing costs, optimizing operations, and ensuring profitability. This discipline enabled Apple to invest in research and development, marketing, and other areas critical to its long-term success.

Legacy in Modern Business Practices

Steve Jobs's leadership and management style have left an enduring legacy in modern business practices. His principles and approaches continue to influence leaders and organizations worldwide.

- Innovation-Driven Culture: Jobs's legacy is most evident in the emphasis on innovation-driven culture. Many companies have adopted his approach to fostering creativity and encouraging bold ideas. The focus on innovation as a core value has become a standard in the technology industry and beyond.

- User Experience Focus: Jobs's obsession with user experience has become a benchmark for product development. Companies now prioritize creating products that are not only functional but also intuitive and enjoyable to use. This user-centric approach has transformed industries, from consumer electronics to software development and beyond.

- Design Thinking: Jobs's emphasis on design has popularized the concept of design thinking, which integrates empathy, creativity, and rationality to solve complex problems. Design thinking has become a widely adopted methodology in various fields, including business, education, and healthcare.

- Integrated Ecosystem: The concept of an integrated ecosystem of products and services, pioneered by Jobs, has been emulated by many companies. The idea of creating a seamless and cohesive user experience across multiple devices and platforms is now a common strategy in the technology industry.

- Visionary Leadership: Jobs's visionary leadership style has inspired a new generation of leaders who seek to combine creativity with strategic acumen. His ability to articulate a clear vision, inspire innovation, and drive execution is studied in business schools and leadership programs worldwide.

- Resilience and Adaptability: Jobs's resilience in the face of setbacks and his ability to adapt and learn from failures have become key lessons in leadership. His story of overcoming challenges and returning to lead Apple to unprecedented success serves as a powerful example of perseverance and adaptability.

Steve Jobs's leadership and management style were characterized by visionary leadership, an ability to build and manage high-performing teams, resilience in dealing with failures, a balance of creativity and business strategy, and a lasting impact on modern business practices. His approach to design and user experience set new standards for the industry, while his strategies for innovation and market disruption transformed Apple into a global leader.

Jobs's legacy continues to influence leaders and organizations around the world. His principles of innovation, user-centricity, design excellence, and strategic vision have become benchmarks for success in the technology industry and beyond. Steve Jobs's impact on business practices is enduring, and his story serves as an inspiration for future generations of leaders and innovators.

Case Study: The Launch of the iPhone

Development and Design of the iPhone

The development and design of the iPhone were marked by a relentless pursuit of innovation, meticulous attention to detail, and a bold vision for the future of mobile communication. The project began with a simple yet revolutionary idea: to create a device that combined a phone, an iPod, and an internet communicator in one seamless package.

- Concept and Vision: The concept for the iPhone emerged from Apple's desire to enter the mobile phone market with a device that would disrupt existing standards. Steve Jobs envisioned a phone that was not only functional but also intuitive and enjoyable to use. The goal was to create a product that would revolutionize the way people communicated, accessed information, and entertained themselves.

- Multi-Touch Technology: One of the most significant innovations of the iPhone was its multi-touch interface. Apple engineers developed a touch-sensitive screen that could recognize multiple points of contact simultaneously, allowing for gestures such as pinch-to-zoom and swipe. This technology enabled a more natural and intuitive user experience, eliminating the need for physical keyboards and buttons.

- Design Aesthetics: The iPhone's design was a

departure from the clunky, feature-laden phones of the time. It featured a sleek, minimalist design with a large, high-resolution display that dominated the front of the device. The body was made of aluminum and glass, giving it a premium feel. The design emphasized simplicity and elegance, with a focus on user experience.

- Integration of Functions: The iPhone was designed to integrate three primary functions: a phone, an iPod, and an internet communicator. This integration required innovative software and hardware solutions. The development team created a custom operating system, iOS, which supported the seamless integration of these functions and provided a platform for future app development.

- Hardware and Software Synergy: Apple's approach to the iPhone's development involved tight integration between hardware and software. The custom-designed A4 chip ensured optimal performance, while the iOS operating system provided a smooth and responsive user interface. This synergy between hardware and software was key to delivering the seamless experience that defined the iPhone.

Marketing and Product Launch Strategies

The marketing and product launch strategies for the iPhone were masterfully executed, generating unprecedented excitement and anticipation for the device. Apple's approach combined secrecy, strategic partnerships, and compelling storytelling to create a sense of inevitability around the iPhone's success.

- Secrecy and Hype: Apple maintained strict secrecy around the iPhone's development, fueling speculation and anticipation. This approach created a sense of mystery and excitement, making the eventual reveal a highly anticipated event. The secrecy also prevented competitors from copying Apple's innovations before the official launch.

- Iconic Keynote Presentation: The iPhone was unveiled by Steve Jobs on January 9, 2007, during his keynote address at the Macworld Conference & Expo. Jobs's presentation is often cited as one of the most iconic product launches in history. He introduced the iPhone with his signature "one more thing" moment, highlighting its key features and demonstrating its capabilities live on stage. Jobs's charisma and storytelling captivated the audience and set the tone for the iPhone's market entry.

- Strategic Partnerships: Apple secured an exclusive partnership with AT&T (formerly Cingular Wireless) to provide network services for the iPhone in the United States. This partnership ensured that the iPhone had strong carrier support and allowed Apple to leverage AT&T's marketing and distribution channels. The exclusivity deal also created a sense of scarcity and desirability for the device.

- Compelling Advertising: Apple's advertising campaign for the iPhone emphasized its revolutionary features and user-friendly design. The ads showcased the device's multi-touch interface, web browsing capabilities, and integration with iTunes. The tagline "This is only the beginning" conveyed the message that the iPhone was not just a new phone but the start of a new era in mobile communication.

- Retail Experience: The iPhone launch was supported by Apple's retail stores, which provided customers with a hands-on experience of the device. The stores were designed to highlight the iPhone's features and offer personalized assistance from knowledgeable staff. This retail strategy ensured that customers could fully appreciate the iPhone's capabilities and receive excellent customer service.

Impact on the Mobile Phone Industry

The launch of the iPhone had a profound impact on the mobile phone industry, fundamentally changing the way phones were designed, marketed, and used. It set new standards for what consumers expected from their mobile devices and forced competitors to innovate or risk obsolescence.

- Redefining the Smartphone: The iPhone redefined the concept of the smartphone, shifting the focus from a communication device with added features to a versatile computing platform. Its multi-touch interface, intuitive design, and powerful functionality set a new benchmark for the industry. Other manufacturers quickly followed suit, adopting similar design principles and integrating touch interfaces into their devices.

- App Ecosystem: The introduction of the App Store in 2008 revolutionized the mobile phone industry by creating a thriving ecosystem of third-party applications. Developers could create and distribute apps directly to consumers, opening up new possibilities for innovation and utility. The success of the App Store inspired other platforms, such as Google's Android Market (now Google Play), to develop their own app ecosystems.

- User Experience Focus: The iPhone's emphasis on user experience shifted the industry's focus towards creating devices that were not only functional but also enjoyable to use. Manufacturers began prioritizing design, ease of use, and seamless integration of hardware and software. This shift led to significant improvements in the overall quality and usability of smartphones.

- Convergence of Devices: The iPhone's ability to combine multiple functions—phone, music player, and internet communicator—into a single device set a new standard for device convergence. This trend continued with the integration of additional features, such as cameras, GPS, and mobile payments, into smartphones. The convergence of devices streamlined consumers' digital lives and reduced the need for multiple gadgets.

- Industry Disruption: The iPhone disrupted established players in the mobile phone industry, such as Nokia, BlackBerry, and Motorola. Companies that failed to adapt to the new paradigm of touchscreen smartphones and app ecosystems saw their market share decline. The disruption caused by the iPhone led to a major shift in the competitive landscape, with Apple and later Google's Android platform emerging as dominant forces.

Competition and Market Disruption

The introduction of the iPhone intensified competition in the mobile phone market and led to significant market disruption. Competitors were forced to innovate rapidly to keep up with the new standard set by Apple.

- Rise of Android: In response to the iPhone, Google accelerated the development of its Android operating system, which was designed to offer a flexible and open alternative to iOS. Android's open-source nature attracted a wide range of manufacturers, leading to a proliferation of Android devices. The competition between iOS and Android became a defining feature of the smartphone market, driving innovation and diversity in device offerings.

- Hardware Innovation: Competing manufacturers, such as Samsung, HTC, and LG, introduced their own flagship smartphones with advanced features to challenge the iPhone. Innovations included larger screens, higher-resolution cameras, and advanced processing power. The competition drove rapid advancements in hardware technology, benefiting consumers with more powerful and versatile devices.

- Ecosystem Wars: The battle for ecosystem dominance extended beyond hardware to include software and services. Companies like Google, Microsoft, and Amazon developed their own app stores, cloud services, and digital content platforms to compete with Apple's ecosystem. The competition led to a rich diversity of apps, services, and content available to consumers, enhancing the overall smartphone experience.

- Market Penetration Strategies: Competitors adopted various strategies to penetrate the market and gain a foothold against the iPhone. These strategies included offering devices at different price points, targeting emerging markets, and forming strategic partnerships with carriers. The competitive landscape became increasingly dynamic, with companies vying for market share through innovation, pricing, and distribution tactics.

- Legal Battles: The intense competition between Apple and its rivals also led to numerous legal battles over intellectual property and patents. Apple engaged in high-profile lawsuits with companies like Samsung, alleging patent infringement related to design and functionality. These legal disputes highlighted the high stakes involved in the smartphone market and the importance of protecting intellectual property.

Apple's Enduring Influence on Technology and Innovation

The launch of the iPhone not only transformed the mobile phone industry but also had a lasting impact on technology and innovation across various sectors. Apple's influence extended beyond smartphones, shaping the future of consumer electronics and digital experiences.

- Consumer Electronics Design: Apple's emphasis on sleek, minimalist design and premium materials set new standards for consumer electronics. The design principles introduced with the iPhone influenced a wide range of products, from tablets and laptops to wearable devices and smart home technology. Apple's design ethos became synonymous with quality, elegance, and user-centricity.

- User Interface Innovation: The multi-touch interface and intuitive user experience of the iPhone inspired innovations in user interface design across multiple industries. Touchscreens became ubiquitous in devices such as tablets, kiosks, ATMs, and automotive infotainment systems. The principles of simplicity and ease of use pioneered by Apple continue to guide user interface design in diverse applications.

- App Economy Growth: The success of the App Store demonstrated the potential of mobile apps as a powerful business model. The app economy grew exponentially, creating opportunities for developers, entrepreneurs, and businesses. Mobile apps became essential tools for communication, productivity, entertainment, and commerce, transforming the way people interact with technology and access services.

- Innovation Culture: Apple's culture of innovation, driven by Steve Jobs's vision and leadership, inspired other companies to prioritize creativity and bold thinking. The emphasis on continuous innovation, even at the risk of disrupting one's own products, became a guiding principle for many technology companies. Apple's success story encouraged a new generation of entrepreneurs and innovators to pursue ambitious goals and challenge established norms.

- Ecosystem Integration: The concept of an integrated ecosystem of devices and services, exemplified by Apple, influenced the strategies of numerous technology companies. The seamless connectivity and interoperability between devices, along with the integration of hardware, software, and cloud services, became a benchmark for creating cohesive and compelling user experiences. This approach extended to various sectors, including smart home technology, wearable devices, and connected vehicles.

- Impact on Digital Transformation: The iPhone played a significant role in driving digital transformation across industries. Mobile technology became a catalyst for innovation in sectors such as healthcare, education, finance, and retail. Mobile apps and services enabled new business models, enhanced customer experiences, and improved operational efficiency. The iPhone's influence on digital transformation continues to shape the future of technology and innovation.

The launch of the iPhone was a defining moment in the history of technology and innovation. Steve Jobs's visionary leadership and Apple's relentless pursuit of excellence led to the creation of a product that revolutionized the mobile phone industry and set new standards for design, user experience, and functionality.

The iPhone's development and design showcased Apple's commitment to innovation and attention to detail. The marketing and product launch strategies generated unprecedented excitement and anticipation, establishing the iPhone as a cultural and technological phenomenon. The impact of the iPhone on the mobile phone industry was profound, redefining the concept of the smartphone and driving significant advancements in hardware and software.

The competition and market disruption caused by the iPhone led to a dynamic and rapidly evolving industry landscape. Apple's enduring influence on technology and innovation extended beyond smartphones, shaping the future of consumer electronics and digital experiences. The legacy of the iPhone continues to inspire and drive innovation, demonstrating the transformative power of visionary leadership and groundbreaking technology.

Chapter 8:

Mary Barra
Leading General Motors

Mary Barra was born on December 24, 1961, in Waterford, Michigan. Her full name is Mary Teresa Makela Barra, and she grew up in a family deeply connected to the automotive industry. Her father, Ray Makela, worked as a die maker for Pontiac, a division of General Motors (GM), which gave Mary an early exposure to the world of cars and manufacturing.

From a young age, Mary demonstrated a strong interest in engineering and problem-solving. She excelled academically and was particularly drawn to mathematics and science. This inclination towards technical subjects paved the way for her future career in the automotive industry. Barra attended Waterford Mott High School, where she continued to cultivate her interest in engineering and technology.

After high school, Barra enrolled at the General Motors Institute (now Kettering University), a co-op university that allowed students to alternate between academic coursework and practical work experience at GM. She graduated in 1985 with a Bachelor of Science degree in Electrical Engineering. This education provided her with a solid foundation in engineering principles and a deep understanding of the automotive industry.

Barra's commitment to furthering her education led her to Stanford University, where she earned a Master of Business Administration (MBA) degree in 1990. The combination of her engineering background and business acumen would later prove invaluable in her ascent to the top of General Motors.

Entry into the Automotive Industry

Mary Barra's entry into the automotive industry began at a young age, thanks to her co-op position at GM during her time at the General Motors Institute. This hands-on experience allowed her to gain practical knowledge and develop a strong work ethic. Barra started her career at GM in 1980 as a co-op student, working in various engineering and administrative roles. This early exposure to different facets of the company provided her with a broad perspective on GM's operations.

After completing her MBA, Barra returned to GM and took on a series of increasingly responsible positions. She worked in several engineering and manufacturing roles, gaining a reputation for her technical expertise and leadership abilities. Barra's ability to navigate complex technical challenges and her commitment to continuous improvement set her apart from her peers.

In the mid-1990s, Barra moved into management roles, where she was responsible for overseeing vehicle manufacturing and quality control. Her leadership in these areas demonstrated her ability to balance technical knowledge with effective management practices. Barra's focus on quality and efficiency helped improve GM's manufacturing processes and product reliability.

Rise through the Ranks at General Motors

Mary Barra's rise through the ranks at General Motors was marked by her ability to take on challenging assignments and deliver exceptional results. Her career trajectory at GM is a testament to her leadership skills, technical expertise, and dedication to the company's success.

- Director of Internal Communications: In the early 2000s, Barra served as the Director of Internal Communications for GM, where she was responsible for managing communication strategies within the company. This role allowed her to develop a deep understanding of GM's corporate culture and the importance of effective communication in driving organizational change.

- Vice President of Global Manufacturing Engineering: Barra's technical acumen and leadership abilities earned her the position of Vice President of Global Manufacturing Engineering in 2008. In this role, she was responsible for overseeing GM's global manufacturing processes and ensuring that the company maintained high standards of quality and efficiency. Barra's focus on innovation and continuous improvement helped GM enhance its manufacturing capabilities.

- Vice President of Global Human Resources: In 2009, Barra was appointed Vice President of

Global Human Resources, a role that allowed her to leverage her engineering background and business knowledge to drive organizational transformation. She played a key role in restructuring GM's workforce and implementing initiatives to improve employee engagement and development. Barra's efforts in this role helped create a more agile and performance-driven culture at GM.

- Senior Vice President of Global Product Development: Barra's success in human resources led to her promotion as Senior Vice President of Global Product Development in 2011. In this role, she was responsible for overseeing the design, engineering, and development of GM's vehicle lineup. Barra's emphasis on innovation, quality, and customer focus resulted in the introduction of several successful new models and helped GM regain its competitive edge in the global automotive market.

- Executive Vice President of Global Product Development, Purchasing, and Supply Chain: In 2013, Barra's responsibilities were expanded to include global purchasing and supply chain management. This comprehensive role allowed her to integrate product development with procurement and logistics, ensuring that GM's supply chain operations were aligned with its strategic goals. Barra's leadership in this role further solidified her reputation as a visionary and effective leader.

Vision for the Future of GM

Mary Barra's vision for the future of General Motors is centered on innovation, sustainability, and customer-centricity. As the automotive industry undergoes a profound transformation driven by technological advancements and changing consumer preferences, Barra has positioned GM to lead in several key areas.

- Electric and Autonomous Vehicles: Barra has been a strong advocate for the development and adoption of electric and autonomous vehicles. Under her leadership, GM has committed to an all-electric future, with plans to introduce a comprehensive lineup of electric vehicles (EVs) across different segments. The Chevrolet Bolt EV, introduced in 2016, was one of the first affordable long-range electric vehicles on the market. Barra's vision includes making EVs accessible to a broad range of consumers and reducing the environmental impact of GM's vehicles.

- Sustainability and Environmental Responsibility: Barra has emphasized the importance of sustainability in GM's operations. The company has set ambitious goals to reduce its carbon footprint, increase the use of renewable energy, and promote sustainable manufacturing practices. GM's commitment to sustainability is reflected in its efforts to improve fuel efficiency, reduce emissions, and develop innovative technologies that contribute to a cleaner and greener future.

- Technological Innovation: Barra recognizes that technological innovation is key to GM's long-term success. The company has invested heavily in research and development to advance its capabilities in areas such as battery technology, autonomous driving, and connected vehicles. GM's acquisition of autonomous vehicle startup Cruise Automation and its partnership with companies like Honda and LG Chem highlight Barra's commitment to staying at the forefront of technological advancements.

- Customer Experience: Barra's vision for GM places a strong emphasis on delivering exceptional customer experiences. She understands that customer satisfaction and loyalty are critical to the company's success. GM has implemented initiatives to enhance the ownership experience, including improved vehicle connectivity, personalized services, and a focus on quality and reliability. Barra's customer-centric approach aims to build lasting relationships with GM's customers.

- Diversity and Inclusion: Barra is a champion of diversity and inclusion within GM. She believes that a diverse workforce fosters innovation and better decision-making. Under her leadership, GM has implemented programs to promote diversity at all levels of the organization, create an inclusive work environment, and ensure equal opportunities for all employees. Barra's commitment to diversity extends to GM's suppliers and business partners, promoting a culture of inclusion across the automotive industry.

Initial Challenges and Leadership Transition

Mary Barra's appointment as CEO of General Motors in January 2014 marked a historic milestone, as she became the first woman to lead a major global automaker. Her early tenure as CEO was marked by several significant challenges that tested her leadership and resilience.

- Ignition Switch Recall Crisis: Shortly after Barra took the helm, GM faced a major crisis related to defective ignition switches in several of its vehicles. The defect, which could cause the engine to shut off and disable safety features like airbags, was linked to numerous accidents and fatalities. The ignition switch recall affected millions of vehicles and resulted in significant financial and reputational damage for GM.

Barra responded to the crisis with transparency and accountability. She ordered a comprehensive internal investigation, led by former U.S. Attorney Anton Valukas, to understand the root causes of the defect and identify areas for improvement. Barra also took steps to enhance GM's safety culture, including the establishment of a new Global Vehicle Safety organization and the implementation of rigorous safety protocols. Her handling of the crisis demonstrated her commitment to integrity and her willingness to make difficult decisions to protect customers and rebuild trust.

- Restructuring and Cost Management: Barra faced the challenge of restructuring GM's operations to ensure long-term sustainability and profitability. This included making tough decisions to close underperforming plants, streamline product lines, and reduce costs. Barra's focus on operational efficiency and cost management helped GM navigate a competitive and rapidly changing industry landscape.

- Adapting to Market Trends: The automotive industry was undergoing significant shifts, including the rise of electric and autonomous vehicles, changing consumer preferences, and increasing regulatory requirements. Barra's leadership was instrumental in positioning GM to adapt to these trends and capitalize on new opportunities. Her vision for an all-electric future and investment in autonomous driving technology reflected her forward-thinking approach.

- Cultural Transformation: Barra recognized the need for cultural transformation within GM to foster innovation, agility, and collaboration. She implemented initiatives to empower employees, encourage open communication, and promote a culture of continuous improvement. Barra's leadership style, characterized by empathy and inclusiveness, helped create a more dynamic and resilient organization.

- Global Expansion and Market Presence:

Barra's leadership also involved navigating the complexities of global markets. She focused on strengthening GM's presence in key regions, such as China and South America, while also addressing challenges in markets with declining sales. Barra's strategic decisions on global expansion and market presence were aimed at ensuring GM's growth and competitiveness on a global scale.

Mary Barra's early life and career laid the foundation for her remarkable journey to become the CEO of General Motors. Her technical expertise, business acumen, and leadership skills enabled her to rise through the ranks and take on increasingly responsible roles within the company. Barra's vision for the future of GM is characterized by innovation, sustainability, and customer-centricity.

As CEO, Barra has faced significant challenges, including the ignition switch recall crisis and the need for organizational restructuring. Her response to these challenges demonstrated her resilience, integrity, and commitment to excellence. Barra's leadership has positioned GM to thrive in a rapidly evolving industry, with a focus on electric and autonomous vehicles, technological innovation, and exceptional customer experiences.

Mary Barra's legacy as a trailblazer in the automotive industry and a visionary leader continues to inspire future generations of leaders. Her ability to navigate complex challenges, drive transformative change, and lead with empathy and inclusiveness has solidified her place as one of the most influential figures in the history of General Motors and the broader automotive industry.

Innovations and Strategic Initiatives

Development of Electric and Autonomous Vehicles

Mary Barra's leadership at General Motors (GM) has been marked by a strong commitment to the development of electric and autonomous vehicles. Recognizing the significant shift in the automotive industry towards sustainability and advanced technologies, Barra has positioned GM to be at the forefront of these innovations.

- Electric Vehicles (EVs): Barra has championed the transition to electric vehicles as a core part of GM's strategy. Under her leadership, GM has set ambitious goals to introduce a comprehensive lineup of electric vehicles across various segments. The Chevrolet Bolt EV, launched in 2016, was one of the first affordable long-range electric vehicles on the market, offering a range of over 200 miles on a single charge. The success of the Bolt EV demonstrated GM's capability to produce competitive electric vehicles.

- Ultium Battery Technology: A key component of GM's electric vehicle strategy is the development of Ultium battery technology. This innovative battery platform is designed to be flexible and scalable, allowing it to power a wide range of vehicles, from compact cars to large trucks. Ultium batteries offer improved energy density, longer range, and faster charging times. By investing in advanced battery technology, GM aims to make electric vehicles more accessible and appealing to consumers.

- Autonomous Vehicles: Barra has also driven GM's efforts in the development of autonomous vehicles. The acquisition of Cruise Automation in 2016 marked a significant step in GM's pursuit of self-driving technology. Cruise, a San Francisco-based startup, has been working on developing fully autonomous vehicles capable of navigating urban environments. GM's investment in autonomous technology aligns with Barra's vision of creating safer, more efficient, and sustainable transportation solutions.

- Future Models and Concepts: GM has announced plans to launch 30 new electric vehicles globally by 2025, including the GMC Hummer EV, Cadillac LYRIQ, and Chevrolet Silverado EV. These models showcase GM's commitment to innovation and its ability to adapt to changing market demands. The Hummer EV, for example, reimagines the iconic Hummer brand as a high-performance electric truck with advanced off-road capabilities.

- Collaborations and Partnerships: To accelerate the development and deployment of electric and autonomous vehicles, GM has formed strategic partnerships with other companies. Collaborations with Honda, LG Chem, and other industry leaders have enabled GM to leverage external expertise and resources. These partnerships have facilitated the sharing of technology and knowledge, helping GM to stay at the cutting edge of innovation.

Expansion into New Markets and Technologies

Under Mary Barra's leadership, GM has expanded into new markets and embraced emerging technologies to drive growth and enhance its competitive position. This strategic expansion has allowed GM to diversify its revenue streams and capitalize on new opportunities.

- Global Market Expansion: Barra has focused on strengthening GM's presence in key international markets, such as China and South America. China, in particular, represents a significant growth opportunity for GM, given its status as the world's largest automotive market. GM has introduced a range of models tailored to Chinese consumers and invested in local manufacturing facilities to support its operations in the region.

- Electric Commercial Vehicles: Recognizing the potential of electric vehicles in the commercial sector, GM has launched initiatives to develop electric delivery vans and trucks. The BrightDrop division, introduced in 2021, aims to provide integrated solutions for commercial delivery and logistics. BrightDrop's EV600 electric van and EP1 electric pallet are designed to improve efficiency and reduce emissions in last-mile delivery operations.

- Mobility Services: GM has ventured into the mobility services market with the launch of Maven, a car-sharing service that offers on-demand access to GM vehicles. Maven provides flexible mobility solutions for urban residents and businesses, reflecting GM's commitment to adapting to changing consumer preferences and urban mobility trends. Although Maven's operations were scaled back in 2020, GM continues to explore opportunities in the mobility services sector.

- Connected Vehicle Technology: GM has been a pioneer in the development of connected vehicle technology, which enhances safety, convenience, and entertainment for drivers and passengers. The introduction of OnStar in the late 1990s marked the beginning of GM's journey in connected services. Today, GM's vehicles are equipped with advanced connectivity features, such as 4G LTE Wi-Fi, remote diagnostics, and over-the-air updates. These technologies enable GM to offer a seamless and integrated driving experience.

- Investments in Startups and Innovation: GM has established a venture capital arm, GM Ventures, to invest in startups and innovative technologies that align with its strategic goals.

Through GM Ventures, the company has invested in companies working on electric vehicles, autonomous driving, battery technology, and other cutting-edge innovations. These investments allow GM to stay ahead of industry trends and leverage emerging technologies to enhance its product offerings.

Innovations in Manufacturing and Sustainability

Mary Barra has championed innovations in manufacturing and sustainability, positioning GM as a leader in environmentally responsible production practices and advanced manufacturing techniques.

- Sustainable Manufacturing Practices: Under Barra's leadership, GM has implemented initiatives to reduce its environmental footprint and promote sustainability across its operations. The company has set ambitious goals to achieve carbon neutrality by 2040 and source 100% of its global electricity from renewable energy by 2035. GM's commitment to sustainability is reflected in its efforts to improve energy efficiency, reduce waste, and minimize water usage in its manufacturing facilities.

- Advanced Manufacturing Technologies: GM has embraced advanced manufacturing technologies, such as 3D printing, robotics, and artificial intelligence, to enhance its production processes. The use of 3D printing allows GM to produce complex components more efficiently and cost-effectively. Robotics and automation improve precision and reduce production times, while artificial intelligence helps optimize supply chain management and quality control.

- Flexible Manufacturing: GM has developed flexible manufacturing systems that allow for the production of multiple vehicle models on the same assembly line. This flexibility enables GM to respond quickly to changes in consumer demand and market trends. It also supports the company's transition to electric vehicles by allowing for the integration of EV production within existing facilities.

- Recycling and Circular Economy: GM is committed to promoting a circular economy by increasing the use of recycled materials and reducing waste. The company has implemented programs to recycle scrap metal, plastics, and other materials used in vehicle production. GM's efforts to incorporate recycled content into its vehicles help reduce the environmental impact of manufacturing and support the development of a sustainable supply chain.

- Sustainable Supply Chain: GM works closely with its suppliers to ensure that sustainability practices are integrated throughout the supply chain. The company has established guidelines and standards for its suppliers, encouraging them to adopt environmentally responsible practices. GM's commitment to sustainability extends to sourcing raw materials, with a focus on ethical and sustainable mining practices for key materials like cobalt and lithium used in electric vehicle batteries.

Impact on the Automotive Industry

Mary Barra's leadership and strategic initiatives have had a profound impact on the automotive industry, driving significant advancements in technology, sustainability, and market dynamics.

- Accelerating the Shift to Electric Vehicles: GM's commitment to an all-electric future has accelerated the industry's transition to electric vehicles. The company's investments in battery technology, EV production, and charging infrastructure have set new standards for the industry. GM's ambitious plans and innovative products have influenced other automakers to prioritize the development of electric vehicles, contributing to a broader shift towards sustainable transportation.

- Advancing Autonomous Driving: GM's focus on autonomous vehicle technology has positioned the company as a leader in the development of self-driving cars. The progress made by Cruise Automation in creating safe and reliable autonomous vehicles has set benchmarks for the industry. GM's advancements in this area have the potential to transform urban mobility, improve road safety, and reduce traffic congestion.

- Innovative Business Models: Barra's strategic initiatives, such as the development of BrightDrop and Maven, have introduced new business models to the automotive industry. These initiatives reflect GM's ability to adapt to changing market dynamics and consumer preferences. By exploring opportunities in electric commercial vehicles and mobility services, GM is diversifying its revenue streams and staying ahead of industry trends.

- Sustainability Leadership: GM's commitment to sustainability has set an example for the automotive industry. The company's efforts to reduce emissions, promote renewable energy, and implement sustainable manufacturing practices have raised the bar for environmental responsibility. GM's leadership in sustainability has influenced other automakers to adopt similar practices, contributing to a more sustainable industry.

- Technological Innovation: GM's investments in advanced manufacturing technologies, connected vehicle services, and cutting-edge research have driven technological innovation in the automotive industry. The company's focus on integrating new technologies into its vehicles has enhanced the driving experience and set new standards for safety, convenience, and performance. GM's leadership in technological innovation continues to shape the future of the industry.

Long-Term Growth and Sustainability

Mary Barra's strategic vision for GM emphasizes long-term growth and sustainability, ensuring that the company remains competitive and resilient in a rapidly changing industry.

- Commitment to Innovation: Barra's leadership is characterized by a commitment to continuous innovation. GM's investments in research and development, strategic partnerships, and new technologies ensure that the company remains at the forefront of industry advancements. By fostering a culture of innovation, Barra has positioned GM to capitalize on emerging opportunities and drive long-term growth.

- Sustainable Business Practices: Barra's focus on sustainability extends to all aspects of GM's operations. The company's efforts to reduce its environmental impact, promote ethical sourcing, and support a circular economy contribute to its long-term sustainability. GM's commitment to sustainability aligns with consumer expectations and regulatory requirements, enhancing the company's reputation and competitiveness.

- Diversification and Flexibility: Barra has led GM in diversifying its product offerings and exploring new business models. The development of electric and autonomous vehicles, expansion into commercial mobility services, and investment in connected technologies provide multiple avenues for growth. GM's flexible manufacturing systems and agile operations enable the company to adapt to changing market conditions and consumer demands.

- Customer-Centric Approach: Barra's emphasis on delivering exceptional customer experiences is central to GM's long-term success. By prioritizing quality, reliability, and innovation, GM aims to build lasting relationships with its customers. The company's focus on understanding and meeting customer needs drives brand loyalty and supports sustained growth.

- Global Market Presence: Barra's strategic initiatives to strengthen GM's presence in key global markets ensure that the company remains competitive on a global scale. By tailoring products and services to meet the needs of diverse markets, GM can capture new growth opportunities and expand its customer base. The company's global footprint positions it to navigate geopolitical challenges and capitalize on regional trends.

Mary Barra's leadership at General Motors has been marked by a visionary approach to innovation, sustainability, and strategic growth. Her commitment to the development of electric and autonomous vehicles, expansion into new markets and technologies, and implementation of sustainable manufacturing practices has positioned GM as a leader in the automotive industry.

Barra's impact on the industry extends beyond GM, influencing broader trends in technology, sustainability, and market dynamics. Her strategic initiatives have accelerated the shift towards electric vehicles, advanced autonomous driving technology, and introduced innovative business models. GM's leadership in sustainability and technological innovation continues to shape the future of the automotive industry.

Barra's vision for long-term growth and sustainability ensures that GM remains competitive and resilient in a rapidly changing industry. Her focus on continuous innovation, customer-centricity, and global market presence drives the company's success and positions it for sustained growth. Mary Barra's legacy as a trailblazer and visionary leader continues to inspire and set new benchmarks for the automotive industry and beyond.

Corporate Culture and Employee Engagement

Barra's Approach to Leadership and Management

Mary Barra's leadership and management style have been pivotal in shaping the corporate culture at General Motors (GM). Her approach is characterized by transparency, accountability, inclusiveness, and a strong focus on innovation and continuous improvement.

- Transparency and Accountability: Barra emphasizes transparency and accountability in her leadership. She believes in open communication and sharing information across all levels of the organization. This approach fosters trust and ensures that employees are well-informed about the company's goals, challenges, and progress. Barra's handling of the ignition switch recall crisis, where she openly addressed the issues and took responsibility, exemplifies her commitment to accountability.

- Inclusive Leadership: Barra's leadership style is inclusive, valuing diverse perspectives and encouraging collaboration. She fosters an environment where all employees feel valued and heard, promoting a sense of belonging and teamwork. This inclusive approach helps harness the collective intelligence and creativity of the workforce, driving innovation and better decision-making.

- Focus on Innovation: Barra is a strong advocate for innovation and continuous improvement. She encourages employees to think creatively and challenge the status quo. By promoting a culture of innovation, Barra ensures that GM remains competitive in a rapidly evolving industry. Her support for research and development initiatives and investment in new technologies reflect her commitment to innovation.

- Empowerment and Trust: Barra believes in empowering employees by giving them the autonomy to make decisions and take ownership of their work. This empowerment fosters a sense of responsibility and motivates employees to perform at their best. Barra's trust in her team encourages them to take initiative and contribute to the company's success.

- Empathy and Compassion: Barra's leadership is also marked by empathy and compassion. She understands the importance of supporting employees' well-being and work-life balance. Her empathetic approach helps create a positive and supportive work environment, where employees feel cared for and motivated to excel.

Building a Strong Corporate Culture

Mary Barra has been instrumental in building a strong corporate culture at GM that aligns with the company's values and strategic goals. Her efforts have focused on creating a culture of excellence, collaboration, and integrity.

- Cultural Transformation: When Barra became CEO, she recognized the need for cultural transformation at GM. She initiated programs to modernize the company's culture, shifting from a hierarchical and siloed organization to one that is more agile and collaborative. This transformation aimed to break down barriers, promote cross-functional teamwork, and foster a culture of continuous learning and improvement.

- Core Values: Barra has reinforced GM's core values of integrity, respect, and accountability. These values are embedded in the company's operations and decision-making processes. By consistently emphasizing these values, Barra has created a culture where ethical behavior and mutual respect are paramount.

- Innovation and Agility: Barra's focus on innovation has permeated GM's corporate culture. She encourages employees to embrace change and be agile in their approach. This mindset has enabled GM to quickly adapt to industry trends and technological advancements, maintaining its competitive edge.

- Recognition and Rewards: Recognizing and rewarding employees for their contributions is a key aspect of GM's corporate culture under Barra's leadership. The company has implemented various recognition programs to celebrate achievements and motivate employees. These programs help reinforce positive behaviors and encourage a culture of excellence.

- Communication and Engagement: Effective communication is central to building a strong corporate culture. Barra has prioritized open and transparent communication, ensuring that employees are informed and engaged. Regular town hall meetings, internal newsletters, and other communication channels facilitate dialogue and keep employees connected to the company's vision and goals.

Employee Engagement and Motivation

Employee engagement and motivation are critical to GM's success, and Mary Barra has implemented several initiatives to enhance these aspects of the corporate culture.

- Employee Development: Barra places a strong emphasis on employee development and career growth. GM offers a range of training and development programs to help employees build their skills and advance their careers. These programs include leadership development, technical training, and mentorship opportunities. By investing in employee development, Barra ensures that GM's workforce remains skilled and motivated.

- Empowerment and Autonomy: Barra's leadership style empowers employees by giving them the autonomy to make decisions and take ownership of their work. This empowerment fosters a sense of responsibility and accountability, motivating employees to perform at their best. Barra's trust in her team encourages them to take initiative and contribute to the company's success.

- Work-Life Balance: Recognizing the importance of work-life balance, Barra has implemented policies to support employees' well-being. Flexible work arrangements, wellness programs, and family-friendly benefits help employees manage their personal and professional lives. These initiatives contribute to higher levels of job satisfaction and employee engagement.

- Feedback and Recognition: Providing regular feedback and recognition is essential for employee motivation. GM has established processes for continuous performance feedback, allowing employees to understand their strengths and areas for improvement. Recognition programs, such as awards and incentives, celebrate employees' achievements and reinforce a culture of appreciation.

- Inclusive and Supportive Environment: Barra's commitment to inclusiveness and support creates a positive work environment where employees feel valued and motivated. GM's focus on diversity and inclusion, along with initiatives to support mental health and well-being, fosters a sense of belonging and engagement among employees.

Diversity and Inclusion Initiatives

Mary Barra has made diversity and inclusion a top priority at GM, recognizing that a diverse and inclusive workforce drives innovation and better business outcomes.

- Diversity and Inclusion Strategy: Under Barra's leadership, GM has developed a comprehensive diversity and inclusion strategy. This strategy includes goals for increasing representation of underrepresented groups, promoting inclusive leadership, and creating an equitable work environment. GM's diversity and inclusion efforts are integrated into its business strategy and operations.

- Employee Resource Groups: GM supports various Employee Resource Groups (ERGs) that provide a platform for employees to connect, share experiences, and advocate for diversity and inclusion. These ERGs focus on different dimensions of diversity, including race, gender, sexual orientation, and veteran status. ERGs play a crucial role in fostering a sense of community and promoting an inclusive culture at GM.

- Inclusive Leadership Training: Barra has implemented inclusive leadership training programs to equip leaders with the skills to manage diverse teams and create an inclusive work environment. These programs focus on unconscious bias, cultural competence, and inclusive decision-making. By training leaders to be inclusive, GM ensures that diversity and inclusion are embedded in the company's leadership practices.

- Equitable Hiring Practices: GM has revised its hiring practices to ensure equity and inclusiveness. The company has implemented strategies to attract diverse talent, such as partnering with diverse professional organizations and universities. GM also uses structured interview processes and diverse hiring panels to reduce bias in hiring decisions.

- Supplier Diversity: Barra's commitment to diversity extends beyond GM's workforce to its suppliers. GM has a robust supplier diversity program that seeks to do business with diverse suppliers, including minority-owned, women-owned, and veteran-owned businesses. This program supports economic inclusion and reflects GM's broader commitment to diversity and inclusion.

Long-Term Impact on Corporate Culture

Mary Barra's initiatives and leadership have had a long-term impact on GM's corporate culture, positioning the company for sustained success in a dynamic and competitive industry.

- Culture of Innovation: Barra's emphasis on innovation has created a culture where creativity and continuous improvement are valued. This culture of innovation drives GM to develop cutting-edge technologies and stay ahead of industry trends. The long-term impact is a company that is agile, forward-thinking, and capable of leading in a rapidly changing market.

- Sustainable Practices: Barra's commitment to sustainability has instilled a culture of environmental responsibility at GM. Employees are encouraged to consider the environmental impact of their work and contribute to GM's sustainability goals. This focus on sustainability not only enhances GM's reputation but also supports long-term business resilience.

- Employee Engagement and Retention: The initiatives implemented under Barra's leadership have led to higher levels of employee engagement and retention. By fostering a positive work environment, supporting employee development, and promoting work-life balance, GM has become an employer of choice. Engaged and motivated employees are more likely to stay with the company and contribute to its long-term success.

- Diverse and Inclusive Workforce: Barra's efforts to promote diversity and inclusion have created a more diverse and inclusive workforce at GM. This diversity brings a range of perspectives and ideas, driving innovation and better decision-making. The long-term impact is a company that is more adaptable, creative, and reflective of the diverse markets it serves.

- Reputation and Brand Value: Barra's leadership has enhanced GM's reputation as a forward-thinking, responsible, and inclusive company. This positive reputation strengthens GM's brand value and supports its ability to attract top talent, customers, and business partners. The long-term impact is a stronger and more competitive company with a solid foundation for growth.

Mary Barra's approach to leadership and management has been instrumental in transforming GM's corporate culture. Her focus on transparency, inclusiveness, innovation, and accountability has created a positive and dynamic work environment. Barra's initiatives to build a strong corporate culture, enhance employee engagement and motivation, and promote diversity and inclusion have positioned GM for sustained success.

The long-term impact of Barra's leadership is evident in the culture of innovation, sustainability, and inclusiveness that permeates GM. Her efforts have not only improved employee satisfaction and retention but also strengthened GM's reputation and competitive position. Mary Barra's legacy as a visionary and inclusive leader continues to inspire and set new benchmarks for corporate culture and employee engagement in the automotive industry and beyond.

Business Strategies and Market Positioning

Strategies for Competing in a Global Market

Mary Barra's tenure as CEO of General Motors (GM) has been marked by a strategic focus on competing in the global automotive market. Understanding that the automotive industry is increasingly interconnected and competitive, Barra has implemented several key strategies to strengthen GM's global market position.

- Global Product Portfolio: Barra has emphasized the importance of a diverse and competitive global product portfolio. GM offers a range of vehicles that cater to different markets and consumer preferences, from affordable compact cars to luxury SUVs and electric vehicles. This strategy ensures that GM can capture a broad customer base and respond to varying market demands.

- Localization of Production: To compete effectively in global markets, GM has localized production in key regions, such as China, South America, and Europe. By establishing manufacturing facilities close to major markets, GM can reduce costs, improve supply chain efficiency, and better tailor products to local consumer preferences. Localization also helps GM navigate trade barriers and currency fluctuations.

- Market-Specific Strategies: Barra has recognized the importance of developing market-specific strategies to address the unique characteristics of each region. For example, in China, GM has focused on developing vehicles that meet local regulations and consumer preferences, such as electric vehicles (EVs) to align with the government's push for cleaner transportation. In North America, GM continues to capitalize on the popularity of trucks and SUVs while expanding its EV offerings.

- Brand Differentiation: GM's strategy includes clear differentiation of its brands to cater to different market segments. Chevrolet, Buick, Cadillac, and GMC each have distinct brand identities and value propositions. This brand differentiation allows GM to target specific consumer groups effectively and build strong brand loyalty.

- Technology and Innovation Leadership: Competing in a global market requires leadership in technology and innovation. Barra has positioned GM as a leader in electric and autonomous vehicle technology, advanced manufacturing processes, and connected vehicle services. This focus on innovation not only differentiates GM from competitors but also prepares the company for the future of mobility.

Innovations in Product Development and Design

Innovation in product development and design has been a cornerstone of GM's strategy under Mary Barra's leadership. Recognizing that the automotive industry is evolving rapidly, Barra has driven efforts to develop cutting-edge vehicles that meet the demands of modern consumers.

- Electric Vehicles (EVs): One of GM's most significant innovations under Barra has been the development of electric vehicles. The Chevrolet Bolt EV, introduced in 2016, was one of the first affordable long-range electric cars, setting a new standard in the industry. GM's commitment to an all-electric future is evident in its Ultium battery technology, which offers improved range, efficiency, and scalability. The upcoming launch of the GMC Hummer EV, Cadillac LYRIQ, and other electric models underscores GM's leadership in the EV market.

- Autonomous Vehicles: GM has made substantial investments in autonomous vehicle technology through its subsidiary, Cruise Automation. Cruise is developing fully autonomous vehicles capable of navigating complex urban environments without human intervention. This innovation positions GM at the forefront of the autonomous driving revolution, with the potential to transform transportation and mobility.

- Advanced Design and Manufacturing: GM has leveraged advanced design and manufacturing techniques to enhance vehicle performance, safety, and aesthetics. The use of lightweight materials, such as high-strength steel and aluminum, improves fuel efficiency and handling. Advanced manufacturing technologies, including 3D printing and robotics, streamline production processes and reduce costs.

- Connected Vehicle Technology: GM has been a pioneer in connected vehicle technology, offering features that enhance the driving experience and provide added safety and convenience. OnStar, GM's telematics service, offers features like emergency assistance, remote diagnostics, and vehicle tracking. The integration of 4G LTE Wi-Fi, advanced infotainment systems, and over-the-air software updates further enhances connectivity and user experience.

- Sustainable Design: Sustainability is a key focus in GM's product development and design. The company is committed to reducing the environmental impact of its vehicles through improved fuel efficiency, reduced emissions, and the use of sustainable materials. GM's efforts to develop electric and hybrid vehicles, along with its focus on sustainable manufacturing practices, reflect this commitment.

Strategic Partnerships and Collaborations

Strategic partnerships and collaborations have been crucial to GM's success in navigating the complexities of the global automotive industry. Mary Barra has fostered partnerships that enhance GM's capabilities, expand its market reach, and drive innovation.

- Collaborations with Technology Companies: To accelerate the development of advanced technologies, GM has formed strategic partnerships with leading technology companies. For example, GM's collaboration with LG Chem has been instrumental in advancing battery technology for electric vehicles. The partnership with Honda to develop fuel cell technology and electric vehicles demonstrates GM's commitment to leveraging external expertise to drive innovation.

- Joint Ventures in Key Markets: In China, GM has established successful joint ventures with local partners such as SAIC Motor Corporation. These joint ventures enable GM to navigate regulatory requirements, access local market knowledge, and tailor products to meet Chinese consumer preferences. The success of these collaborations has made China one of GM's largest and most important markets.

- Partnerships in Autonomous Driving: GM's acquisition of Cruise Automation and subsequent collaborations with companies like Honda and Microsoft have bolstered its efforts in autonomous driving. These partnerships provide access to additional resources, technological expertise, and capital, accelerating the development and deployment of self-driving vehicles.

- Supplier Relationships: Strong relationships with suppliers are essential for GM's success. Barra has emphasized collaboration with suppliers to ensure quality, innovation, and efficiency in the supply chain. GM's supplier diversity program also supports relationships with minority-owned, women-owned, and veteran-owned businesses, promoting inclusiveness and economic development.

- Industry Alliances: GM participates in industry alliances and consortia to address common challenges and drive collective progress. For example, GM is a member of the Zero Emission Transportation Association (ZETA), which advocates for policies that support the transition to electric vehicles. These alliances enable GM to collaborate with other industry leaders, share best practices, and influence regulatory frameworks.

Response to Market Changes and Challenges

The automotive industry is subject to rapid changes and significant challenges, and Mary Barra's leadership has been pivotal in ensuring GM's agility and resilience in response to these dynamics.

- Adapting to Technological Advances: As technology evolves, GM has proactively adapted to incorporate advancements into its products and operations. The shift towards electric and autonomous vehicles, connected car technology, and advanced manufacturing techniques reflects GM's ability to stay ahead of technological trends and meet the changing demands of consumers.

- Navigating Economic Fluctuations: The automotive industry is cyclical and sensitive to economic fluctuations. Barra has implemented strategies to ensure GM's financial stability and resilience, such as cost management initiatives, operational efficiencies, and strategic investments. These measures help GM weather economic downturns and capitalize on growth opportunities during economic upswings.

- Regulatory Compliance: The automotive industry is subject to stringent regulatory requirements related to safety, emissions, and environmental standards. GM has invested in technologies and processes to ensure compliance with these regulations. Barra's leadership emphasizes proactive engagement with regulators and policymakers to anticipate and influence regulatory changes.

- Market Shifts and Consumer Preferences: GM has demonstrated agility in responding to shifts in market demand and consumer preferences. For example, the growing demand for SUVs and trucks has led GM to expand its lineup of these vehicles, while also investing in electric and hybrid models to meet the increasing preference for sustainable transportation options.

- Crisis Management: Barra's leadership during crises, such as the ignition switch recall and the COVID-19 pandemic, has showcased her ability to navigate challenging situations effectively. Her focus on transparency, accountability, and swift action has helped GM maintain trust and credibility with stakeholders. During the COVID-19 pandemic, GM pivoted production to manufacture ventilators and personal protective equipment, demonstrating agility and social responsibility.

Lessons for Modern Automotive Businesses

Mary Barra's leadership and the strategies implemented at GM offer valuable lessons for modern automotive businesses seeking to navigate the complexities of the industry and achieve long-term success.

- Embrace Innovation and Change: The automotive industry is undergoing significant transformations, and businesses must embrace innovation and change to stay competitive. Barra's focus on electric and autonomous vehicles, advanced manufacturing, and connected technology highlights the importance of staying ahead of industry trends and investing in future-oriented innovations.

- Foster a Strong Corporate Culture: Building a strong corporate culture that values inclusiveness, innovation, and accountability is essential for driving employee engagement and organizational success. Barra's efforts to transform GM's culture demonstrate the impact of effective leadership in shaping a positive and dynamic work environment.

- Leverage Strategic Partnerships: Collaborations and partnerships can enhance capabilities, expand market reach, and drive innovation. GM's strategic partnerships with technology companies, joint ventures in key markets, and supplier relationships illustrate the benefits of leveraging external expertise and resources.

- Adapt to Market Dynamics: Agility and resilience are critical in responding to market changes and challenges. GM's ability to adapt to technological advances, economic fluctuations, regulatory requirements, and consumer preferences showcases the importance of being flexible and responsive to external dynamics.

- Commit to Sustainability: Sustainability is increasingly important to consumers, regulators, and investors. Barra's commitment to sustainability in product development, manufacturing practices, and corporate strategy underscores the value of integrating environmental responsibility into business operations.

- Focus on Customer Experience: Delivering exceptional customer experiences is key to building brand loyalty and long-term success. GM's emphasis on quality, reliability, and innovation in its vehicles, along with enhanced connectivity and personalized services, highlights the importance of prioritizing customer needs and preferences.

Mary Barra's leadership at General Motors has been characterized by strategic initiatives and innovations that have strengthened the company's market positioning and competitive edge. By focusing on competing in a global market, driving innovation in product development and design, fostering strategic partnerships, and responding effectively to market changes and challenges, Barra has positioned GM for sustained success in a rapidly evolving industry.

The lessons from Barra's leadership and GM's strategies offer valuable insights for modern automotive businesses. Embracing innovation, fostering a strong corporate culture, leveraging strategic partnerships, adapting to market dynamics, committing to sustainability, and focusing on customer experience are essential elements for achieving long-term growth and resilience in the automotive industry.

Mary Barra's vision and strategic leadership continue to inspire and set new benchmarks for excellence in the automotive sector, demonstrating the transformative power of innovation, inclusiveness, and adaptability.

Case Study: The Revival of General Motors

Challenges and Strategies During the Financial Crisis

The 2008 financial crisis presented unprecedented challenges for the global economy, and the automotive industry was among the hardest hit. General Motors (GM), one of the world's largest automakers, faced severe financial difficulties that threatened its survival. The crisis underscored the need for urgent and comprehensive restructuring to restore GM's financial health and competitive position.

- Financial Collapse and Bankruptcy: By 2008, GM was struggling with declining sales, high production costs, and an unsustainable debt load. The company's outdated business model, over-reliance on gas-guzzling vehicles, and inability to adapt to changing market demands contributed to its precarious financial state. In

June 2009, GM filed for Chapter 11 bankruptcy protection, marking one of the largest corporate bankruptcies in history. The U.S. government intervened with a $49.5 billion bailout to help GM restructure and emerge from bankruptcy.

- Government Intervention and Bailout: The U.S. Treasury provided GM with the financial support needed to undergo a comprehensive restructuring. This intervention aimed to prevent a collapse of the U.S. auto industry and save hundreds of thousands of jobs. The bailout came with conditions, including the replacement of GM's CEO, the reduction of the company's debt, and significant cost-cutting measures.

- Cost-Cutting Measures: To address its financial woes, GM implemented aggressive cost-cutting measures. The company closed several plants, eliminated thousands of jobs, and discontinued underperforming brands such as Pontiac, Saturn, and Hummer. These steps were necessary to streamline operations, reduce excess capacity, and focus on profitable core brands.

- Operational Restructuring: GM's restructuring involved a thorough re-evaluation of its operational strategy. The company aimed to become more agile and responsive to market changes. This included reducing its reliance on high-margin trucks and SUVs and increasing investment in fuel-efficient vehicles and technology. The restructuring also involved renegotiating labor contracts to reduce costs and improve flexibility.

- Focus on Core Brands: As part of its revival strategy, GM concentrated on strengthening its core brands: Chevrolet, Cadillac, Buick, and GMC. This focus allowed GM to allocate resources more effectively and build a stronger brand identity in the market. Chevrolet, in particular, played a central role in GM's recovery, with models like the Chevrolet Cruze and Chevrolet Volt leading the charge.

Leadership Transition and Restructuring

The leadership transition and restructuring at GM were critical to the company's revival. The appointment of Mary Barra as CEO in January 2014 marked a significant milestone in GM's journey towards recovery and transformation.

- Leadership Changes: In the wake of the financial crisis, GM underwent several leadership changes to steer the company towards a more sustainable future. Mary Barra, with her extensive experience within GM and her reputation for driving change, was chosen to lead the company. Her appointment as CEO made her the first woman to head a major global automaker, signaling a new era for GM.

- Cultural Transformation: Barra recognized that GM's revival required not only financial and operational restructuring but also a cultural transformation. She aimed to break down the hierarchical and siloed structure of the company and foster a more collaborative, innovative, and accountable culture. Barra's focus on transparency, integrity, and continuous improvement helped instill a sense of purpose and direction within the organization.

- Product Portfolio Revamp: Under Barra's leadership, GM embarked on an ambitious plan to revamp its product portfolio. The company prioritized the development of vehicles that met evolving consumer preferences and regulatory standards. This included a greater emphasis on fuel efficiency, safety, and advanced technology. Barra's vision for GM's future involved leading the industry in electric and autonomous vehicles.

- Investment in Technology and Innovation: Barra spearheaded significant investments in technology and innovation to position GM as a leader in the automotive industry. This included advancements in electric vehicle (EV) technology, autonomous driving, and connected car services. Barra's commitment to innovation ensured that GM remained competitive in a rapidly evolving market.

- Streamlining Operations: Barra continued the process of streamlining GM's operations to improve efficiency and reduce costs. This involved consolidating manufacturing facilities, optimizing the supply chain, and leveraging global platforms to enhance production flexibility. Barra's focus on operational excellence helped GM achieve better financial performance and sustainability.

Development of New Product Lines

The development of new product lines was a cornerstone of GM's revival strategy under Mary Barra's leadership. The company introduced a range of innovative vehicles that addressed changing consumer preferences and positioned GM as a leader in the industry.

- Electric Vehicles (EVs): One of the most significant developments during Barra's tenure was GM's commitment to electric vehicles. The introduction of the Chevrolet Bolt EV in 2016 marked a major milestone, offering an affordable long-range electric vehicle to the mass market. The success of the Bolt EV demonstrated GM's capability to produce competitive electric vehicles. GM's Ultium battery technology further advanced the company's EV strategy, providing scalable and efficient battery solutions for a wide range of vehicles.

- Autonomous Vehicles: GM made substantial progress in the development of autonomous vehicles through its subsidiary, Cruise Automation. The acquisition of Cruise in 2016 positioned GM at the forefront of autonomous driving technology. Cruise has been developing fully autonomous vehicles with the potential to revolutionize urban transportation. The Chevrolet Bolt EV was chosen as the platform for Cruise's autonomous fleet, highlighting GM's commitment to integrating advanced technology into its vehicles.

- Fuel-Efficient Models: GM also focused on developing fuel-efficient models to meet stricter emissions standards and address consumer demand for environmentally friendly vehicles. The Chevrolet Malibu and Chevrolet Cruze, equipped with advanced fuel-saving technologies, catered to the growing market for efficient and reliable sedans. GM's efforts to improve fuel efficiency extended across its entire product lineup.

- Luxury and Performance Vehicles: The revitalization of GM's luxury brand, Cadillac, played a key role in the company's product strategy. Cadillac introduced several new models, including the XT5 and XT6 SUVs, which combined luxury, performance, and advanced technology. The launch of the Cadillac CT6, with its innovative Super Cruise hands-free driving system, showcased GM's leadership in autonomous driving technology for the luxury segment.

- Trucks and SUVs: GM continued to capitalize on the strong demand for trucks and SUVs, a segment where it traditionally held a competitive advantage. The introduction of new models such as the Chevrolet Silverado, GMC Sierra, and GMC Yukon reinforced GM's position in the market. These vehicles featured advanced safety, connectivity, and performance features, appealing to a broad range of consumers.

Impact on the Automotive Industry

The revival of GM under Mary Barra's leadership had a significant impact on the automotive industry, setting new standards for innovation, sustainability, and corporate governance.

- Leadership in Electric Vehicles: GM's commitment to electric vehicles influenced the broader automotive industry, encouraging other automakers to accelerate their EV development plans. GM's investments in battery technology and EV infrastructure set benchmarks for the industry. The company's goal of an all-electric future by 2035 positioned it as a leader in the transition to sustainable transportation.

- Advancements in Autonomous Driving: GM's progress in autonomous driving technology through Cruise Automation pushed the industry towards the development of self-driving cars. The focus on safety, reliability, and scalability of autonomous systems set high standards for competitors. GM's collaboration with companies like Honda and Microsoft further underscored the importance of partnerships in advancing autonomous technology.

- **Cultural and Operational Transformation:** The cultural and operational transformation led by Barra became a model for other automakers facing similar challenges. GM's emphasis on transparency, accountability, and collaboration demonstrated the value of strong leadership and a clear vision. The company's ability to adapt to market changes and invest in future-oriented technologies provided a blueprint for resilience and growth.

- **Sustainability Initiatives:** GM's sustainability initiatives, including its commitment to carbon neutrality by 2040 and sourcing 100% renewable energy, set new environmental standards for the industry. The company's focus on reducing emissions, improving fuel efficiency, and promoting sustainable practices influenced other automakers to adopt similar goals.

- **Technological Integration:** GM's integration of advanced technologies, such as connected car services, over-the-air updates, and hands-free driving systems, showcased the potential of technological innovation in enhancing the driving experience. These advancements highlighted the importance of continuous investment in research and development to stay competitive in a rapidly evolving industry.

Barra's Enduring Influence on General Motors and the Industry

Mary Barra's leadership has left an enduring influence

on GM and the automotive industry, shaping the future of mobility and setting new benchmarks for excellence.

- Visionary Leadership: Barra's visionary leadership has positioned GM as a leader in electric and autonomous vehicles. Her strategic initiatives and investments in advanced technologies have ensured that GM remains at the forefront of industry innovation. Barra's ability to articulate a clear vision and inspire her team has been instrumental in driving the company's transformation.

- Commitment to Diversity and Inclusion: Barra's commitment to diversity and inclusion has had a lasting impact on GM's corporate culture. By promoting a diverse and inclusive workforce, Barra has fostered an environment where creativity and innovation can thrive. GM's diversity and inclusion initiatives have set an example for the industry, demonstrating the value of embracing diverse perspectives.

- Sustainability Leadership: Barra's focus on sustainability has positioned GM as a leader in environmental responsibility. The company's ambitious goals for carbon neutrality and renewable energy use reflect Barra's commitment to addressing climate change and promoting sustainable practices. GM's sustainability leadership has influenced other automakers to prioritize environmental goals.

- Operational Excellence: Barra's emphasis on

operational excellence and efficiency has strengthened GM's financial performance and competitiveness. Her efforts to streamline operations, optimize the supply chain, and leverage global platforms have improved the company's agility and resilience. Barra's leadership in operational excellence has set a standard for other companies to follow.

- Industry Influence: Barra's influence extends beyond GM to the broader automotive industry. Her leadership has inspired other automakers to prioritize innovation, sustainability, and diversity. Barra's role as a trailblazer and advocate for change has had a profound impact on the industry, driving progress and setting new benchmarks for excellence.

The revival of General Motors under Mary Barra's leadership is a testament to the power of visionary leadership, strategic innovation, and cultural transformation. Facing unprecedented challenges during the financial crisis, GM emerged stronger and more competitive, thanks to Barra's focus on operational excellence, product innovation, and sustainability.

Barra's leadership has had a significant impact on the automotive industry, setting new standards for electric and autonomous vehicles, cultural and operational transformation, and environmental responsibility. Her enduring influence continues to shape the future of GM and the industry, inspiring other automakers to embrace change, prioritize sustainability, and drive innovation.

Mary Barra's legacy as a transformative leader demonstrates the importance of resilience, vision, and strategic action in navigating complex challenges and achieving long-term success in the automotive industry. Her contributions have positioned GM for sustained growth and leadership in the rapidly evolving world of mobility.

Chapter 9:

Robert Noyce
The Integrated Circuit Pioneer

Robert Noyce, born on December 12, 1927, in Burlington, Iowa, grew up in a nurturing environment that fostered his curiosity and creativity. His father, Ralph Brewster Noyce, was a Congregational clergyman, and his mother, Harriet May Norton, was a schoolteacher. This combination of intellectual rigor and moral grounding influenced Noyce's character and approach to life.

Noyce exhibited a keen interest in mechanical and electrical devices from a young age. His early fascination with tinkering and building things laid the foundation for his future career in electronics. Noyce's talent for understanding complex systems became evident during his childhood, as he frequently dismantled and reassembled household items to understand how they worked.

He attended Grinnell College in Iowa, where he majored in physics and mathematics. Noyce's academic prowess was matched by his enthusiasm for extracurricular activities. He was an avid athlete, participating in swimming and gymnastics, and he also demonstrated leadership qualities as the president of his fraternity. During his time at Grinnell, Noyce's interest in electronics deepened, and he conducted various experiments that further honed his technical skills.

After graduating from Grinnell College in 1949, Noyce pursued a Ph.D. in physics at the Massachusetts Institute of Technology (MIT). At MIT, he worked under the guidance of Julius Stratton and Karl Taylor Compton, two prominent figures in the field of physics. Noyce's doctoral research focused on semiconductor physics, a burgeoning area of study at the time. His work at MIT laid the groundwork for his future contributions to the semiconductor industry.
Early Interest in Electronics

Noyce's early interest in electronics was sparked by a combination of innate curiosity and exposure to the rapidly evolving field of technology. As a child, he built radios and other electronic devices, experimenting with circuits and components to understand their functionality. This hands-on experience provided Noyce with a practical understanding of electronics, complementing his formal education.

During his undergraduate years at Grinnell College, Noyce's passion for electronics continued to grow. He conducted experiments in the college's physics lab, exploring the properties of materials and the behavior of electrical currents. Noyce's ability to think creatively and approach problems from multiple angles set him apart from his peers. His innovative mindset would later become a hallmark of his career in the semiconductor industry.

Noyce's time at MIT further solidified his interest in electronics. The research environment at MIT, coupled with the mentorship of leading physicists, provided Noyce with the opportunity to delve deeper into semiconductor physics. He became particularly interested in the properties of silicon and germanium, two materials that would play a crucial role in the development of semiconductor devices.
Entry into the Semiconductor Industry

After completing his Ph.D. at MIT in 1953, Noyce joined the Philco Corporation in Philadelphia as a research engineer. At Philco, he worked on the development of transistors, which were rapidly replacing vacuum tubes in electronic devices. Noyce's work at Philco provided him with valuable experience in semiconductor technology and solidified his reputation as a talented engineer.

In 1956, Noyce joined Shockley Semiconductor Laboratory, a division of Beckman Instruments, founded by William Shockley, one of the inventors of the transistor. Shockley's lab was located in Mountain View, California, in what would later become known as Silicon Valley. The lab attracted some of the brightest minds in the field, and Noyce found himself among a group of highly skilled and ambitious engineers.

However, working under Shockley proved challenging. Shockley's management style was often autocratic, and his erratic behavior led to conflicts with his team. In 1957, Noyce and seven other engineers, later known as the "Traitorous Eight," decided to leave Shockley Semiconductor Laboratory and start their own company. This decision marked a pivotal moment in the history of the semiconductor industry and the birth of Fairchild Semiconductor.

Founding of Fairchild Semiconductor

In 1957, Robert Noyce, along with Gordon Moore, Julius Blank, Victor Grinich, Jean Hoerni, Eugene Kleiner, Jay Last, and Sheldon Roberts, co-founded Fairchild Semiconductor. The company was initially funded by Sherman Fairchild, an investor and inventor who recognized the potential of the semiconductor industry.

Fairchild Semiconductor quickly established itself as a leader in the development and manufacturing of semiconductor devices. The company's success was driven by the innovative ideas and technical expertise of its founders, as well as a collaborative and entrepreneurial culture that encouraged risk-taking and experimentation.

One of the most significant contributions of Fairchild Semiconductor was the development of the planar process, pioneered by Jean Hoerni. The planar process revolutionized the manufacturing of transistors by enabling the production of multiple transistors on a single silicon wafer. This breakthrough laid the foundation for the development of integrated circuits, a concept that Noyce would soon bring to fruition.

Vision for Integrated Circuits

Robert Noyce's vision for integrated circuits (ICs) was inspired by the limitations and challenges of existing semiconductor technology. At the time, electronic devices relied on discrete transistors, resistors, and capacitors, which were individually assembled into circuits. This approach was labor-intensive, prone to errors, and limited the complexity and performance of electronic systems.

Noyce recognized that integrating multiple transistors and other components onto a single silicon chip could significantly improve the performance, reliability, and scalability of electronic devices. In 1959, he conceptualized the idea of the integrated circuit, where all the components of an electronic circuit could be fabricated simultaneously on a single piece of silicon.

Noyce's approach to integrated circuits involved the use of the planar process to create interconnected layers of transistors, resistors, and capacitors on a silicon wafer. This method allowed for the mass production of complex circuits with a high degree of precision and consistency. Noyce's invention of the integrated circuit was a monumental breakthrough that revolutionized the electronics industry.

In 1961, Fairchild Semiconductor produced the first commercial integrated circuits, marking the beginning of a new era in electronics. The impact of Noyce's vision was profound, leading to the miniaturization of electronic devices, the proliferation of consumer electronics, and the advent of the digital age.

Legacy and Impact on the Semiconductor Industry

Robert Noyce's contributions to the semiconductor industry extended far beyond the invention of the integrated circuit. His vision and leadership helped shape the industry and paved the way for future innovations.

- Founding of Intel: In 1968, Noyce and Gordon Moore left Fairchild Semiconductor to co-found Intel Corporation. Intel quickly became a dominant force in the semiconductor industry, pioneering the development of microprocessors. Noyce's leadership and vision were instrumental in establishing Intel as a technology leader and driving the growth of the computer industry.

- Mentorship and Industry Influence: Noyce was known for his collaborative and supportive leadership style. He mentored many young engineers and entrepreneurs, inspiring a culture of innovation and entrepreneurship in Silicon Valley. Noyce's influence extended beyond his own companies, as he played a key role in fostering the growth of the semiconductor industry and shaping its future direction.

- Technological Advancements: The invention of the integrated circuit set the stage for countless technological advancements. Integrated circuits enabled the development of powerful and compact electronic devices, from computers and smartphones to medical equipment and communication systems. Noyce's work laid the foundation for the digital revolution and the modern information age.

- Industry Standards and Practices: Noyce's contributions to semiconductor manufacturing processes and industry standards helped establish best practices that are still in use today. His emphasis on precision, reliability, and scalability in manufacturing has influenced the entire semiconductor industry and ensured the continued advancement of technology.

- Philanthropy and Education: Noyce was committed to giving back to the community and supporting education and research. He was involved in various philanthropic activities and served on the boards of educational institutions. Noyce's legacy includes not only his technological contributions but also his dedication to fostering the next generation of scientists and engineers.

Robert Noyce's early life and career were marked by a relentless curiosity, a passion for innovation, and a visionary approach to technology. From his childhood fascination with electronics to his pioneering work in the semiconductor industry, Noyce's contributions have had a lasting impact on the world.

The founding of Fairchild Semiconductor and the invention of the integrated circuit revolutionized the electronics industry, enabling the development of complex and powerful electronic devices. Noyce's vision for integrated circuits laid the foundation for the digital age and transformed the way we live and work.

As a co-founder of Intel, Noyce continued to drive innovation and shape the future of technology. His leadership and mentorship inspired a culture of entrepreneurship and creativity in Silicon Valley, leaving an enduring legacy that continues to influence the semiconductor industry and beyond.

Robert Noyce's contributions to technology, industry standards, and education have left an indelible mark on the world. His vision, leadership, and dedication to innovation serve as an inspiration to future generations of engineers and entrepreneurs, ensuring that his legacy will continue to shape the future of technology for years to come.

Innovations in Semiconductor Technology

Development of the First Integrated Circuit

The development of the first integrated circuit (IC) by Robert Noyce was a landmark achievement that revolutionized the semiconductor industry and laid the groundwork for modern electronics. This innovation was driven by the need to improve the performance, reliability, and scalability of electronic circuits, which, at the time, were composed of discrete components like transistors, resistors, and capacitors.

- Conceptualization of the Integrated Circuit: In

the late 1950s, as electronic devices became more complex, the limitations of discrete component circuits became evident. These circuits were not only bulky but also prone to errors and inefficiencies due to the manual assembly process. Noyce, who was working at Fairchild Semiconductor, envisioned a solution where multiple components could be fabricated simultaneously on a single piece of silicon.

- Planar Process Innovation: The breakthrough that enabled the development of integrated circuits was the planar process, pioneered by Jean Hoerni at Fairchild Semiconductor. This process involved creating a flat, planar surface on a silicon wafer and diffusing impurities into the surface to form transistors. The planar process allowed for the precise placement of components and the creation of interconnected layers on the same chip, which was essential for building integrated circuits.

- Noyce's Invention: In 1959, Noyce conceived the idea of interconnecting transistors, resistors, and capacitors on a single silicon wafer using the planar process. He proposed using a layer of metal (typically aluminum) to connect the components, effectively creating an integrated circuit. This approach not only improved the performance and reliability of electronic circuits but also allowed for the miniaturization of devices.

- Patent and Commercialization: Noyce filed a patent for his invention of the integrated circuit in 1959, and by 1961, Fairchild Semiconductor produced the first commercial integrated circuits. These early ICs were used in military applications, computers, and communication systems, demonstrating their versatility and potential.

Impact on Computing and Electronics

The invention of the integrated circuit had a profound and far-reaching impact on computing and electronics, transforming industries and paving the way for the digital age.

- Miniaturization of Devices: Integrated circuits enabled the miniaturization of electronic devices, making it possible to create smaller, more compact, and portable products. This miniaturization revolutionized consumer electronics, leading to the development of devices such as personal computers, calculators, and mobile phones.

- Increased Performance and Reliability: ICs significantly improved the performance and reliability of electronic systems. The precise fabrication process reduced the likelihood of errors and inconsistencies, resulting in more dependable and efficient circuits. This reliability was crucial for applications in aerospace, defense, and telecommunications.

- Advancement of Computers: The development of integrated circuits was instrumental in advancing computer technology. Early computers relied on vacuum tubes and discrete transistors, which were bulky and consumed a lot of power. ICs allowed for the creation of smaller, faster, and more powerful computers. This innovation laid the foundation for the development of microprocessors, which are at the heart of modern computing.

- Economic Growth and Innovation: The impact of integrated circuits extended beyond technology, driving economic growth and innovation across various sectors. The semiconductor industry became a critical component of the global economy, with applications in consumer electronics, automotive, healthcare, and industrial automation. The widespread adoption of ICs spurred new business opportunities and technological advancements.

- Consumer Electronics Revolution: Integrated circuits transformed the consumer electronics market by enabling the production of affordable and high-performance devices. Products like radios, televisions, and home appliances became more accessible to the general public. The advent of personal computing in the 1970s and 1980s, driven by IC technology, further democratized access to technology and information.

Overcoming Technical Challenges

The development and commercialization of integrated circuits were not without significant technical challenges. Noyce and his colleagues at Fairchild Semiconductor had to overcome numerous obstacles to realize the potential of this groundbreaking technology.

- Material and Process Innovation: One of the key challenges was developing materials and processes that could reliably produce integrated circuits. The planar process, which involved creating a flat surface on a silicon wafer, was critical to this effort. Innovations in photolithography and chemical etching allowed for the precise patterning of components on the wafer.

- Thermal Management: Managing the heat generated by densely packed components was another significant challenge. Integrated circuits had to be designed to dissipate heat effectively to prevent damage and ensure reliable operation. Advances in packaging and thermal management techniques were essential to addressing this issue.

- Yield and Scalability: Producing integrated circuits with high yield and scalability was crucial for commercial viability. Early production runs often faced low yields due to defects and inconsistencies in the manufacturing process. Continuous improvements in fabrication techniques, quality control, and testing helped increase yields and reduce costs.

- Interconnection and Integration: Ensuring

reliable electrical connections between components on the same chip was a technical hurdle. Noyce's innovation of using metal interconnects (typically aluminum) to connect transistors and other components was a critical solution. This approach allowed for the integration of complex circuits on a single chip.

- Industry Collaboration and Standards: Overcoming these technical challenges required collaboration and the establishment of industry standards. Fairchild Semiconductor worked closely with other companies, research institutions, and government agencies to advance semiconductor technology. The creation of standards for semiconductor manufacturing and testing helped ensure compatibility and reliability across the industry.

Collaboration with Other Innovators

The success of integrated circuits was not solely the result of Robert Noyce's efforts; it was also due to collaboration with other innovators and the collective contributions of the semiconductor community.

- The Traitorous Eight: The founding of Fairchild Semiconductor by Noyce and his seven colleagues, known as the "Traitorous Eight," was a collaborative effort that brought together some of the brightest minds in the field. Each member contributed unique skills and expertise, creating a dynamic and innovative environment that drove the development of integrated circuits.

- Jean Hoerni and the Planar Process: Jean Hoerni's invention of the planar process was a critical enabler for the development of integrated circuits. His work at Fairchild Semiconductor laid the foundation for Noyce's vision of integrating multiple components on a single chip. The collaboration between Noyce and Hoerni exemplifies the importance of teamwork in advancing technology.

- Jack Kilby and Texas Instruments: Around the same time that Noyce was developing the integrated circuit at Fairchild Semiconductor, Jack Kilby at Texas Instruments was independently working on a similar concept. Kilby's approach used germanium and wire connections, whereas Noyce's used silicon and metal interconnects. Both inventions were crucial to the advancement of IC technology, and their simultaneous development highlights the collaborative and competitive nature of innovation in the semiconductor industry.

- Industry and Academic Partnerships: The semiconductor industry's growth was fueled by partnerships between companies, research institutions, and government agencies. Collaborations with universities and research labs provided access to cutting-edge research and talent. Government funding and support for semiconductor research played a significant role in advancing the technology.

- Formation of Silicon Valley: The collaborative environment fostered by Noyce and other pioneers led to the formation of Silicon Valley, a hub of innovation and entrepreneurship. The culture of knowledge-sharing, risk-taking, and collaboration in Silicon Valley attracted top talent and spurred the growth of numerous technology companies. This ecosystem continues to drive advancements in semiconductor technology and beyond.

Long-Term Implications for Technology

The invention of the integrated circuit by Robert Noyce and the subsequent advancements in semiconductor technology have had profound long-term implications for technology and society.

- Digital Revolution: Integrated circuits were the catalyst for the digital revolution, transforming how information is processed, stored, and communicated. The development of microprocessors, powered by IC technology, enabled the creation of personal computers, smartphones, and the internet. These advancements have reshaped industries, economies, and daily life.

- Advancements in Computing Power: The continuous improvement in integrated circuit technology, often described by Moore's Law (coined by Gordon Moore, Noyce's colleague at Fairchild Semiconductor and Intel), has led to exponential increases in computing power. This progress has enabled the development of sophisticated software, artificial intelligence, and data analytics, driving innovation across various fields.

- Impact on Healthcare: Integrated circuits have revolutionized healthcare by enabling the development of advanced medical devices and diagnostic tools. Technologies such as MRI machines, pacemakers, and wearable health monitors rely on ICs for their functionality. These innovations have improved patient care, diagnostics, and treatment outcomes.

- Consumer Electronics: The proliferation of integrated circuits has driven the growth of the consumer electronics market. From televisions and gaming consoles to smart home devices and wearable technology, ICs are at the core of modern consumer electronics. The affordability and accessibility of these devices have transformed entertainment, communication, and lifestyle.

- Industrial and Automotive Applications: Integrated circuits have had a significant impact on industrial automation and automotive technology. ICs are used in manufacturing processes, robotics, and control systems, improving efficiency and precision. In the automotive industry, ICs power advanced driver-assistance systems (ADAS), engine control units, and infotainment systems, enhancing safety and driving experience.

- Global Connectivity: The advancements in

integrated circuit technology have facilitated global connectivity through the development of communication networks and the internet. ICs enable the operation of telecommunications infrastructure, satellites, and network devices, supporting seamless communication and data exchange worldwide.

- Future Prospects: The long-term implications of integrated circuits continue to evolve as technology advances. Emerging fields such as quantum computing, nanotechnology, and biotechnology hold the promise of further breakthroughs, with IC technology playing a crucial role in their development. The ongoing innovation in semiconductor technology will continue to shape the future of technology and society.

Robert Noyce's invention of the integrated circuit marked a turning point in the history of technology, revolutionizing the semiconductor industry and laying the foundation for the digital age. The development of ICs enabled the miniaturization, increased performance, and reliability of electronic devices, transforming computing, consumer electronics, healthcare, and industrial applications.

Noyce's ability to overcome technical challenges and collaborate with other innovators was instrumental in realizing the potential of integrated circuits. The collaborative spirit of Silicon Valley, fostered by Noyce and his peers, continues to drive advancements in semiconductor technology and beyond.

The long-term implications of integrated circuits are far-reaching, impacting virtually every aspect of modern life. As technology continues to evolve, the legacy of Robert Noyce and the innovation of integrated circuits will remain a cornerstone of progress and innovation in the 21st century and beyond.

Founding Intel Corporation

Transition from Fairchild to Intel

In the late 1960s, Robert Noyce and Gordon Moore, both pivotal figures at Fairchild Semiconductor, recognized the need to address the growing challenges and opportunities in the semiconductor industry. Fairchild, despite its pioneering achievements, was struggling with internal conflicts and a lack of strategic direction. This environment prompted Noyce and Moore to consider a new venture that would allow them to pursue their innovative visions without the constraints they faced at Fairchild.

- Dissatisfaction at Fairchild: By the late 1960s, Fairchild Semiconductor was experiencing significant internal strife. The company, which had been a leader in the semiconductor industry, was suffering from management issues, bureaucracy, and an inability to retain its top talent. Noyce and Moore were particularly frustrated with the lack of support for new and risky projects, which stifled innovation.

- Founding of Intel: In July 1968, Noyce and

Moore decided to leave Fairchild Semiconductor and co-founded Intel Corporation (originally named NM Electronics). They aimed to create a company that was agile, innovative, and focused on cutting-edge semiconductor technology. With an initial investment of $2.5 million from Arthur Rock, a prominent venture capitalist, and other investors, Intel was established with a clear mission to push the boundaries of semiconductor technology.

- Initial Focus and Vision: Intel's initial focus was on developing semiconductor memory products. Noyce and Moore identified a significant market opportunity in replacing magnetic core memory with semiconductor memory. Their vision was to leverage their expertise in silicon technology to create faster, more reliable, and scalable memory solutions for computers and other electronic devices.

- Early Challenges and Successes: Transitioning from Fairchild to Intel was not without its challenges. The founders had to build a new team, establish manufacturing facilities, and develop new products from scratch. However, their experience and reputation in the industry helped them attract top talent and secure strategic partnerships. Intel's first product, the 3101 Schottky bipolar random-access memory (RAM) chip, was introduced in 1969 and marked the beginning of Intel's success in semiconductor memory.

Innovations in Microprocessor Technology

Intel's most transformative contribution to the semiconductor industry was the development of microprocessors. The microprocessor revolutionized computing by integrating the functions of a computer's central processing unit (CPU) onto a single chip, enabling the creation of smaller, more powerful, and more efficient computers.

- The Intel 4004: In 1971, Intel introduced the world's first commercially available microprocessor, the Intel 4004. This 4-bit microprocessor, designed for use in calculators, could perform complex calculations that previously required multiple chips. The 4004 contained 2,300 transistors and was capable of executing approximately 92,000 instructions per second. This innovation demonstrated the feasibility of integrating a CPU on a single chip and laid the groundwork for future advancements in microprocessor technology.

- The Intel 8008 and 8080: Building on the success of the 4004, Intel released the 8008 microprocessor in 1972. The 8008 was an 8-bit microprocessor that offered greater processing power and memory addressing capabilities. This was followed by the Intel 8080 in 1974, which became the first widely used microprocessor in personal computers. The 8080's performance and versatility made it a popular choice for early computer manufacturers and hobbyists, cementing Intel's reputation as a leader in microprocessor technology.

- The Intel 8086 and x86 Architecture: In 1978, Intel introduced the 8086 microprocessor, which featured a 16-bit architecture. The 8086 was significant not only for its technical advancements but also for its role in establishing the x86 architecture, which would become the foundation for future generations of microprocessors. The x86 architecture provided a scalable and compatible platform that allowed for continuous improvements in performance and capabilities.

- Advancements in Semiconductor Technology: Intel's innovations in microprocessor technology were complemented by advancements in semiconductor manufacturing. The company pioneered new fabrication processes, such as the use of complementary metal-oxide-semiconductor (CMOS) technology, which improved the efficiency, speed, and power consumption of microprocessors. These technological advancements enabled Intel to maintain its leadership position and drive the evolution of computing.

Market Strategies and Product Development

Intel's market strategies and product development initiatives played a crucial role in establishing its dominance in the semiconductor industry. The company's approach to innovation, strategic partnerships, and marketing helped it stay ahead of competitors and meet the evolving needs of the market.

- Strategic Partnerships: Intel forged strategic partnerships with key players in the computer industry to drive the adoption of its microprocessors. One of the most significant partnerships was with IBM, which chose Intel's 8088 microprocessor for its first personal computer (PC), the IBM PC, launched in 1981. This decision had a profound impact on the industry, as IBM's choice set a standard that many other PC manufacturers followed, leading to widespread adoption of Intel processors.

- Branding and Marketing: Intel's marketing strategies played a pivotal role in building its brand and increasing market share. The "Intel Inside" campaign, launched in 1991, was particularly successful in raising consumer awareness and preference for Intel processors. By placing the Intel logo on PCs, the campaign highlighted the importance of the microprocessor in overall system performance and created a strong brand identity for Intel.

- Continuous Innovation: Intel maintained its competitive edge through continuous innovation and product development. The company invested heavily in research and development to advance microprocessor technology and introduce new products that met the increasing demands for performance and efficiency. The introduction of the Pentium processor in 1993 exemplified Intel's commitment to innovation, offering significant improvements in speed and capabilities over previous generations.

- Diversification of Product Lines: While Intel's core business was centered around microprocessors, the company also diversified its product lines to include other semiconductor products, such as chipsets, motherboards, and networking components. This diversification allowed Intel to capture additional market segments and provide integrated solutions to its customers.

- Global Expansion: Intel expanded its operations globally to meet the growing demand for its products. The company established manufacturing facilities and research centers in various regions, including Europe, Asia, and Latin America. This global presence enabled Intel to leverage regional expertise, reduce production costs, and better serve its international customer base.

Competition with Other Tech Companies

As Intel grew in prominence, it faced increasing competition from other tech companies. Navigating this competitive landscape required strategic planning, innovation, and adaptability.

- Competition with AMD: Advanced Micro Devices (AMD) emerged as one of Intel's primary competitors in the microprocessor market. AMD's introduction of x86-compatible processors, such as the Athlon and Ryzen series, challenged Intel's dominance by offering competitive performance and pricing. The rivalry between Intel and AMD spurred innovation and advancements in microprocessor technology, benefiting consumers with a wider range of choices and improved products.

- RISC vs. CISC Architectures: In the 1980s and 1990s, the debate between Reduced Instruction Set Computing (RISC) and Complex Instruction Set Computing (CISC) architectures influenced the industry. While Intel's x86 architecture was based on CISC, competitors like Sun Microsystems and IBM promoted RISC-based processors. Intel responded by enhancing its CISC architecture with features that improved performance and efficiency, ensuring its continued relevance in the market.

- Emergence of ARM: The rise of ARM Holdings and its ARM architecture introduced new competition in the form of low-power, high-efficiency processors used primarily in mobile and embedded devices. Intel's attempts to enter the mobile market with products like the Atom processor faced challenges, as ARM-based processors dominated the space. This competition highlighted the need for Intel to diversify and innovate beyond its traditional markets.

- Technological Advancements and Adaptation: Intel faced the challenge of keeping pace with rapid technological advancements and changing market dynamics. The company's ability to adapt to new trends, such as the shift towards mobile computing, cloud computing, and artificial intelligence, was crucial in maintaining its competitive position. Intel's investments in new technologies, acquisitions, and strategic initiatives demonstrated its commitment to staying at the forefront of innovation.

- Legal and Regulatory Challenges: Intel's competitive practices sometimes led to legal and regulatory challenges. The company faced antitrust investigations and lawsuits related to its business practices, including allegations of monopolistic behavior and unfair competition. Navigating these legal challenges required careful strategy and compliance with regulatory requirements.

Building a Dominant Industry Position

Intel's success in building a dominant industry position can be attributed to its strategic vision, relentless innovation, and ability to execute effectively. The company's leadership in microprocessor technology and its impact on the broader tech industry have solidified its position as a key player in the semiconductor market.

- Leadership in Microprocessors: Intel's pioneering work in microprocessor technology established it as a leader in the semiconductor industry. The continuous development of advanced microprocessors, from the Intel 4004 to the latest generations of Core and Xeon processors, showcased Intel's commitment to innovation and excellence.

- Influence on Personal Computing: Intel's microprocessors played a critical role in the development and proliferation of personal computing. The adoption of Intel processors by major PC manufacturers, including IBM, Dell, HP, and Apple, helped drive the growth of the PC market and made computing accessible to millions of people worldwide.

- Contribution to Technological Advancements: Intel's advancements in semiconductor technology have had a profound impact on various industries. The company's innovations have enabled the development of powerful and efficient computing systems, driving progress in fields such as artificial intelligence, data analytics, cloud computing, and the Internet of Things (IoT).

- Strategic Acquisitions and Investments: Intel's strategic acquisitions and investments have played a key role in expanding its capabilities and market presence. Acquisitions of companies like Altera (FPGA technology), Mobileye (autonomous driving technology), and Habana Labs (AI accelerators) have diversified Intel's product portfolio and positioned it for future growth in emerging technologies.

- Corporate Culture and Leadership: Intel's corporate culture, characterized by a focus on innovation, collaboration, and excellence, has been instrumental in its success. Leadership figures like Robert Noyce, Gordon Moore, and Andy Grove set the tone for a company that values technological advancement and strategic vision. This culture has fostered a dynamic and resilient organization capable of adapting to industry changes.

- Global Impact and Industry Standards: Intel's influence extends beyond its products to its role in setting industry standards and shaping the future of technology. The company has been involved in various industry consortia and standards organizations, contributing to the development of technologies such as Wi-Fi, USB, and PCIe. Intel's leadership in these areas has helped drive interoperability and innovation across the tech ecosystem.

The founding of Intel Corporation by Robert Noyce and Gordon Moore marked a significant milestone in the history of the semiconductor industry. Intel's pioneering work in microprocessor technology, strategic market positioning, and relentless pursuit of innovation have established it as a dominant player in the industry.

Intel's transition from Fairchild Semiconductor to a leading global technology company was driven by a clear vision and the ability to execute on that vision.

The development of groundbreaking products, strategic partnerships, and effective market strategies helped Intel navigate competition and build a strong industry position.

The long-term impact of Intel's innovations extends beyond the semiconductor industry, influencing the broader technology landscape and driving advancements in computing, consumer electronics, and various other fields. The company's commitment to continuous improvement and strategic foresight ensures that it will remain at the forefront of technological innovation for years to come.

Leadership and Management Style

Noyce's Approach to Innovation and Leadership

Robert Noyce's approach to innovation and leadership was characterized by a unique blend of technical brilliance, visionary thinking, and an egalitarian management style that fostered creativity and collaboration. Noyce, often referred to as the "Mayor of Silicon Valley," played a pivotal role in shaping the culture of innovation that has become synonymous with the region.

- Visionary Thinking: Noyce had a remarkable ability to foresee the future potential of technology. His visionary thinking was evident in his early work at Fairchild Semiconductor and later at Intel. He recognized the transformative potential of integrated circuits (ICs) and microprocessors long before they became mainstream. This foresight allowed him to steer his companies towards groundbreaking innovations that changed the technology landscape.

- Technical Expertise: As a physicist and engineer, Noyce possessed deep technical expertise, which he leveraged to drive innovation. His understanding of semiconductor physics and his ability to solve complex technical problems were crucial in the development of the first ICs and microprocessors. Noyce's technical acumen earned him the respect of his peers and the confidence of his teams.

- Inclusive Leadership: Noyce's leadership style was inclusive and democratic. He believed in empowering his employees and giving them the autonomy to pursue their ideas. Noyce fostered an open-door policy, encouraging employees at all levels to share their thoughts and contribute to decision-making processes. This inclusive approach created a sense of ownership and commitment among his teams.

- Focus on Collaboration: Collaboration was a cornerstone of Noyce's leadership approach. He understood that complex technological challenges could best be addressed through teamwork and the sharing of knowledge. Noyce encouraged cross-functional collaboration and the formation of interdisciplinary teams, which led to the creation of innovative solutions and products.

- Ethical Leadership: Noyce was known for his ethical leadership and integrity. He believed in conducting business with honesty and transparency. Noyce's ethical standards set a positive example for his employees and helped build a culture of trust and respect within his organizations. His commitment to ethical behavior also earned him the admiration of his peers in the industry.

Building a Collaborative Corporate Culture

Noyce's emphasis on collaboration was instrumental in building a corporate culture that valued teamwork, open communication, and collective problem-solving. This collaborative culture became a defining characteristic of both Fairchild Semiconductor and Intel, and it influenced the broader culture of Silicon Valley.

- Team-Oriented Environment: Noyce created a team-oriented environment where employees were encouraged to work together towards common goals. He recognized that the complexity of semiconductor technology required the combined efforts of diverse experts. By fostering a collaborative atmosphere, Noyce ensured that employees felt supported and motivated to contribute their best work.

- Open Communication: Transparent and open communication was a hallmark of Noyce's management style. He believed that sharing information freely across the organization was essential for innovation. Noyce held regular meetings and encouraged informal interactions to keep communication lines open. This practice helped break down silos and facilitated the flow of ideas.

- Flat Organizational Structure: Noyce favored a flat organizational structure over a rigid hierarchy. He believed that reducing layers of management allowed for quicker decision-making and greater agility. This structure also empowered employees by giving them direct access to leadership and the ability to influence the direction of the company.

- Empowering Employees: Noyce was committed to empowering his employees by providing them with the resources and autonomy they needed to succeed. He trusted his teams to make decisions and take ownership of their projects. This empowerment not only boosted morale but also encouraged employees to take initiative and innovate.

- Fostering Innovation Through Collaboration: Noyce understood that collaboration was key to fostering innovation. He promoted interdisciplinary collaboration, bringing together experts from different fields to tackle complex challenges. This approach led to breakthrough innovations, such as the development of the integrated circuit and the microprocessor, which required the combined expertise of engineers, physicists, and material scientists.

Encouraging Risk-Taking and Experimentation

Noyce's willingness to take risks and his encouragement of experimentation were crucial factors in driving innovation at Fairchild Semiconductor and Intel. He believed that innovation often required venturing into uncharted territory and that failure was an inevitable part of the process.

- Cultivating a Risk-Tolerant Culture: Noyce cultivated a culture that was tolerant of risk and failure. He understood that not all experiments would lead to success, but he valued the learning that came from failure. This risk-tolerant culture encouraged employees to pursue bold ideas without fear of repercussions, fostering an environment where innovation could thrive.

- Supporting Experimentation: Noyce actively supported experimentation by providing the necessary resources and time for research and development. He encouraged his teams to explore new concepts and technologies, even if they seemed unconventional or risky. This support for experimentation led to significant technological advancements and kept the companies at the forefront of innovation.

- Learning from Failure: Noyce viewed failure as a valuable learning experience. He encouraged his employees to analyze and learn from their mistakes, rather than dwelling on them. This approach helped create a culture of continuous improvement, where setbacks were seen as opportunities for growth and development.

- Encouraging Intrapreneurship: Noyce fostered a sense of intrapreneurship within his organizations, encouraging employees to think and act like entrepreneurs. He provided the freedom and support for individuals to develop their own projects and initiatives. This intrapreneurial spirit led to the creation of new products and technologies that drove the companies' success.

- Balancing Risk and Reward: While Noyce encouraged risk-taking, he also emphasized the importance of balancing risk with potential reward. He guided his teams to assess the feasibility and impact of their projects, ensuring that resources were allocated to the most promising ideas. This strategic approach to risk management helped maximize the chances of success.

Balancing Technical Expertise with Business Acumen

Noyce's ability to balance technical expertise with business acumen was a key factor in his success as a leader. He recognized that technological innovation needed to be aligned with business objectives to drive sustainable growth and profitability.

- Technical Vision and Business Strategy: Noyce

had a clear technical vision for the future of semiconductor technology, but he also understood the importance of aligning this vision with a sound business strategy. He worked closely with business leaders to develop strategies that leveraged technological advancements to create market opportunities and competitive advantages.

- Market Awareness: Noyce was acutely aware of market trends and customer needs. He used this market awareness to guide the development of new products and technologies. By aligning technical innovation with market demands, Noyce ensured that the companies' offerings were relevant and valuable to customers.

- Financial Acumen: Noyce possessed strong financial acumen, which he used to make informed decisions about resource allocation and investment. He understood the importance of managing finances effectively to support long-term growth and sustainability. Noyce's financial discipline helped the companies navigate economic challenges and invest in future innovations.

- Strategic Partnerships: Noyce leveraged strategic partnerships to enhance both technical capabilities and business opportunities. Collaborations with other companies, research institutions, and government agencies provided access to new technologies, markets, and resources. These partnerships were instrumental in driving innovation and expanding the companies' reach.

- **Leadership Development:** Noyce recognized the importance of developing leaders who could balance technical expertise with business acumen. He mentored and supported emerging leaders within the organization, providing them with the skills and knowledge needed to navigate both technical and business challenges. This focus on leadership development ensured a strong pipeline of talent for the companies' future success.

Legacy in Modern Technology Leadership

Robert Noyce's leadership and management style have left an enduring legacy in the technology industry. His contributions to semiconductor technology, corporate culture, and innovation continue to influence modern technology leadership.

- **Pioneering Silicon Valley Culture:** Noyce played a pivotal role in shaping the culture of Silicon Valley, which has become a global hub of innovation and entrepreneurship. The collaborative, risk-tolerant, and inclusive culture that Noyce fostered at Fairchild Semiconductor and Intel has become a model for technology companies worldwide.

- **Influence on Corporate Culture:** Noyce's emphasis on collaboration, open communication, and empowerment has influenced the corporate culture of many technology companies. These principles are now widely recognized as essential for fostering innovation and driving business success. Noyce's legacy is evident in the organizational practices of leading technology firms.

- Advancements in Semiconductor Technology: Noyce's contributions to semiconductor technology have had a lasting impact on the industry. The development of integrated circuits and microprocessors revolutionized computing and electronics, enabling the digital age. Noyce's innovations laid the foundation for the development of powerful and compact electronic devices that have transformed modern life.

- Mentorship and Leadership Development: Noyce's commitment to mentorship and leadership development has inspired generations of technology leaders. His approach to nurturing talent and fostering a culture of innovation has been emulated by many successful technology entrepreneurs and executives. Noyce's influence continues to shape the leadership practices of the technology industry.

- Enduring Principles of Innovation: The principles of innovation that Noyce championed—visionary thinking, risk-taking, collaboration, and ethical leadership—remain relevant and influential in the modern technology landscape. These principles guide technology companies as they navigate the challenges and opportunities of a rapidly evolving industry.

Robert Noyce's leadership and management style were characterized by visionary thinking, technical expertise, inclusive leadership, and a commitment to innovation. His approach to building a collaborative corporate culture, encouraging risk-taking and experimentation, and balancing technical expertise with business acumen played a crucial role in the success of Fairchild Semiconductor and Intel.

Noyce's legacy extends beyond his technological contributions to the broader impact he had on corporate culture and innovation in the technology industry. His influence continues to shape the practices and principles of modern technology leadership, inspiring future generations of innovators and entrepreneurs.

Noyce's contributions to semiconductor technology and his visionary leadership have left an indelible mark on the world, driving advancements that have transformed modern life and paved the way for the digital age. His legacy as a pioneer of innovation and a leader of Silicon Valley endures, ensuring that his impact will be felt for many years to come.

Case Study: The Microprocessor Revolution

Development and Impact of the Intel 4004

The development of the Intel 4004, the world's first commercially available microprocessor, marked the beginning of the microprocessor revolution. This groundbreaking innovation transformed the computing industry and laid the foundation for modern electronics.

- Origins of the Intel 4004: The Intel 4004 was developed in response to a request from the Japanese calculator company Busicom. In 1969, Busicom sought a set of custom integrated circuits for their new line of calculators. Federico Faggin, Marcian "Ted" Hoff, and Stan Mazor at Intel proposed a different solution: a single chip that could be programmed to perform various functions, reducing the complexity and cost of the design. This idea led to the creation of the 4004 microprocessor.

- Technical Specifications: The Intel 4004 was a 4-bit microprocessor that operated at a clock speed of 740 kHz and contained 2,300 transistors. It could execute approximately 92,000 instructions per second and was capable of addressing up to 4 KB of memory. The 4004's design included a 16-pin dual in-line package, which allowed for easy integration into various electronic systems.

- Innovative Design: The innovation behind the 4004 lay in its ability to perform the functions of a central processing unit (CPU) on a single chip. This integration of multiple functions onto one silicon chip was a significant advancement over previous designs, which relied on multiple discrete components. The

4004's design simplified the architecture of electronic devices and paved the way for the development of more complex microprocessors.

- Commercial Release and Impact: The Intel 4004 was released in November 1971 and quickly garnered attention for its versatility and performance. Its ability to be programmed for different tasks made it applicable to a wide range of applications beyond calculators, including embedded systems and industrial control systems. The 4004 demonstrated the potential of microprocessors to revolutionize electronic design and computation.

- Catalyst for the Microprocessor Industry: The success of the 4004 established Intel as a leader in microprocessor technology and set the stage for further innovations. The development of the 4004 proved that complex computing functions could be integrated into a single chip, leading to the rapid advancement of microprocessor technology. The 4004's impact extended beyond Intel, as it inspired other companies to explore and develop their own microprocessor designs.

Market Disruption and Competition

The introduction of the Intel 4004 and subsequent microprocessors disrupted the existing market for electronic components and computing devices. This disruption led to increased competition and accelerated innovation in the semiconductor industry.

- Disruption of Existing Technologies: Before the advent of microprocessors, electronic devices relied on discrete transistors, resistors, and capacitors to perform computing functions. These components were bulky, consumed more power, and were less reliable. The microprocessor's ability to integrate these functions onto a single chip disrupted the market for discrete components, offering a more efficient and compact solution.

- Emergence of New Applications: The versatility of microprocessors opened up new applications in various industries. Consumer electronics, telecommunications, automotive, and industrial automation sectors began to adopt microprocessors to enhance the functionality and performance of their products. This broad applicability fueled demand for microprocessors and drove market growth.

- Rise of Competitors: The success of Intel's microprocessors attracted numerous competitors to the market. Companies such as Motorola, Texas Instruments, and AMD began developing their own microprocessors, leading to increased competition and innovation. Each company sought to differentiate itself through advancements in processing power, energy efficiency, and cost-effectiveness.

- Moore's Law and Technological Progress: The rapid pace of innovation in microprocessor technology was encapsulated by Moore's Law, proposed by Intel co-founder Gordon Moore. Moore's Law predicted that the number of transistors on a microprocessor would double approximately every two years, leading to exponential increases in computing power. This principle drove the semiconductor industry to continuously push the boundaries of technology and deliver more powerful and efficient microprocessors.

- Market Dynamics and Pricing: The competitive landscape of the microprocessor market led to dynamic pricing strategies. Companies had to balance the cost of research and development with the need to offer competitive prices. The competition also spurred advancements in manufacturing techniques, such as photolithography, which improved yield and reduced production costs.

Evolution of Microprocessor Technology

The microprocessor technology that began with the Intel 4004 evolved rapidly, leading to significant advancements in computing power, efficiency, and functionality. This evolution was marked by several key developments and innovations.

- Intel 8008 and 8080: Building on the success of the 4004, Intel released the 8008 in 1972 and the 8080 in 1974. The 8008 was an 8-bit microprocessor that offered greater processing power and memory addressing capabilities. The 8080 further improved performance and became widely adopted in early personal computers, such as the Altair 8800. The 8080's success demonstrated the potential of microprocessors in computing and solidified Intel's position as a leader in the industry.

- Intel 8086 and x86 Architecture: In 1978, Intel introduced the 8086 microprocessor, which featured a 16-bit architecture. The 8086 was significant not only for its technical advancements but also for establishing the x86 architecture, which became the foundation for future generations of microprocessors. The x86 architecture provided a scalable and compatible platform that allowed for continuous improvements in performance and capabilities.

- Advancements in Semiconductor Technology: The evolution of microprocessors was closely tied to advancements in semiconductor manufacturing technology. Innovations such as complementary metal-oxide-semiconductor (CMOS) technology improved the efficiency, speed, and power consumption of microprocessors. These advancements enabled the creation of smaller, more powerful, and energy-efficient chips.

- Introduction of the Pentium Processor: In 1993, Intel introduced the Pentium processor, which represented a significant leap in microprocessor technology. The Pentium featured a superscalar architecture, allowing it to execute multiple instructions per clock cycle. This innovation led to substantial improvements in performance and marked the beginning of the era of high-performance computing for personal computers.

- Multi-Core Processors: The development of multi-core processors in the early 2000s marked another milestone in the evolution of microprocessor technology. Multi-core processors integrated multiple processing units (cores) onto a single chip, allowing for parallel processing and increased performance. This innovation addressed the limitations of single-core processors and enabled more efficient handling of complex and resource-intensive applications.

Impact on the Computing Industry

The microprocessor revolution had a profound impact on the computing industry, transforming how computers were designed, manufactured, and used. This transformation drove the growth of the personal computer market and enabled the development of new technologies and applications.

- Rise of Personal Computing: The advent of microprocessors made it possible to create affordable and powerful personal computers. Early personal computers, such as the Apple II, IBM PC, and Commodore 64, were powered by microprocessors and brought computing capabilities to homes, schools, and small businesses. The widespread adoption of personal computers revolutionized how people accessed information, performed tasks, and communicated.

- Advancements in Software Development: The increased processing power and capabilities of microprocessors enabled the development of more sophisticated software applications. Operating systems, productivity software, and programming languages evolved to take advantage of the new hardware capabilities. The growth of the software industry was closely linked to advancements in microprocessor technology.

- Expansion of the Internet: The microprocessor revolution played a crucial role in the expansion of the internet. The development of powerful and affordable computers enabled more people to connect to the internet and access online services. The growth of the internet, in turn, drove demand for faster and more capable microprocessors to handle the increasing complexity and volume of online activities.

- Innovation in Embedded Systems: Microprocessors became a key component in embedded systems, which are specialized computing systems integrated into other devices. Embedded systems are used in a wide range of applications, including automotive systems, medical devices, industrial automation, and consumer electronics. The versatility and performance of microprocessors enabled the creation of smarter and more efficient embedded systems.

- Advances in Artificial Intelligence and Machine Learning: The evolution of microprocessor technology has been instrumental in advancing artificial intelligence (AI) and machine learning. Modern microprocessors, with their high processing power and parallel processing capabilities, enable the training and execution of complex machine learning models. These advancements have led to significant breakthroughs in AI applications, such as natural language processing, computer vision, and autonomous systems.

Intel's Enduring Influence on Modern Technology

Intel's contributions to the development and advancement of microprocessor technology have had a lasting impact on modern technology. The company's innovations have shaped the evolution of computing and influenced a wide range of industries.

- Leadership in Microprocessor Technology: Intel has maintained its leadership in microprocessor technology through continuous innovation and a commitment to advancing the state of the art. The company's microprocessors are used in a wide range of devices, from personal computers and servers to mobile devices and embedded systems. Intel's processors continue to set benchmarks for performance, efficiency, and reliability.

- Influence on Industry Standards: Intel has played a key role in establishing industry standards for microprocessor architecture and computing technologies. The x86 architecture, introduced with the Intel 8086, has become the dominant architecture for personal computers and servers. Intel's influence extends to other technologies, such as USB, PCI Express, and Thunderbolt, which have become standard interfaces in the industry.

- Investment in Research and Development: Intel's significant investment in research and development has driven innovation and technological progress. The company's focus on developing new fabrication processes, such as FinFET and Extreme Ultraviolet (EUV) lithography, has enabled the creation of smaller, faster, and more efficient microprocessors. Intel's R&D efforts continue to push the boundaries of semiconductor technology.

- Strategic Acquisitions and Partnerships: Intel has expanded its capabilities and market presence through strategic acquisitions and partnerships. Acquisitions of companies like Altera (FPGA technology), Mobileye (autonomous driving technology), and Habana Labs (AI accelerators) have diversified Intel's product portfolio and positioned it for growth in emerging technologies. Partnerships with other technology companies and research institutions have also been instrumental in driving innovation.

- Commitment to Sustainability: Intel has

demonstrated a commitment to sustainability and environmental responsibility. The company has implemented initiatives to reduce its carbon footprint, improve energy efficiency, and promote responsible sourcing of materials. Intel's efforts in sustainability reflect its broader commitment to corporate social responsibility and its role as a leader in the technology industry.

- Impact on the Global Economy: Intel's contributions to the semiconductor industry have had a significant impact on the global economy. The company's innovations have driven the growth of the technology sector, created jobs, and enabled new industries and applications. Intel's influence extends beyond technology, shaping the economic landscape and driving progress in various fields.

The development of the Intel 4004 and the subsequent microprocessor revolution transformed the computing industry and laid the foundation for modern technology. The 4004's innovative design demonstrated the potential of integrating complex computing functions onto a single chip, leading to rapid advancements in microprocessor technology.

Intel's leadership in microprocessor development, market strategies, and continuous innovation have established it as a dominant player in the semiconductor industry. The company's contributions have driven the growth of personal computing, advanced software development, and enabled the expansion of the internet and embedded systems.

The impact of the microprocessor revolution extends beyond computing, influencing a wide range of industries and applications. Intel's enduring influence on modern technology is evident in its leadership in microprocessor technology, establishment of industry standards, and commitment to sustainability.

Robert Noyce's vision and leadership, along with the efforts of his colleagues at Intel, have left a lasting legacy that continues to shape the future of technology. The microprocessor revolution has transformed how we live, work, and communicate, driving progress and innovation in the 21st century and beyond.

Chapter 10:

Fred Smith Revolutionizing Logistics

Fred Smith was born on August 11, 1944, in Marks, Mississippi. He grew up in a family that valued hard work and entrepreneurship. His father, James Frederick Smith, founded the Dixie Greyhound Lines, a regional bus service that was later incorporated into the Greyhound Bus Company. This entrepreneurial spirit in the family likely influenced Fred's future endeavors.

As a child, Smith faced significant health challenges. He was diagnosed with a congenital bone disease that caused him to use crutches until he was ten years old. Despite this, he was an active and determined child who developed a keen interest in aviation at an early age. By the time he was 15, Smith had learned to fly airplanes, a skill that would later play a crucial role in his career.

Smith attended Memphis University School, a private all-boys school where he excelled both academically and athletically. After graduating high school, he went on to attend Yale University. It was at Yale that Smith's interest in logistics and business began to take shape more formally. He majored in economics and was a member of the Skull and Bones society, one of Yale's most prestigious secret societies.

During his time at Yale, Smith wrote a term paper that outlined his vision for an integrated air-to-ground system for overnight deliveries. This concept, which he detailed for his economics class, would later become the foundation for Federal Express. The paper argued that with the rise of computers and the need for fast and reliable delivery of parts and products, an integrated delivery system that used both air and ground transportation would be essential. Despite receiving a mediocre grade for the paper, Smith was convinced of its potential.

Early Interest in Aviation and Logistics

Fred Smith's early interest in aviation was not just a hobby but a passion that significantly influenced his future career. His childhood fascination with flying led him to become a skilled pilot, and this experience gave him a deep understanding of the aviation industry. This knowledge proved invaluable when he later founded Federal Express.

After graduating from Yale in 1966, Smith enlisted in the U.S. Marine Corps. He served two tours of duty in Vietnam, where he flew over 200 combat missions. His time in the Marines further honed his leadership skills and deepened his understanding of logistics. The military's emphasis on efficiency, precision, and the importance of timely supply deliveries left a lasting impression on Smith. He saw firsthand how critical reliable logistics were in high-stakes situations, and this experience reinforced his belief in the potential for a civilian overnight delivery service.

Upon his return from Vietnam, Smith took over the family business, Smith Motor Coach Company, and expanded its operations. However, his vision for a revolutionary logistics company continued to occupy his thoughts. He was determined to bring his idea of an integrated air-to-ground delivery system to life.

Founding of Federal Express

In 1971, with a clear vision and a plan in hand, Fred Smith founded Federal Express (now FedEx). He used his inheritance, estimated at around $4 million, and raised an additional $91 million from venture capitalists and investors to launch the company. This initial funding was one of the largest amounts ever raised for a startup at that time, reflecting the boldness and potential of Smith's vision.

Federal Express began operations in April 1973, with its headquarters in Memphis, Tennessee. Memphis was chosen for its central location, which allowed the company to efficiently service the entire United States. The company started with 14 Dassault Falcon 20 jets, 389 employees, and 186 packages to be delivered on its first night.

Smith's vision for Federal Express was revolutionary. He wanted to create a system where packages could be delivered overnight anywhere in the United States. This required not only a fleet of airplanes but also a network of ground vehicles and sorting facilities that could handle large volumes of packages quickly and efficiently. The hub-and-spoke model, where packages are routed through a central hub (Memphis in this case), was central to this vision. This model allowed for greater efficiency and reliability in delivery times. Vision for Overnight Delivery Services

Fred Smith's vision for Federal Express was based on the premise that there was a growing need for overnight delivery services, particularly for high-priority items such as medical supplies, electronics, and important documents. He believed that businesses would be willing to pay a premium for a reliable and fast delivery service that could guarantee next-day delivery.

Smith's innovative approach to logistics included several key components:

- Integrated Air-to-Ground System: Smith envisioned a system that combined air and ground transportation seamlessly. Packages would be picked up from customers, transported by ground to the nearest airport, flown to the central hub, sorted, and then flown to their destination cities, where they would be delivered by ground transportation.

- Central Hub-and-Spoke Model: The use of a central hub in Memphis allowed Federal Express to optimize flight schedules and minimize the time packages spent in transit. This model ensured that packages could be routed efficiently and reliably, reducing the likelihood of delays and errors.

- Real-Time Tracking and Data Management: Smith understood the importance of information management in logistics. Federal

Express invested heavily in technology to track packages in real-time and manage logistics data. This investment allowed the company to provide customers with accurate delivery times and improved overall efficiency.

- Focus on Reliability and Customer Service: Smith emphasized the importance of reliability and customer service. Federal Express offered a money-back guarantee for on-time delivery, which was a bold move that demonstrated confidence in their service and built trust with customers.

Initial Business Challenges

Despite the innovative vision and substantial initial investment, Federal Express faced significant challenges in its early years. The logistics business is capital-intensive, and the company struggled with cash flow issues as it tried to scale its operations.

- Financial Struggles: Federal Express burned through its initial funding quickly. The cost of maintaining a fleet of aircraft, building sorting facilities, and managing a growing workforce was immense. By 1974, just a year after launching, the company was losing $1 million a month and was on the brink of bankruptcy.

- Operational Challenges: Coordinating a nationwide overnight delivery service was a massive logistical challenge. Federal Express had to develop new processes and systems to ensure packages were picked up, transported, and delivered on time. This required significant trial and error, and the company faced numerous operational setbacks in its early days.

- Skepticism from Investors and the Market: Many investors and market analysts were skeptical about the feasibility of Smith's vision. The idea of a nationwide overnight delivery service seemed overly ambitious and fraught with risk. Convincing stakeholders to continue supporting the company financially was a constant struggle.

- Competition and Market Conditions: The logistics and delivery market was highly competitive, with established players like UPS and the U.S. Postal Service dominating the industry. Federal Express had to carve out its niche and prove that it could offer a superior service to justify its higher prices.

- Fuel Prices and Economic Conditions: The 1970s were marked by economic volatility, including fluctuating fuel prices and inflation. These factors added to the financial pressures on Federal Express, as the cost of operating a fleet of aircraft was heavily influenced by fuel prices.

Overcoming Challenges and Achieving Success

Fred Smith's determination and innovative thinking played crucial roles in overcoming these initial challenges and steering Federal Express towards success. Several key strategies and pivotal moments helped the company turn the corner.

- Securing Additional Funding: In a now-legendary move, Fred Smith personally took a desperate measure to keep the company afloat. Faced with the prospect of insolvency, Smith took the last $5,000 of the company's money to Las Vegas and won $27,000 playing blackjack. While this was a risky and unconventional move, it provided a brief respite and demonstrated Smith's willingness to do whatever it took to save his company. More importantly, Smith managed to secure additional funding from investors by presenting a compelling vision and demonstrating early operational successes.

- Improving Operational Efficiency: Federal Express continuously refined its operations to improve efficiency and reliability. Investments in technology, such as the Digitally Assisted Dispatch System (DADS), allowed for better coordination of deliveries and real-time tracking of packages. These technological advancements helped Federal Express enhance its service quality and build a reputation for reliability.

- Building a Strong Corporate Culture: Smith understood the importance of a motivated and dedicated workforce. He fostered a corporate culture that emphasized teamwork, innovation, and a commitment to customer service. This culture was instrumental in driving the company's success, as employees were motivated to go above and beyond to meet customer expectations.

- Expanding Services and Market Reach: Federal Express expanded its services to include international deliveries and freight services. This diversification allowed the company to tap into new markets and revenue streams. Strategic acquisitions and partnerships further enhanced the company's capabilities and global reach.

- Marketing and Brand Building: Federal Express invested in marketing and brand-building efforts to differentiate itself from competitors. The company's iconic "When it absolutely, positively has to be there overnight" campaign emphasized reliability and urgency, resonating with business customers who valued timely deliveries.

Vision for the Future and Enduring Impact

Fred Smith's vision for Federal Express extended beyond its initial success. He continued to innovate and expand the company's services, positioning it as a leader in the logistics industry. Smith's forward-thinking approach and commitment to excellence have left a lasting impact on the industry.

- Embracing Technological Advancements: Smith recognized the importance of technology in driving operational efficiency and customer satisfaction. Federal Express was an early adopter of computer systems, barcoding, and later, internet-based tracking and customer service tools. These technological advancements have become industry standards, shaping the way logistics companies operate today.

- Focus on Sustainability: In recent years, Federal Express (now FedEx) has placed a strong emphasis on sustainability. The company has invested in fuel-efficient aircraft, electric vehicles, and renewable energy sources to reduce its environmental footprint. Smith's leadership in sustainability reflects a broader industry trend towards more eco-friendly logistics practices.

- Global Expansion and Diversification: Under Smith's leadership, FedEx has grown into a global logistics powerhouse with a diverse portfolio of services. The company's international network spans over 220 countries and territories, offering a wide range of shipping, freight, and supply chain solutions. This global reach has solidified FedEx's position as a leader in the logistics industry.

- Innovations in Supply Chain Management: Smith's vision for logistics has extended to supply chain management, with FedEx offering comprehensive solutions that integrate transportation, warehousing, and distribution. These innovations have helped businesses optimize their supply chains and improve efficiency.

- Influence on Modern Logistics and E-commerce: FedEx's innovations have had a profound impact on modern logistics and e-commerce. The company's reliable and efficient delivery services have enabled the growth of online retail, allowing businesses to reach customers quickly and effectively. Smith's contributions have fundamentally changed the way goods are transported and delivered, shaping the modern economy.

Fred Smith's journey from his early interest in aviation and logistics to founding Federal Express is a testament to his visionary thinking, determination, and innovative spirit. His concept of an integrated air-to-ground delivery system revolutionized the logistics industry and set new standards for reliability and efficiency.

Despite facing significant challenges in the early years, Smith's leadership and commitment to excellence propelled Federal Express to success. The company's impact on the logistics industry has been profound, with innovations that have transformed how goods are transported and delivered worldwide.

Smith's enduring legacy in the logistics industry is evident in the continued success and growth of FedEx. His vision for overnight delivery services, emphasis on technological advancements, and commitment to sustainability have left a lasting impact on the industry, influencing modern logistics practices and shaping the future of global commerce.

Fred Smith's story is one of innovation, resilience, and

visionary leadership. His contributions have not only revolutionized logistics but have also paved the way for the modern e-commerce landscape, making him a true pioneer in the world of business and logistics.

Innovations in Logistics and Delivery

Development of the Hub-and-Spoke Distribution Model

One of the most significant innovations introduced by Fred Smith and Federal Express (now FedEx) was the hub-and-spoke distribution model. This model revolutionized the logistics industry by optimizing the efficiency and reliability of package delivery services.

- Concept of the Hub-and-Spoke Model: The hub-and-spoke model is designed to streamline the transportation of packages by routing them through a central hub before they are delivered to their final destinations. In this system, all packages are first transported to a central sorting facility (the hub), where they are sorted and then sent out to their respective delivery locations (the spokes).

- Implementation at FedEx: Fred Smith chose Memphis, Tennessee, as the central hub for Federal Express. Memphis was strategically located near the geographic center of the continental United States, allowing for efficient overnight distribution to most parts of the country. The Memphis hub became the heart of FedEx's operations, where packages were sorted and redistributed for delivery.

- Efficiency and Reliability: The hub-and-spoke model significantly improved the efficiency of package delivery. By centralizing sorting operations, FedEx could ensure that packages were routed correctly and delivered on time. This model also allowed for more predictable and consistent delivery schedules, which was critical for the company's promise of overnight delivery.

- Scalability: The hub-and-spoke model proved to be highly scalable, allowing FedEx to expand its operations without compromising efficiency. As the company grew, it established additional regional hubs to complement the central hub in Memphis. This expansion enabled FedEx to handle increasing volumes of packages while maintaining high levels of service reliability.

- Impact on the Industry: The success of the hub-and-spoke model at FedEx set a new standard for the logistics industry. Other companies adopted similar models to improve their own distribution networks. The hub-and-spoke system became a fundamental principle in logistics and transportation, influencing the design of airline networks, freight transportation, and even public transportation systems.

Innovations in Tracking and Information Systems

FedEx's commitment to innovation extended beyond its distribution model to the development of advanced tracking and information systems. These technologies transformed the way packages were managed and tracked, providing greater visibility and control for both the company and its customers.

- Digitally Assisted Dispatch System (DADS): One of the early innovations at FedEx was the implementation of the Digitally Assisted Dispatch System (DADS). This system used computers to optimize the routing and dispatching of delivery vehicles. By analyzing traffic patterns, package volumes, and delivery routes, DADS helped FedEx improve the efficiency and speed of its ground operations.

- COSMOS (Customer, Operations, and Services Master Online System): In the 1980s, FedEx introduced COSMOS, a comprehensive information system that integrated all aspects of the company's operations. COSMOS allowed for real-time tracking of packages, inventory management, and customer service. This system provided unprecedented visibility into the status of each package, enabling FedEx to offer accurate and timely updates to customers.

- Barcoding and Scanning Technology: FedEx was a pioneer in adopting barcoding and scanning technology to improve the accuracy and efficiency of package handling. Barcodes were applied to packages, and handheld scanners were used to record each movement through the distribution network. This technology reduced errors, streamlined sorting processes, and provided real-time tracking information.

- Tracking and Tracing Systems: FedEx's development of advanced tracking and tracing systems allowed customers to monitor the progress of their shipments from pickup to delivery. The company's tracking system provided detailed information about the location and status of packages, giving customers confidence in the reliability of the service. This level of transparency set FedEx apart from its competitors and became an industry standard.

- Internet-Based Tracking: With the advent of the internet, FedEx introduced online tracking tools that allowed customers to track their packages via the company's website. This innovation made it even easier for customers to access real-time information about their shipments, enhancing the overall customer experience. The ability to track packages online became a critical feature in the logistics industry.

Expansion into Global Markets

Under Fred Smith's leadership, FedEx expanded its operations beyond the United States to become a global logistics powerhouse. This expansion involved establishing a presence in international markets, building a global network, and adapting to the unique challenges of operating in different regions.

- Early International Expansion: FedEx's first step towards international expansion was the launch of its service to Canada in 1981. This move marked the beginning of the company's efforts to establish a global presence. In the following years, FedEx continued to expand its operations to Europe, Asia, and Latin America, providing comprehensive international shipping services.

- Global Network Development: Building a global network required significant investment in infrastructure, including regional hubs, sorting facilities, and fleets of aircraft and vehicles. FedEx established regional hubs in key locations such as Paris, Hong Kong, and Dubai, enabling efficient transportation and distribution of packages worldwide. This network allowed FedEx to offer reliable and timely delivery services to customers around the globe.

- Acquisitions and Partnerships: To accelerate its global expansion, FedEx pursued strategic acquisitions and partnerships. Notable acquisitions included the purchase of Flying Tigers, an international cargo airline, in 1989, and TNT Express, a European logistics company, in 2016. These acquisitions expanded FedEx's capabilities and market reach, allowing it to better serve international customers.

- Adapting to Local Markets: Expanding into global markets required FedEx to adapt its operations to meet the unique needs and regulations of different regions. This involved understanding local customs, navigating regulatory requirements, and tailoring services to local customer preferences. FedEx's ability to adapt and operate effectively in diverse markets was a key factor in its success.

- Global Trade Facilitation: FedEx played a crucial role in facilitating global trade by providing reliable and efficient logistics services. The company's global network enabled businesses to expand their reach, access new markets, and compete internationally. FedEx's services supported the growth of e-commerce, enabling small and medium-sized enterprises to engage in cross-border trade.

Overcoming Regulatory and Logistical Challenges

Expanding globally and innovating in logistics came with numerous regulatory and logistical challenges. FedEx's ability to navigate these challenges was instrumental in its growth and success.

- Navigating Regulatory Frameworks: Operating in multiple countries meant dealing with a complex web of regulations, including customs, trade policies, and aviation laws. FedEx invested in building a robust regulatory compliance framework to ensure it adhered to local laws and regulations. The company worked closely with government agencies and industry associations to facilitate smoother operations and address regulatory challenges.

- Customs Clearance and Trade Compliance: Efficient customs clearance was critical for timely delivery of international shipments. FedEx developed expertise in customs brokerage and trade compliance, helping customers navigate the complexities of international trade. The company's investments in technology and processes streamlined customs procedures, reducing delays and improving the overall efficiency of cross-border shipments.

- Infrastructure Development: Building the necessary infrastructure to support a global logistics network was a significant logistical challenge. FedEx invested heavily in constructing state-of-the-art sorting facilities, regional hubs, and distribution centers. The company also expanded its fleet of aircraft and ground vehicles to ensure reliable transportation of packages across vast distances.

- Supply Chain Management: Managing a global supply chain required precise coordination and integration of various components, including transportation, warehousing, and distribution. FedEx leveraged advanced supply chain management practices to optimize its operations and ensure seamless movement of goods. This included using real-time data and analytics to make informed decisions and improve operational efficiency.

- Overcoming Geographic and Environmental Challenges: Operating in diverse geographic regions presented unique challenges, such as extreme weather conditions, varying infrastructure quality, and geopolitical risks. FedEx developed contingency plans and robust risk management strategies to mitigate these challenges. The company's ability to adapt and maintain service continuity in the face of disruptions was a testament to its resilience and operational excellence.

Long-Term Impact on the Logistics Industry

Fred Smith's innovations in logistics and delivery have had a profound and lasting impact on the industry. FedEx's pioneering approaches set new standards for efficiency, reliability, and customer service, influencing the way logistics companies operate today.

- Setting Industry Standards: FedEx's introduction of the hub-and-spoke model, real-time tracking systems, and commitment to overnight delivery set new benchmarks for the logistics industry. These innovations became industry standards, adopted by competitors and shaping the expectations of customers worldwide.

- Driving Technological Advancements: FedEx's investments in technology, such as barcoding, scanning, and internet-based tracking, drove technological advancements in the logistics industry. The company's focus on leveraging technology to improve operations and customer experience influenced the development of new tools and systems that are now widely used across the industry.

- Enhancing Customer Experience: FedEx's emphasis on reliability, transparency, and customer service revolutionized the customer experience in logistics. The ability to track packages in real-time, receive accurate delivery estimates, and rely on timely deliveries built trust and loyalty among customers. This customer-centric approach became a key differentiator for logistics companies.

- Facilitating Global Trade and E-Commerce: FedEx's global network and efficient logistics services played a crucial role in facilitating global trade and the growth of e-commerce. The company's services enabled businesses of all sizes to reach international markets, driving economic growth and expanding opportunities for cross-border trade.

- Promoting Sustainability: FedEx's commitment to sustainability and environmental responsibility has influenced the logistics industry to adopt more eco-friendly practices. The company's investments in fuel-efficient aircraft, electric vehicles, and renewable energy sources set an example for other logistics companies to follow, promoting a more sustainable approach to logistics.

- Shaping Future Innovations: The legacy of Fred Smith and FedEx continues to shape future innovations in logistics and delivery. The company's pioneering spirit and focus on continuous improvement inspire ongoing advancements in technology, supply chain management, and customer service. FedEx remains a leader in the industry, driving innovation and setting the pace for the future of logistics.

Fred Smith's innovations in logistics and delivery transformed the industry, setting new standards for efficiency, reliability, and customer service. The development of the hub-and-spoke distribution model, advancements in tracking and information systems, expansion into global markets, and overcoming regulatory and logistical challenges were key factors in FedEx's success.

Smith's vision and leadership have had a lasting impact on the logistics industry, influencing the way companies operate and driving technological advancements. The legacy of FedEx's innovations continues to shape the future of logistics, facilitating global trade, enhancing customer experience, and promoting sustainability.

Fred Smith's contributions to logistics and delivery exemplify the power of innovation, resilience, and visionary leadership. His story is a testament to the transformative impact that one individual's vision can have on an entire industry, paving the way for future generations of innovators and entrepreneurs.

Business Strategies and Market Positioning

Strategies for Rapid Growth and Expansion

Fred Smith's strategic vision for Federal Express (now FedEx) was rooted in the need for rapid growth and expansion to achieve economies of scale and establish market dominance. Several key strategies were instrumental in driving the company's early growth and long-term success.

- Aggressive Market Penetration: From the outset, Smith recognized the importance of quickly establishing a strong market presence. FedEx invested heavily in marketing and sales to build brand awareness and attract customers. The company's focus on overnight delivery services, combined with a money-back guarantee for on-time delivery, helped differentiate it from competitors and build a loyal customer base.

- Capital Investment in Infrastructure: FedEx's growth strategy involved significant capital investment in infrastructure. The company built state-of-the-art sorting facilities, acquired a fleet of aircraft, and developed a robust ground transportation network. These investments enabled FedEx to handle large volumes of packages efficiently and expand its

service offerings.
- Geographic Expansion: Rapid geographic expansion was a key component of FedEx's growth strategy. The company quickly expanded its service area to cover the entire United States and, later, international markets. Strategic acquisitions, such as the purchase of Flying Tigers, an international cargo airline, helped accelerate this expansion and enhance FedEx's global capabilities.

- Service Diversification: To drive growth, FedEx diversified its service offerings beyond overnight delivery. The company introduced a range of services, including two-day and ground delivery, freight services, and logistics solutions. This diversification allowed FedEx to tap into new revenue streams and better meet the needs of its customers.

- Strategic Partnerships and Alliances: FedEx formed strategic partnerships and alliances to support its growth objectives. These partnerships provided access to new markets, enhanced operational capabilities, and facilitated the development of innovative solutions. Collaborations with technology companies, suppliers, and other logistics providers helped FedEx stay ahead of the competition.

Competing with Established Logistics Companies

Competing with established logistics companies like

United Parcel Service (UPS) and the U.S. Postal Service (USPS) required FedEx to develop strategies that leveraged its unique strengths and differentiated it from its competitors.

- Focus on Speed and Reliability: FedEx's core value proposition was based on speed and reliability. The company's commitment to overnight delivery with a money-back guarantee set it apart from competitors. By consistently delivering packages on time, FedEx built a reputation for reliability that became a key competitive advantage.

- Technological Innovation: FedEx invested heavily in technology to enhance its operations and customer experience. The implementation of advanced tracking systems, barcoding, and real-time data management provided FedEx with a technological edge. These innovations improved operational efficiency and allowed customers to track their packages in real-time, offering greater transparency and peace of mind.

- Customer-Centric Approach: FedEx's customer-centric approach was a critical factor in its success. The company focused on understanding and meeting the needs of its customers, offering tailored solutions and exceptional customer service. FedEx's willingness to go above and beyond for its customers helped build strong relationships and foster loyalty.

- Niche Market Targeting: FedEx identified and targeted niche markets where it could provide unique value. For example, the company focused on serving industries that required urgent and reliable delivery, such as medical supplies, electronics, and high-value documents. By catering to these specific needs, FedEx was able to carve out a niche and build a loyal customer base.

- Continuous Improvement: FedEx adopted a philosophy of continuous improvement, constantly seeking ways to enhance its services and operations. This commitment to innovation and excellence allowed FedEx to stay ahead of competitors and adapt to changing market conditions.

Building a Strong Brand and Customer Loyalty

Building a strong brand and cultivating customer loyalty were central to FedEx's market positioning and long-term success. The company's branding and marketing strategies played a crucial role in establishing its identity and reputation.

- Iconic Advertising Campaigns: FedEx's advertising campaigns were instrumental in building brand recognition and trust. The company's iconic "When it absolutely, positively has to be there overnight" campaign emphasized its commitment to reliability and urgency. These campaigns resonated with customers and reinforced FedEx's value proposition.

- Consistent Brand Messaging: FedEx maintained consistent brand messaging across all its marketing and communications efforts. This consistency helped build a strong and recognizable brand identity. The FedEx logo and color scheme became synonymous with reliability and speed, further strengthening the company's brand equity.

- Exceptional Customer Service: FedEx's focus on exceptional customer service was key to building customer loyalty. The company invested in training and empowering its employees to provide top-notch service. Customer feedback was actively sought and used to improve service offerings. This customer-centric approach fostered strong relationships and repeat business.

- Loyalty Programs and Incentives: FedEx introduced loyalty programs and incentives to reward repeat customers and encourage continued use of its services. Programs like FedEx Rewards offered discounts, special offers, and other benefits to loyal customers. These initiatives helped increase customer retention and foster long-term loyalty.

- Corporate Social Responsibility: FedEx's commitment to corporate social responsibility (CSR) also contributed to its strong brand reputation. The company engaged in various CSR initiatives, including environmental sustainability efforts, community involvement, and disaster relief. These actions demonstrated FedEx's commitment to making a positive impact, enhancing its brand image and customer loyalty.

Innovations in Supply Chain Management

FedEx's innovations in supply chain management have had a profound impact on the logistics industry. The company's focus on efficiency, technology, and integrated solutions set new standards for supply chain management.

- Integrated Logistics Solutions: FedEx developed integrated logistics solutions that combined transportation, warehousing, and distribution services. These solutions provided customers with end-to-end supply chain management, streamlining operations and reducing costs. FedEx's ability to offer comprehensive logistics solutions helped it become a strategic partner for many businesses.

- Real-Time Tracking and Visibility: FedEx's investment in real-time tracking and visibility systems revolutionized supply chain management. Customers could track their shipments at every stage of the journey, providing greater transparency and control. This real-time visibility allowed businesses to make informed decisions and respond quickly to any issues.

- Optimized Transportation Networks: FedEx optimized its transportation networks to improve efficiency and reduce transit times. The company's hub-and-spoke model, combined with advanced routing algorithms, ensured that packages were delivered quickly and reliably. This optimization was critical for just-in-time inventory management and other time-sensitive supply chain operations.

- Collaboration and Partnership: FedEx collaborated with suppliers, customers, and other logistics providers to enhance supply chain efficiency. These partnerships facilitated the sharing of information and resources, improving overall supply chain performance. FedEx's collaborative approach helped create more resilient and responsive supply chains.

- Sustainability Initiatives: FedEx's commitment to sustainability extended to its supply chain management practices. The company implemented initiatives to reduce its carbon footprint, such as using fuel-efficient vehicles, optimizing delivery routes, and investing in renewable energy. These sustainability efforts not only benefited the environment but also resonated with customers who valued eco-friendly practices.

Lessons for Modern Logistics Businesses

FedEx's success offers valuable lessons for modern logistics businesses looking to thrive in a competitive and dynamic industry. Key takeaways from FedEx's strategies and market positioning include:

- Embrace Innovation: Innovation is crucial for staying ahead in the logistics industry. Modern logistics businesses should invest in technology and explore new ways to enhance efficiency, improve customer experience, and reduce costs. Embracing innovation can provide a competitive edge and drive long-term growth.

- Focus on Customer Experience: A customer-centric approach is essential for building loyalty and differentiating from competitors. Logistics businesses should prioritize understanding customer needs, offering tailored solutions, and providing exceptional service. Building strong relationships with customers can lead to repeat business and positive word-of-mouth.

- Invest in Infrastructure: Building and maintaining robust infrastructure is key to ensuring reliable and efficient operations. Logistics businesses should invest in state-of-the-art facilities, transportation networks, and technology to support their growth and service offerings. A well-developed infrastructure can enhance operational efficiency and customer satisfaction.

- Leverage Data and Analytics: Data-driven decision-making is critical for optimizing logistics operations and improving supply chain management. Businesses should leverage data and analytics to gain insights, identify trends, and make informed decisions. Real-time tracking and visibility systems can enhance transparency and control, leading to better outcomes.

- Adapt to Market Changes: The logistics industry is constantly evolving, and businesses must be agile and adaptable to stay competitive. Modern logistics businesses should be proactive in responding to market changes, regulatory developments, and customer demands. Flexibility and resilience are key to navigating challenges and seizing opportunities.

- Commit to Sustainability: Sustainability is becoming increasingly important in the logistics industry. Businesses should implement eco-friendly practices and strive to reduce their environmental impact. Sustainability initiatives can enhance brand reputation, meet regulatory requirements, and appeal to environmentally conscious customers.

- Build Strong Partnerships: Collaboration and partnerships can enhance capabilities and drive growth. Logistics businesses should seek strategic alliances with suppliers, technology providers, and other stakeholders to create more efficient and resilient supply chains. Building strong partnerships can facilitate innovation and improve overall performance.

Fred Smith's strategic vision and innovative

approaches to logistics and delivery transformed FedEx into a global leader in the industry. The company's strategies for rapid growth and expansion, competing with established logistics companies, building a strong brand and customer loyalty, and innovations in supply chain management set new standards for the logistics industry.

FedEx's success offers valuable lessons for modern logistics businesses, emphasizing the importance of innovation, customer-centricity, infrastructure investment, data-driven decision-making, adaptability, sustainability, and strong partnerships. By embracing these principles, logistics businesses can thrive in a competitive and dynamic industry, delivering exceptional value to their customers and driving long-term growth.

Fred Smith's contributions to the logistics industry have had a lasting impact, shaping the future of logistics and setting the stage for continued innovation and excellence. His legacy as a visionary leader and pioneer in logistics serves as an inspiration for future generations of entrepreneurs and business leaders.

Leadership and Corporate Culture

Smith's Approach to Leadership and Management

Fred Smith, the founder of FedEx, is renowned for his distinctive approach to leadership and management. His philosophy combines visionary thinking, a strong emphasis on innovation, and a deep commitment to employee empowerment and customer service.

- Visionary Leadership: Smith's leadership is characterized by his ability to envision the future of logistics and to transform that vision into reality. He foresaw the demand for overnight delivery services long before it became apparent to others and developed FedEx based on that insight. His clear vision provided a guiding star for the company and inspired employees to work towards a common goal.

- Empowerment and Delegation: Smith believes in empowering his employees and delegating responsibility. He trusts his team to make decisions and encourages a culture of ownership and accountability. This approach not only fosters innovation but also ensures that employees feel valued and motivated to contribute their best work.

- Focus on Innovation: Innovation has always been at the heart of Smith's management style. He encourages a culture where new ideas are welcomed and explored. This commitment to innovation has led FedEx to pioneer many technological advancements in the logistics industry, such as real-time tracking systems and the hub-and-spoke distribution model.

- Customer-Centric Approach: Smith's leadership emphasizes the importance of customer satisfaction. He instilled a philosophy of "putting the customer first" within FedEx, ensuring that the company's services consistently meet or exceed customer expectations. This customer-centric approach has been a cornerstone of FedEx's success.

- Resilience and Adaptability: Smith's military background taught him the importance of resilience and adaptability. He applies these principles to his leadership style, ensuring that FedEx can navigate challenges and changes in the market effectively. His ability to remain calm under pressure and to make strategic decisions has helped FedEx weather various crises and emerge stronger.

Building a Strong Corporate Culture

A strong corporate culture has been fundamental to FedEx's success, and Fred Smith has played a pivotal role in shaping and nurturing this culture.

- People-Service-Profit (PSP) Philosophy: At the core of FedEx's corporate culture is the People-Service-Profit (PSP) philosophy. This principle posits that if the company takes care of its employees (People), they will provide exceptional service (Service), which in turn will lead to profitability (Profit). This holistic approach ensures that all stakeholders are valued and that the company's operations are aligned towards achieving sustainable success.

- Open Communication: Smith has always promoted open communication within the company. FedEx fosters an environment where employees can freely share their ideas, concerns, and feedback. This open communication helps identify issues early, encourages innovation, and builds trust among employees.

- Inclusivity and Diversity: FedEx places a strong emphasis on inclusivity and diversity. Smith believes that a diverse workforce brings a variety of perspectives and ideas, which are crucial for innovation and problem-solving. FedEx's commitment to diversity is reflected in its hiring practices, employee resource groups, and inclusion initiatives.

- Recognition and Rewards: Recognizing and rewarding employees' contributions is a key aspect of FedEx's corporate culture. The company has various programs to acknowledge employees' efforts, from formal awards to informal recognition. This practice boosts morale, encourages high performance, and fosters loyalty.

- Training and Development: FedEx invests heavily in the training and development of its employees. The company offers a range of programs to enhance employees' skills and career prospects. This focus on development not only benefits employees but also ensures that FedEx has a capable and skilled workforce ready to meet future challenges.

Employee Engagement and Motivation

Employee engagement and motivation are critical to

FedEx's success. Fred Smith's leadership and the company's corporate culture have created an environment where employees feel engaged, motivated, and committed to the company's mission.

- Empowerment and Autonomy: By empowering employees and giving them autonomy in their roles, FedEx ensures that employees feel a sense of ownership and responsibility. This empowerment leads to higher job satisfaction and motivation as employees see the direct impact of their work on the company's success.

- Clear Vision and Purpose: Smith's clear vision for FedEx and its purpose provides employees with a sense of direction and meaning. Understanding how their work contributes to the company's goals and the broader impact on customers and society helps keep employees engaged and motivated.

- Supportive Work Environment: FedEx strives to create a supportive work environment where employees feel valued and respected. This includes offering support for work-life balance, providing resources for professional growth, and fostering a culture of collaboration and mutual respect.

- Competitive Compensation and Benefits: FedEx offers competitive compensation and benefits packages to attract and retain top talent. This includes not only salaries but also health benefits, retirement plans, and other perks. Providing fair and attractive compensation is key to maintaining high levels of employee motivation and engagement.

- Opportunities for Advancement: FedEx provides numerous opportunities for career advancement within the company. By promoting from within and offering pathways for career development, FedEx ensures that employees have long-term career prospects, which increases their commitment to the company.

Dealing with Competition and Market Changes

Fred Smith's strategic vision and adaptability have enabled FedEx to navigate competition and market changes effectively.

- Innovation and Technology: FedEx's continuous investment in innovation and technology has been a key strategy in staying ahead of the competition. By adopting and developing cutting-edge technologies, such as real-time tracking systems and automated sorting facilities, FedEx has maintained a competitive edge in the logistics industry.

- Agility and Adaptability: Smith's leadership emphasizes the importance of agility and adaptability. FedEx has demonstrated the ability to quickly respond to market changes, whether it's shifting customer demands, economic fluctuations, or technological advancements. This adaptability has allowed FedEx to remain relevant and competitive in a dynamic industry.

- Strategic Acquisitions: To expand its capabilities and market presence, FedEx has pursued strategic acquisitions. Notable acquisitions, such as the purchase of Flying Tigers and TNT Express, have enhanced FedEx's global reach and service offerings. These strategic moves have strengthened FedEx's position in the market and provided new growth opportunities.

- Customer Focus: Maintaining a strong focus on customer needs and preferences has been critical for FedEx in dealing with competition. By continuously improving service quality, expanding service offerings, and providing exceptional customer service, FedEx has built strong customer loyalty and differentiated itself from competitors.

- Sustainability Initiatives: FedEx's commitment to sustainability has also helped it navigate market changes. As environmental concerns and regulations increase, FedEx's investments in fuel-efficient vehicles, renewable energy, and sustainable practices have positioned the company as a leader in green logistics. This focus on sustainability appeals to environmentally conscious customers and meets regulatory requirements.

Legacy in Modern Logistics and Business Practices

Fred Smith's leadership and the corporate culture he cultivated at FedEx have left a lasting legacy in modern logistics and business practices.

- Revolutionizing Logistics: Smith's vision and innovative approach revolutionized the logistics industry. The hub-and-spoke distribution model, real-time tracking systems, and commitment to overnight delivery set new standards for efficiency and reliability. These innovations have been widely adopted across the industry, shaping modern logistics practices.

- People-Service-Profit (PSP) Philosophy: The PSP philosophy introduced by Smith has had a profound impact on corporate culture and business practices. This holistic approach, which prioritizes employees, customer service, and profitability, has been emulated by many companies seeking to achieve sustainable success. The PSP philosophy underscores the importance of balancing the needs of all stakeholders in driving long-term growth.

- Technology and Innovation: FedEx's focus on technology and innovation has influenced the broader logistics and transportation industry. The company's adoption of advanced technologies, such as barcoding, scanning, and real-time tracking, has become industry standards. FedEx's commitment to innovation continues to inspire other companies to explore new ways to enhance efficiency and service quality.

- Customer-Centric Approach: Smith's emphasis on customer satisfaction has set a benchmark for service excellence. The importance of understanding and meeting customer needs, providing reliable service, and building strong customer relationships has become a guiding principle for businesses across industries.

- Sustainability and Corporate Responsibility: FedEx's leadership in sustainability and corporate responsibility has had a lasting impact on business practices. The company's efforts to reduce its environmental footprint, engage in community initiatives, and promote ethical business practices have set an example for others to follow. FedEx's commitment to sustainability demonstrates the importance of integrating social and environmental considerations into business strategies.

- Leadership Development: Fred Smith's approach to leadership development, which emphasizes empowerment, innovation, and continuous improvement, has influenced modern leadership practices. By fostering a culture of mentorship, training, and development, Smith has ensured that FedEx remains a leader in cultivating talented and capable leaders.

Fred Smith's leadership and the corporate culture he established at FedEx have been instrumental in the company's success and have left a lasting legacy in the logistics industry and beyond. Smith's visionary approach, emphasis on innovation, and commitment to empowering employees and delivering exceptional customer service have set new standards for leadership and corporate culture.

The strong corporate culture at FedEx, built on the People-Service-Profit philosophy, open communication, inclusivity, and recognition, has created an environment where employees feel engaged, motivated, and valued. This culture has been key to FedEx's ability to attract and retain top talent and to drive continuous improvement and innovation.

Smith's ability to navigate competition and market changes through strategic investments in technology, agility, customer focus, and sustainability has ensured that FedEx remains a leader in the logistics industry. The lessons from FedEx's success, including the importance of innovation, customer-centricity, employee empowerment, and sustainability, offer valuable insights for modern businesses seeking to thrive in a competitive and dynamic environment.

Fred Smith's legacy in modern logistics and business practices continues to influence and inspire future generations of leaders and entrepreneurs. His contributions have not only transformed the logistics industry but have also set a benchmark for excellence in leadership, corporate culture, and business strategy.

Case Study: The Launch of FedEx Overnight

Development and Implementation of Overnight Delivery

The launch of FedEx Overnight was a groundbreaking moment in the history of logistics, transforming how goods were transported and delivered. Fred Smith's vision for an overnight delivery service that combined air and ground transportation to achieve unparalleled speed and reliability was the cornerstone of Federal Express (now FedEx).

- Conceptualization of Overnight Delivery: The idea for overnight delivery was born out of Smith's realization during his college years at Yale that existing logistics services were inefficient and unreliable. His term paper, which proposed an integrated air-to-ground system, became the blueprint for Federal Express. Smith envisioned a system where packages could be delivered overnight, reliably and consistently, to meet the needs of businesses and consumers in an increasingly fast-paced world.

- Designing the Network: The implementation of overnight delivery required the creation of a network that could support rapid and reliable transportation. Smith and his team designed a hub-and-spoke distribution model, with a central sorting hub located in Memphis, Tennessee. This model allowed for the efficient consolidation and redistribution of packages, minimizing transit times and ensuring that deliveries could be made overnight.

- Acquiring the Fleet: To execute the overnight delivery service, FedEx needed a fleet of aircraft that could handle the transportation of packages between the hub and various destinations. The company initially leased 14 Dassault Falcon 20 jets, which were capable of carrying the volume of packages necessary for the operation. The choice of aircraft was critical, as they needed to be reliable and capable of quick turnaround times to meet the overnight schedule.

- Operational Readiness: FedEx's first night of operations began on April 17, 1973. The company had to ensure that all aspects of the operation were ready, including sorting facilities, aircraft, ground transportation, and staffing. This involved extensive planning and coordination to ensure that packages could be picked up, transported to the hub, sorted, and delivered to their final destinations within a single night.

- Technology and Systems: FedEx invested in advanced technology to support the overnight delivery service. This included computer systems for tracking packages, managing logistics, and optimizing routes. The implementation of the Digitally Assisted Dispatch System (DADS) helped streamline ground operations and improve efficiency, ensuring that packages were delivered on time.

Marketing and Customer Acquisition Strategies

The success of FedEx Overnight depended not only on operational efficiency but also on effective marketing and customer acquisition strategies. Fred Smith and his team employed several innovative approaches to build awareness and attract customers.

- Targeting Businesses: FedEx's initial marketing efforts focused on businesses that required reliable and fast delivery services. This included industries such as healthcare, technology, legal, and financial services, where timely delivery of documents and products was critical. By targeting these high-priority sectors, FedEx was able to demonstrate the value of its overnight delivery service and attract early adopters.

- Money-Back Guarantee: One of the most significant marketing strategies was the introduction of a money-back guarantee for on-time delivery. This bold move underscored FedEx's confidence in its service and built trust with customers. The guarantee assured businesses that they could rely on FedEx to meet their urgent delivery needs, which was a compelling value proposition.

- Advertising Campaigns: FedEx launched a series of advertising campaigns to build brand awareness and communicate the benefits of its overnight delivery service. The iconic slogan

"When it absolutely, positively has to be there overnight" resonated with businesses and consumers alike, reinforcing the company's commitment to reliability and speed.

- Building Relationships with Customers: FedEx invested in building strong relationships with its customers. The company provided personalized service, assigned account managers to key clients, and offered customized solutions to meet specific needs. This customer-centric approach helped FedEx retain clients and generate positive word-of-mouth referrals.

- Demonstrations and Promotions: To showcase the effectiveness of its service, FedEx conducted demonstrations and promotional events. These activities allowed potential customers to see firsthand how FedEx's overnight delivery worked and the benefits it offered. Demonstrations included live tracking of packages, showcasing the efficiency of the hub-and-spoke model, and highlighting the company's technological capabilities.

Overcoming Initial Challenges and Setbacks

Launching an innovative service like FedEx Overnight came with significant challenges and setbacks. Fred Smith and his team had to navigate financial difficulties, operational hurdles, and skepticism from the market.

- Financial Struggles: In the early years, FedEx

faced severe financial difficulties. The company was losing money rapidly, burning through its initial investment, and struggling to cover operational costs. At one point, FedEx was on the brink of bankruptcy, with Fred Smith famously resorting to a high-stakes gamble in Las Vegas to secure emergency funds. This desperate measure underscored the financial pressures the company faced.

- Operational Challenges: Implementing an overnight delivery service required overcoming numerous operational challenges. Coordinating the timely pickup, sorting, and delivery of packages across the country was a complex task. FedEx had to refine its processes, invest in employee training, and continuously improve its operations to ensure reliability.

- Skepticism and Market Acceptance: Convincing businesses to trust and adopt FedEx's new service was another major challenge. Many potential customers were skeptical about the feasibility of overnight delivery and the company's ability to deliver on its promises. Overcoming this skepticism required persistent marketing efforts, building a track record of reliability, and leveraging testimonials from satisfied customers.

- Regulatory Hurdles: Navigating regulatory requirements and securing necessary approvals for operations added another layer of complexity. FedEx had to comply with aviation regulations, customs procedures for international shipments, and various other regulatory frameworks. These hurdles required significant time, effort, and resources to address.

- Technology and Infrastructure Investments: The need for continuous investment in technology and infrastructure was both a challenge and a necessity. FedEx had to keep up with technological advancements, maintain and upgrade its fleet, and expand its facilities to handle growing volumes of packages. These investments were essential for sustaining the quality and efficiency of the service but also added financial strain.

Impact on the Logistics Industry

The successful launch and subsequent growth of FedEx Overnight had a profound impact on the logistics industry, setting new standards for speed, reliability, and customer service.

- Setting Industry Standards: FedEx's commitment to overnight delivery and the introduction of a money-back guarantee set new industry standards. Competitors were forced to improve their own services to meet the expectations set by FedEx, leading to overall improvements in the logistics industry.

- Innovation and Technology Adoption: FedEx's use of advanced technology, such as real-time tracking systems and automated sorting, pushed the industry to adopt similar innovations. The company's investment in technology demonstrated the importance of leveraging digital tools to enhance operational efficiency and customer experience.

- Transformation of Business Practices: The ability to deliver packages overnight transformed how businesses operated. Just-in-time inventory management, same-day repairs, and expedited document deliveries became possible, enabling companies to operate more efficiently and meet the demands of their customers more effectively.

- Growth of E-Commerce: FedEx's reliable and fast delivery service was a catalyst for the growth of e-commerce. Online retailers could promise quick delivery times, which encouraged more consumers to shop online. FedEx's infrastructure and capabilities supported the rapid expansion of the e-commerce sector, changing consumer buying habits.

- Globalization of Trade: As FedEx expanded its services internationally, it played a significant role in the globalization of trade. Businesses could now ship products to international markets quickly and reliably, opening up new opportunities for growth and expansion. FedEx's global network facilitated cross-border commerce and supported the integration of global supply chains.

FedEx's Enduring Influence on Global Commerce

FedEx's innovations and success have had an enduring influence on global commerce, shaping the logistics industry and driving economic growth.

- Revolutionizing Logistics: FedEx's pioneering efforts in overnight delivery revolutionized the logistics industry. The hub-and-spoke model, real-time tracking systems, and commitment to reliability set new benchmarks for logistics services. These innovations have been widely adopted and have become standard practices in the industry.

- Enabling Global Supply Chains: FedEx's global network and efficient logistics services have enabled the development and integration of global supply chains. Businesses can now source materials, manufacture products, and distribute goods on a global scale with confidence. This has led to greater efficiency, cost savings, and access to new markets.

- Supporting Economic Growth: The ability to move goods quickly and reliably has supported economic growth by enabling businesses to operate more efficiently and expand their reach. Small and medium-sized enterprises (SMEs) have particularly benefited from FedEx's services, as they can now compete with larger companies by leveraging reliable logistics solutions.

- Enhancing Consumer Experience: FedEx's commitment to customer service and reliability has enhanced the consumer experience. Customers now expect quick and reliable delivery of their purchases, and businesses have adapted to meet these expectations. This shift has led to higher customer satisfaction and loyalty.

- Promoting Sustainability: FedEx's focus on sustainability has influenced the logistics industry to adopt more environmentally friendly practices. The company's investments in fuel-efficient vehicles, renewable energy, and sustainable operations have set an example for others to follow. FedEx's efforts demonstrate that it is possible to achieve operational excellence while minimizing environmental impact.

- Inspiring Innovation: Fred Smith's vision and leadership have inspired countless entrepreneurs and business leaders to pursue innovation and excellence. FedEx's success story serves as a testament to the power of a clear vision, relentless determination, and the willingness to take risks.

The launch of FedEx Overnight was a transformative moment in the logistics industry, driven by Fred Smith's visionary leadership and innovative approach. The development and implementation of the overnight delivery service required overcoming significant challenges, including financial struggles, operational hurdles, and market skepticism. However, through strategic marketing, customer-centric practices, and continuous improvement, FedEx successfully established itself as a leader in logistics.

The impact of FedEx Overnight on the logistics industry has been profound, setting new standards for speed, reliability, and customer service. FedEx's innovations have revolutionized logistics, enabled the growth of e-commerce, and supported the globalization of trade. The company's enduring influence on global commerce is a testament to its commitment to excellence and innovation.

Fred Smith's legacy and the success of FedEx continue to inspire and shape the future of logistics and business practices, demonstrating the transformative power of visionary leadership and strategic innovation.

www.ingramcontent.com/pod-product-compliance
Lightning Source LLC
Chambersburg PA
CBHW071909210526
45479CB00002B/351